Selected poems of Lord Byron

George Gordon Byron Byron, Matthew Arnold, Nathan Haskell Dole

The Isles of Greece.

SELECTED POEMS

OF

LORD BYRON

EDITED BY

MATTHEW ARNOLD

BIOGRAPHICAL SKETCH

BY

NATHAN HASKELL DOLE

NEW YORK
THOMAS Y. CROWELL COMPANY
PUBLISHERS

Copyright, 1884 and 1893,

By T. Y. Crowell & Co.

BIOGRAPHICAL SKETCH OF LORD BYRON.

GEORGE GORDON BYRON was born in Holles Street, London, Jan. 22, 1788.

On his mother's side he was descended from James I. through his daughter Annabella, married to the second Earl of Huntley.

On his father's side he claimed to be of Norman blood. He wrote Count d'Orsay: "My name and family are both Norman." William the Conqueror had in his train two de Buruns: Sir Erneis and Sir Rodulphus or Ralph, who had grants of land in Yorkshire, Lancashire, and Nottinghamshire.

Making allowance for gaps in the record, which is faulty for several hundred years and during several consecutive generations, it is not hard to believe Byron's assertion that his family were knightly from the time of the Conqueror, and noble from that of Charles the First. The name was common though not distinguished in English history. At Calais, at Cressy, and at Bosworth, Byrons fought, bled, and died. Definite ancestry begins with Sir John, familiarly known as "Sir John the Little with the Great Beard," who at the dissolution of the monasteries received from Henry VIII. the church and priory of Newstead.

iii

The poet had no great reason for pride in this ancestor. His only son, John Byron, was illegitimate, and received Newstead, not by inheritance, but by deed of gift. James I. made the new owner of the abbey a Knight of the Bath. The Earl of Shrewsbury advised him to cut down the enormous expenses of the establishment which his father had carried on by means of borrowed money.

It was probably this man's grandson who for his services at Newbury in 1643 was created Baron of Rochdale by Charles I. The first Lord Byron died without male issue. The Barony went to the eldest of his six brothers, who, having begotten ten children and repurchased " part of the ancient inheritance," died at the age of seventy-three. His oldest son, the third Lord, married a daughter of Viscount Chaworth and wrote execrable doggerel.

The fourth Lord was interested in the fine arts, and painted landscapes, several of which were reproduced in etchings. Of his sons, one, Richard Byron, took " holy orders," and is known to art as having copied Rembrandt's " Three Trees " so cleverly that it was bought as an original. John Byron, the poet's grandfather, became an admiral, and wrote a spirited but somewhat dubious account of his luckless adventures, while the eldest inherited the title, married Frances, second daughter of the fourth Baron Berkeley, and from his fierce murderous duel with his cousin Chaworth and his irregular life was known as the " wicked Lord."

In order to spite his son who married for love against his will, the fifth Lord Byron, who has been described as " a morose husband, tyrannical father, hard landlord, and harsh master," made an illegal sale of his Rochdale property and dismantled Newstead. John Murray, who visited the abbey in 1814, sixteen years after his death, wrote : —

"Lord Byron's immediate predecessor stripped the whole place of all that was splendid and interesting, and you may judge of what he must have done to the mansion when I inform you that he converted the ground which used to be covered with the finest trees, like a forest, into an absolute desert. Not a tree is left standing, and the wood thus shamefully cut down was sold in one day for £60,000 [£6,000?]. The hall of entrance has about eighteen large niches, which had been filled with statues, and the side walls covered with family portraits and armor. All these have been mercilessly torn down, as well as the magnificent fireplace, and sold. All the beautiful paintings which filled the galleries — valued at that day at £80,000 — have disappeared, and the whole place is crumbling into dust."

Admiral Byron, known as " Foul-weather Jack," married his cousin, Sophia Trevanion, also of the mad, impetuous race of the Berkeleys. He died in 1786, a disappointed man, leaving two sons and three daughters. One of his daughters married her cousin, the only son of the " wicked Lord Byron." It was by the death of this only son followed by that of his only son that the barony descended to the poet. From the poet in turn it went to his cousin's son; and thus the present Lord Byron is a descendant of the Admiral.

If heredity explains vagaries of character, it is plain that these crossed and intermingled strains of wild and impetuous blood were a terrible legacy rather than a matter of pride. But the poet was to be even more pitied for his immediate birth and training.

His father, John Byron, known as " Mad Jack," was the Admiral's oldest son. He was sent first to Westminster school, then to a French military academy; entering the army, he served in America. Returning to London, he seduced the Marchioness of Carmarthen, Lady Conyers, whom after her divorce he married, and treated brutally, though, by her death, he lost her income of £4,000 a year.   She died in 1784, leaving a daughter, Augusta, who was an important factor in the poet's life.

Two years later he married Catherine Gordon of Gight, near Aberdeen, who had about £23,000 in her own right. She is described as " a dumpy young woman, with a large waist, florid complexion, and homely features," lacking even a common education, and subject to " frequent fits of uncontrollable fury."   Her father had committed suicide.

Captain Byron quickly ran through all but £3,000 of her small property, and three years after his son's birth· he begged a guinea from her and fled to France, where he died, possibly by suicide, at Valenciennes, August, r791.   Though Mrs. Byron had found it impossible to live with him, it is said that when she heard of his death she disturbed the neighborhood with her shrieks.   Byron claimed to have remembered his father, who, when living apart from his wife, used to waylay the child and play with him, and once took him home to his lodgings for the night.   He idealized the memory of " his sire " in a few pathetic lines in *Lara.*

Byron's childhood was spent in Aberdeen. Perhaps fortunate in being out of the influence of " Mad Jack," he was doubly unfortunate in his mother's management. Caresses of passionate violence often alternated with fierce blows.

He was lame from birth — not club-footed, but unable

to put his right foot flat upon the ground, owing to a painful malformation of the tendon of the heel. He had "to hop about like a bird." His mother used to chase him, trying to hit him with the poker. Once when she poured out her abuse upon him, she ended by calling him "a lame brat." His lips quivered, his face turned pale, his eyes flashed: then he replied: " I was born so, mother."

Curiously enough this unnatural mother, who boasted of the superior birth of her branch of the Gordons, vaunted herself a "democrat" and sympathized with the French people in their struggle with royalty. If the poet owed anything to her it was his abhorrence of tyranny, his generosity toward the poor and the oppressed.

To his nurse, Mary Gray, of whom he was fond, Byron owed his familiarity with the Bible and his strong bent toward Calvinism which survived all his doubts.

His secular education was not neglected. In his recollections of Scotland (written when he was twenty-six) he commemorates three pedagogues who, with more or less success, prepared him for the Aberdeen Grammar School. This he entered in 1794, and distinguished himself by being constantly at the foot of the class. His lameness prevented him from taking part in boyish games. He, therefore, instead of studying his lessons, amused himself by reading, and the list of works, particularly travels and descriptions of the East, which he had devoured before he was ten years old is remarkable. He remembered them, too, and the influence of some of them is directly traceable in his poetical works.

He was not able to take long walks, — his references to climbing the hills are apocryphal, — but he had a Shetland pony and thus "roamed the dusky wild."

While in Aberdeen he fell in love with his cousin, Mary Duff, a charming hazel-eyed, brown-haired little girl. This was a serious matter to the impressionable boy. The memory of it, eight years later, when he was sixteen, was so intense that the report of her unromantic marriage to an Edinburgh wine-merchant almost threw him into convulsions.

He dated his love for the mountains from a visit to Ballater in the Highlands, where his mother took him when he was a boy of ten recovering from the scarlet fever. The lesson of her frenzies was not lost upon him. In his recollections he declares that he did not specially differ from other children, being neither tall nor short, dull nor witty, but rather lively, except in his sullen moods, and then he was always a devil. Once at table he even threatened to kill himself with a knife which he snatched up in his fury.

In May, 1798, the family title devolved upon him from his great-uncle, "the wicked lord," who, though he knew that "the little boy at Aberdeen" was to be his successor, had never done anything to relieve his necessities. It is said that when the schoolmaster in calling the roll prefixed the Latin for lord before Byron's name, he was so affected that he was unable to respond, but burst into tears.

Mrs. Byron's income after her husband's death had not been sufficient to keep her out of debt. Even at its utmost it was only £190 a year. She sold her furniture

for a little less than £75, and went with the young lord
and his nurse to the ruined domain which, though
valued at £90,000, yielded less than two per cent, and
was in chancery. Surely a title given by the Stuarts,
and thus stripped of its material accessories, was little to
awaken pride.

Byron, in the thirteenth canto of *Don Juan*, thus
described the Norman Abbey:—

An old, old monastery once, and now
Still older mansion, — of a rich and rare
    Mixed Gothic, such as artists all allow
Few specimens yet left us can compare
    Withal: it lies perhaps a little low,
Because the monks preferred a hill behind,
To shelter their devotions from the wind.

LVI.

It stood embosomed in a happy valley,
    Crowned by high woodlands, where the Druid oak
Stood like Caractacus in act to rally
    His host, with broad arms 'gainst the thunder-stroke;
And from beneath his boughs were seen to sally
    The dappled foresters — as day awoke,
The branching stag swept down with all his herd,
To quaff a brook which murmured like a bird.

LVII.

Before the mansion lay a lucid lake,
    Broad as transparent, deep, and freshly fed
By a river, which its softened way did take
    In currents through the calmer water spread

Around : the wild fowl nestled in the brake
   And sedges, brooding in their liquid bed :
The woods sloped downwards to its brink, and stood
With their green faces fixed upon the flood.

LVIII.

Its outlet dashed into a deep cascade,
   Sparkling with foam, until again subsiding,
Its shriller echoes — like an infant made
   Quiet — sank into softer ripples, gliding
Into a rivulet ; and thus allayed,
   Pursued its course, now gleaming, and now hiding
Its windings through the woods ; now clear, now blue,
According as the skies their shadows threw.

LIX.

A glorious remnant of the Gothic pile
   (While yet the church was Rome's) stood half apart
In a grand arch, which once screened many an aisle.
   These last had disappeared — a loss to art :
The first yet frowned superbly o'er the soil,
   And kindled feelings in the roughest heart,
Which mourned the power of time's or tempest's march
In gazing on that venerable arch.

LX.

Within a niche, nigh to its pinnacle,
   Twelve saints had once stood sanctified in stone ;
But these had fallen, not when the friars fell,
   But in the war which struck Charles from his throne,
When each house was a fortalice — as tell
   The annals of full many a line undone, —
The gallant cavaliers who fought in vain
For those who knew not to resign or reign.

LXI.

But in a higher niche, alone, but crowned,
   The Virgin Mother of the God-born Child,
With her Son in her blessed arms, looked round,
   Spared by some chance when all beside was spoiled;
She made the earth below seem holy ground.
   This may be superstition, weak or wild,
But even the faintest relics of a shrine
Of any worship wake some thoughts divine

LXII.

A mighty window, hollow in the centre,
   Shorn of its glass of thousand colorings,
Through which the deepened glories once could enter,
   Streaming from off the sun like seraph's wings,
Now yawns all desolate : now loud, now fainter,
   The gale sweeps through its fretwork, and oft sings
The owl his anthem, where the silenced quire
Lie with their hallelujahs quenched like fire.

LXIII.

But in the noontide of the moon, and when
   The wind is wingèd from one point of heaven,
There moans a strange unearthly sound, which then
   Is musical — a dying accent driven
Through the huge arch, which soars and sinks again.
   Some deem it but the distant echo given
Back to the night wind by the waterfall,
And harmonized by the old choral wall :

LXIV.

Others, that some original shape, or form
   Shaped by decay, perchance, hath given the power
(Though less than that of Memnon's statue, warm
   In Egypt's rays, to harp at a fixed hour)

To this gray ruin, with a voice to charm ;
    Sad, but serene, it sweeps o'er tree or tower ;
The cause I know not, nor can solve ; but such
The fact : — I've heard it, — once perhaps too much.

LXV.

Amidst the court a Gothic fountain played,
    Symmetrical, but decked with carvings quaint —
Strange faces, like to men in masquerade,
    And here perhaps a monster, there a saint :
The spring gushed through grim mouths of granite made,
    And sparkled into basins, where it spent
Its little torrent in a thousand bubbles,
Like man's vain glory, and his vainer troubles.

LXVI.

The mansion's self was vast and venerable,
    With more of the monastic than has been
Elsewhere preserved : the cloisters still were stable,
    The cells, too, and refectory, I ween :
An exquisite small chapel had been able,
    Still unimpaired, to decorate the scene ;
The rest had been reformed, replaced, or sunk,
And spoke more of the baron than the monk.

But the " huge halls, long galleries, spacious cham
bers " were scarcely fit for habitation, and Mrs. Byron
took lodgings for a year in Nottingham. During this
time an unskilful surgeon attempted to remedy Byron's
lameness, but with only ill results. It is said that the
boy played a trick upon him by writing some gibberish
words and asking him what the language was. " Italian," replied the quack.

Byron continued his studies with a tutor named Rogers. One day Rogers, noticing that the boy was suffering from his foot, expressed his sympathy.

"Never mind, Mr. Rogers; you shan't see any signs of it again," was the answer.

The next year Mrs. Byron, who was granted a pension of three hundred pounds from the civil list, moved to London. Mary Gray, the nurse, returned to Scotland, and Byron, by the advice of his guardian and cousin, Earl Carlisle, was sent to Dr. Glennie's school at Dulwich. Mrs. Byron constantly interfered with his progress. Dr. Glennie appealed to Lord Carlisle, who remonstrated, but Mrs. Byron was so outrageous that the earl refused to have any more to do with her. Dr. Glennie declared that Mrs. Byron, besides being a total stranger to English society and manners, had a lack of understanding and a mind wholly without cultivation.

"Byron, your mother is a fool," exclaimed one of his schoolmates.

"I know it," was his reply.

He slept in the doctor's library and there browsed on an edition of the English poets from Chaucer to Churchill. He afterwards declared that he "first read Pope's Homer with a rapture which no subsequent work could ever afford."

During this time, when he was about twelve, he fell in love with another cousin, Margaret Parker, daughter of Admiral Parker, a girl with dark eyes, long eyelashes, a "completely Greek cast of face and figure," and an exquisite complexion. He declares that "she was one of the most beautiful of evanescent beings. . . . She looked as if she had been made out of a rainbow — all beauty and peace."

This passion was as real as his first. Moreover, it inspired him to song. Byron says, —

"My passion had its usual effect upon me. I could not sleep, I could not eat, I could not rest; and although I had reason to know that she loved me, it was the texture of my life to think of the time which must elapse before we could meet again, being usually about twelve hours of separation."

Margaret soon died of consumption, and Byron, when he learned of it, wrote an elegy in the style of Pope, beginning

"Hushed are the winds and still the evening gloom,"

which was printed in *Hours of Idleness*.

In the summer of 1801 Byron accompanied his mother to Cheltenham: he afterwards recalled the indescribable sensations with which he watched the Malvern Hills at sunset. Here his mother was alarmed by the words of a fortune-teller who predicted that the lame boy would be in danger from poison before he was of age, and would be twice married — the second time to a foreign lady.

The following autumn Byron was sent to Harrow, where he remained four years. He was at first under the charge of Dr. Joseph Drury, who assured Lord Carlisle that he had talents which would add lustre to his rank.

"Indeed," was the sceptical reply.

Byron stated in his journal that he hated Harrow till the last year and a half of his stay there. He also declared that at first he was a most unpopular boy. It is certain that he was unnaturally fat, inordinately conceited, yet shy, uncouth, quick-tempered, and still afflicted with a Scotch brogue. Miss Pigott called him a perfect " gaby;" Dr. Drury regarded him as a " wild mountain colt." The older boys fagged and tormented him till he at last reached the upper forms, when he stood forth characteristically as the champion of the oppressed.

When Dr. Drury retired in 1805, and was succeeded by Dr. Butler, the boys resented the change, and Byron was a ringleader in the pranks played. He helped tear down the window-gratings, but withstood a wild scheme to set one of the class-rooms on fire, arguing that it would burn up the desks on which their grandfathers had carved their initials. Many of his classmates — Peel, Palmerston, Bankes, Hobhouse, Tavistock — became famous. Byron made little progress in his studies at Harrow, but he was an able declaimer and gave promise of becoming an eloquent orator.

While still at Harrow he made the acquaintance of his half-sister, Augusta, plain and dowdyish, but womanly and pious, and destined to be " from first to last the chief influence for good in her brother's life."

In 1803 he spent his vacation at Nottingham. Lord Grey de Ruthen, the tenant of Newstead, gave him a standing invitation to the Abbey, and put a room at his disposal. He also frequently visited Annesley Hall, where lived his cousins, the Chaworths.

Mary Anne Chaworth — " the bright morning star of Annesley " — then about eighteen, was a beautiful girl.

Byron fell in love with her.   She unquestionably led him on, but she was already engaged to Mr. John Masters.   Her remark, "Do you think I could care anything for that lame boy?" was reported to him.,   Such wounds made in a boy's heart leave never-fading scars. The influence of this third grand passion remained all his life and colored his poetry: "The Dream," "Stanzas to a Lady," the "Epistle to a Friend," and other verses are full of that episode.   Byron declared that he took all his fables about the celestial nature of women from the perfection his imagination created in her.

Byron still spent his vacations with his mother, but quarrels between them were frequent and violent.   On one occasion each went to the apothecary and begged him not to sell the other poison.

He went to Trinity College, Cambridge, in October, 1805, where, as at Harrow, he paid more attention to his friendships than to his studies.   Here also most of his friends were of a social rank lower than his own: he was most intimate with Eddlestone, a member of the college choir, whom, according to his own statement, he "loved more than any human being."

He published his juvenile poems for private circulation in November, 1806; his *Hours of Idleness* appeared in March, 1807.   At that time he weighed over two hundred pounds, but he now began a system of banting which, while it succeeded in reducing his weight, also ruined his digestion.   By vapor baths, vinegar, and a restricted diet he thenceforward kept himself down to about one hundred and fifty pounds.   During his first terms at Cambridge he held aloof from general society, but after the publication of *Hours of Idleness* he began to indulge in the usual dissipations of a wealthy nobleman. He lived much in London, but he had expensive furnished apartments in Cambridge, gave dinners, kept dogs, a couple of saddle horses, and a coronetted carriage, a groom and a valet, and gambled recklessly, as he confessed, with " no coolness of judgment, or calculation."

By the time he was of age he was over ten thousand pounds in debt.

In anticipation of occupying Newstead he had a few rooms put in order for himself and Mrs. Byron. He spent the last month of his minority there, occasionally visited by the Brompton girl, whom, dressed in boy's attire, he introduced to his friends as his brother Gordon. He also entertained some of his Cambridge friends. An historical painter might find a congenial subject in depicting the dinner that Byron arranged when he dressed them all in monks' robes, and toasted them in Burgundy from a cup made out of a polished scull that had been dug up in the garden. The exaggerated rumor of such wild revels perhaps kept the gentry in the neighborhood from calling. The bear and wolf which he kept chained at the front entrance would not attract timid neighbors.

In spite of his pecuniary troubles, he, in the most delicate manner, gave £500 to the widow of the young Lord Falkland, who was killed in a duel with Mr. Powell, leaving his family destitute.

Meantime, *Hours of Idleness*, left to itself, would have sunk out of sight even though it attracted the attention of " her Grace of Gordon " and " the rest of the fashionable world," had it not been for the folly of

Brougham or Jeffrey, or some disgruntled Cambridge don who contributed to the *Edinburgh Review* a bitter criticism of the insignificant volume — what Byron called " a masterpiece of low wit, a tissue of scurrilous abuse.'' ''Never did a great poet,'' says the Honorable Roden Noel, ''produce an early volume that gave so little promise and contained so much doggerel, or weak, conventional, and bumptiously affected verse.'' But the review article lashed him to fury. He drank three bottles of claret at a sitting, and when he next tried his wings they had grown from those of a dove to those of an eagle or a hawk.

In 1809 he came of age, and celebrated it by dining on eggs, bacon, and a bottle of ale. An ox was roasted for the tenantry, and a ball was given, but the neighbors were conspicuous by their absence.

In March he took his seat in the House of Lords, but the Earl of Carlisle, to whom he had dedicated *Hours of Idleness*, instead of offering to introduce him, wrote a cool note telling him what formalities were requisite and necessary. Nor did the earl put himself out to help the poet find certain missing proof that his grandfather, Admiral Byron, had been legally married.

Thus Byron took his oaths as a peer of the realm, unattended by any sponsor, and, in the lonely bitterness of his heart he haughtily repulsed the congratulations of the chancellor, Lord Eldon.

A few days later appeared his satire *English Bards and Scotch Reviewers,* in which he not only paid off old scores, but went out of his way gratuitously to attack every living writer whether of note or not. He afterwards called it " a miserable record of misplaced anger and indiscriminate acrimony," and would have been glad to "suppress even the memory " of it.

The first edition, which appeared anonymously, was exhausted in a month. The second, revised and enlarged, bore his name, and he was apparently disappointed that it did not bring more challenges. Tom Moore, indeed, sent him a " cartel," but instead of a hostile meeting a lifelong friendship ensued.

His financial affairs were going from bad to worse. The Rochdale coal-mine property was burdened with a lawsuit that was not settled for years and was a constant expense: his outlays on Newstead were made with borrowed money ; his expenses were more than double his income, which indeed sufficed not even to pay the interest on his debts.

He was urged to sell Newstead, but his pride forbade. Having taken his honorary degree from Cambridge, he made his plans to go abroad, and to obtain the necessary funds he applied to money-lenders who charged him usurious interest on the risk. With three men-servants and a trunkful of costly clothes, including the "scarlet coat, richly embroidered with gold," which he wore at receptions, he sailed with his friend Hobhouse on the 2d of July, 1809.

At Lisbon, Byron, who even when at Harrow was a famous swimmer, and when at Cambridge had once won a wager by swimming three miles in the Thames, swam across to the old castle of Belem. From Lisbon the two friends rode on horseback through Spain to Cadiz, seeing all the sights and flirting with the gazelle-eyed Spanish ladies. From Spain Byron sailed to the east, taking in Sardinia, Sicily, Malta, Albania, Greece, Asia Minor, and Constantinople — seeing "part of Africa and Asia, and a tolerable portion of Europe," and hobnobbing with "generals and admirals, princes and pashas, governors and ungovernables."

On the morning of May 3, he swam from Sestos to Abydos in an hour and ten minutes. He had tried it the week before and failed. "The immediate distance," he wrote, "is not above a mile, but the current renders it hazardous, so much so that I doubt whether Leander's conjugal affection must not have been a little chilled in his passage to Paradise."

While in southern Greece he shot an eagle, and was so touched by its death that he vowed never to attempt the life of another bird. Hobhouse's notes, Trelawny's Recollections, and Byron's letters and poems give full accounts of his travels and adventures during his two years' absence. He had planned to visit Egypt, Persia, and India, but his funds ran out and he was obliged to return.

"Embarrassed in my private affairs," he wrote, "indifferent to public, solitary without the wish to be social, with a body enfeebled by a succession of fevers, but a spirit, I trust, yet unbroken, I am returning *home* without a hope, and almost without a desire."

His return to Newstead in 1811 was saddened by the sudden death of his mother. Several of his most intimate friends also died about the same time. "Some curse hangs over me and mine," he wrote: "my mother lies a corpse in this house; one of my best friends is drowned in a ditch. '

Under the influence of these melancholy events he made his will, directing that he should be buried without religious ceremony, with his dog Boatswain. He left £7,000 to a Greek boy to whom he had taken a fancy at Athens.

In February of the next year he made his first speech in the House of Lords, and was warmly congratulated. Two days later, John Murray published the first two cantos of *Childe Harold's Pilgrimage*. Byron had presented the manuscript to his friend and relative, Dallas, who made one or two unsuccessful attempts to dispose of it. Murray saw its merit, and brought out an edition of five thousand copies.

" I awoke one morning," wrote Byron, "and found myself famous."

The edition in demi-quarto was exhausted in three days. Three thousand copies of the second and third editions were quickly sold. Mr. Murray paid £600 for the copyright. It brought him a fortune. But Byron at that time refused to touch the money he had earned. " I will never receive money for my writings," he said to Dallas. Afterwards he perceived that this was insensate folly, born of pride, and was sharp enough in claiming guineas instead of pounds, for the sake of the extra shilling. Half in jest, half-serious, he began the twelfth canto of *Don Juan* with a panegyric on miserliness:—

> Love or lust makes man sick, and wine much sicker ;
>   Ambition rends, and gaming gains a loss ;
> But making money, slowly first, then quicker,
>   And adding still a little through each cross

(Which *will* come over things), beats love or liquor,
   The gamester's counter, or the statesman's *dross.*
O Gold! I still prefer thee unto paper
Which makes bank credit like a bark of vapor.

" Love rules the camp, the court, the grove," — "for love
   Is heaven, and heaven is love : " — so sings the bard,
Which it were rather difficult to prove
   (A thing with poetry in general hard).
Perhaps there may be something in " the grove,"
   At least it rhymes to " love : " but I 'm prepared
To doubt (no less than landlords of their rental)
If " courts " and " camps " be quite so sentimental.

But if Love don't, *Cash* does, and Cash alone :
   Cash rules the grove, and fells it too besides ;
Without cash, camps were thin, and courts were none ;
   Without cash, Malthus tells you — take no brides."
So Cash rules Love the ruler, on his own
   High ground, as virgin Cynthia sways the tides :
And as for " Heaven being Love," why not say honey
Is wax ? Heaven is not Love, 't is Matrimony.

Lord Byron immediately became the lion of London.
Even those whom he had lampooned in his satire desired
to make his acquaintance. He was invited everywhere,
and made a member of a dozen clubs. The Prince
Regent wished to talk with him. Women in the highest
society fell in love with him, for if his regimen of soda
water, vinegar, and crackers had spoiled his digestion, it
had given him a complexion of transparent poetic pallor,
and reduced his flesh so his face had delicate and beautiful lines. His marble brow, his brown curly hair, his
gray eyes, shaded by long black lashes, his beautiful

mobile mouth, with small white teeth, his fascinating chin, small, shapely hands, rich, musical voice, and irreproachable manners atoned for his rather thick and artificial-looking nose and his lameness. In public he was cold and reserved; in private, impetuous, confidential, irresistible.

The story of Lady Caroline Lamb's infatuation for him is only a type of the temptations to which he was subjected.

In October, 1812, he wrote to Mr. Murray: "I have a poem on Waltzing, of which I make you a present." Murray did not think highly of it, but published it anonymously. It was not well received; whereupon Byron wrote:—

"I hear that a certain malicious publication on Waltzing is attributed to me. This report, I suppose, you will take care to contradict, as the author, I am sure, will not like that I should wear his cap and bells!"

In May, 1813, appeared *The Giaour*. While correcting the proofs of the fifth edition, he wrote in four nights *The Bride of Abydos*. Murray paid one thousand guineas for the two and for a few miscellaneous poems. Byron thought it too much for a fortnight's lucubrations. Six thousand copies of the *Bride* were sold in less than a month. *The Corsair*, written at the rate of two hundred lines a day, between Dec. 18 and 31, was published in February, 1814. Byron gave Mr. Dallas the copyright of this poem, which brought five hundred guineas. Ten thousand copies were sold on the day of publication.

While the work was in press he added the *Stanzas*

on a Lady Weeping which had been published anonymously before his conversation with the Prince
Regent whom they lampooned. His acknowledgment
of their paternity brought upon him the bitterest attacks
from the newspapers. It was even asserted that he
received large sums of money for his writings, which
was an insult equivalent to saying that he was in trade;
and in his galled pride, he allowed Mr. Dallas publicly
to attest that no money from the sale of his poems had
" ever touched his Lordship's hands or been disposed of
for his use ! "

His *Ode to Napoleon Buonaparte* appeared in April,
1814, and was a comparative failure. Byron was so
cut up by the criticisms it called forth that he deter-
mined to buy back his copyrights and suppress every
line of his works. He assigned to Murray as a reason
only his own caprice, but his publisher's protest availed
to make him relent.

Lara was published early in the following August,
and by the 29th had sold six thousand copies. For this
Murray paid five hundred guineas.

Byron, who had been expecting to sell Newstead for
£140,000, about this time regained it together with a
forfeit of £25,000. This ready money did not suffice to
pay his debts. · In September, 1814, he was in London.
Murray saw him and thus reported the interview : —

" Says he : ' Can you keep a secret ? '

" ' Certainly — positively — my wife is out of town.'

" ' Then — I am going to be MARRIED ! '

" ' The devil ! I shall have no poem this winter then ?

" ' No.'

" ' Who is the lady wh_ is to do me this injury?'

" ' Miss Milbanke.' "

Anne Isabella was the only daughter of Sir Ralph Milbanke. She had a fortune of £10,000 and expectations of seven or eight thousand a year from her uncle, Viscount Wentworth. Byron on his marriage gave her £60,000. It was certainly not a brilliant marriage, though the lady was good-looking, a clever mathematician, a poet, and versed in French, Latin, Italian, and Greek, and was regarded as a paragon of virtue.

There is no doubt Byron was in love with her or thought that he was. The marriage took place Jan. 2, 1815, and as the carriage drove away Lady Byron's words to Hobhouse were, "If I am not happy it will be my own fault."

At first they were happy. Byron wrote to Moore just a month later:—

"The treacle-moon is over and I am awake and find myself married. My spouse and I agree to admiration. . . . I still think one ought to marry upon *lease;* but I am very sure I should renew mine at the expiration, though next term were ninety and nine years."

Byron called his wife "Pippin;" she called him "Duck;" his sister, who called him "Baby," they both called "Goose." It seemed like a happy family.

Lord Wentworth died in April and left the bulk of his property to his sister, to revert on her death to Lady Byron. This did not bring any relief to Lord Byron. During the few months that they lived in London (March 18, 1815,–Jan. 15, 1816) there were nine execution upon them for debt. And yet they lived economically.

Lady Caroline Lamb was Lady Byron's cousin. His renewed intimacy with her at Melbourne house began to be a cause of anxiety. Byron was a great joker, and often his " chaff " was coarse and ungentlemanly. Lady Byron was intensely practical and could not see a joke.

Just before the daughter Ada was born Byron undoubtedly treated his wife with positive unkindness. She was not the only one who thought that he might be insane. When she once asked him if she were in his way, he replied, " Damnably." He more than once " breathed the breath of bitter words." Even if his statement that he married her out of revenge for her having once refused him were a jest, it was a cruel one. Once when pressed for money he flung his watch on the hearth and smashed it with a poker.

He chewed tobacco and partook copiously of opium to soothe the pangs of his outraged stomach: he was suffering from jaundice and his mind was evidently in a highly overwrought state.

But the doctors whom she engaged to investigate his state reported that he was sane. Lady Byron's former governess, Mrs. Clermon, known now as the Mischief-maker, broke into Byron's private desk and found some compromising letters written to a married lady before his marriage.

Lady Byron felt justified in leaving her husband. The decision was made known to him Feb. 2, 1816. He at first refused to sign the private agreement, and only consented when it was threatened that the case would be taken into court.

About this time, Jane Clairmont, a step-daughter of William Godwin, applied at Drury Lane Theatre for a position as an actress. Byron, who was on the so-called Board of Mis-management, took a fancy to her. She become the mother of his favorite natural daughter, Allegra.

The scandal of the separation brought down upon Lord Byron a perfect storm of calumnies. Such storms sour the milk of human kindness.

He was advised not to go to the House of Lords lest he should be mobbed. "I was accused," he wrote, "of every monstrous vice by public rumor and private ran-cor. . . . I felt that if what was whispered and mut-tered and murmured was true, I was unfit for England; if false, England was unfit for me."

As for the reasons for their separation Byron later declared that they were "too simple to be found out." It is certain that Lady Byron kept up her friendship with Augusta Leigh until 1830, so that the story circu-lated by Mrs. Stowe seems to be effectually disproved.

The turning of English society against Lord Byron was one of the most curious phenomena of history. But the explanation is not far to seek. Byron painted a portrait in the blackest colors. The world believed that he himself was the model, and accepted the likeness in spite of his disclaimer. The men of his own order hated him because he did not lead their life. Politically he was dangerous; he had outraged the religious suscepti-bilities of the English Philistines. He became the scapegoat of the nobility — attacked by all classes.

Lady Caroline Lamb wrote a novel showing under a

thin disguise how he treated ladies who compromisec themselves for his sake.

Jus. before he left England, Lady Jersey braved public opinion and gave a party in his honor. Even there he was snubbed and avoided.

He left England, April 25, 1816, never to return. Near Geneva he met Shelley, who, having deserted his wife, was travelling with the brilliant Mary Wollstone- craft Godwin who had already taken his name. Her step-sister, Jane Clairmont, was with them. However subversive of morals such a combination may have been, it was favorable to poetry. During the sojourn on the Swiss lake, Byron wrote much of the third canto of *Childe Harold*, *The Prisoner of Chillon*, and other poems ; Shelley read and meditated ; " Mrs." Shelley produced her tremendous story of *Frankenstein*.

The English tourists, who deliberately cut the poets and their loves, gratified their curiosity by spying upon them through telescopes. All sorts of monstrous stories were reported. Doubtless Byron with his *penchant* for making himself out worse than he was, deliberately contributed to the scandal.

Madame de Staël (who after reading his farewell lines had exclaimed, "How gladly would I have been un- happy in Lady Byron's place ! ") was living at Coppet. Byron went to call upon her. A lady novelist " of mature virtue and maturer years " fainted at the announce- ment of his presence !

In Switzerland Byron tried to arrange for a reconcilia- tion with his wife. She refused it. After that his feel- ings toward her changed to bitterness, and he wrote number of savage lines which would better have been left unwritten. Here also he composed parts of *Manfred, Prometheus,* and other poems inspired by the Alps and showing the influence of Wordsworth and possibly that of Goethe. He now began to take pay for his writings. Between 1816 and 1821 Murray paid him over twelve thousand pounds. For the third and fourth cantos of *Childe Harold* he received £3,675, equivalent probably at the present time to nearly $25,000.

In October, 1816, Byron went down to Italy and settled in Venice.

Old Roger Ascham says of Italy: —

"*She is able to turne a saint into a devil and deprave the best natures, if one will abandon himselfe and become a prey to dissolute courses and wantonesse.*"

There is an old proverb, "An italianate Inglischyeman is an Incarnate Devil." Byron for a time at least proved the truth of this proverb.

It seemed as if he wanted to commit a sort of lingering suicide. A weary, homesick, conscience-stricken exile, he exhausted his strength by low debaucheries. Hitherto, for the most part, abstemious and temperate, he now became a glutton, and imbibed quantities of brandy. His propensity to corpulency returned upon him. At the same time he was troubled with malaria and sleeplessness. His palace was filled with lewd revellers. One of his mistresses was the wife of a gondolier — scarcely more cultured than a fishwife.

This wretched, prodigal life lasted till early in 1819, when he suddenly began to have better thoughts. He wrote Tom Moore: "I was obliged to reform my 'way

of life ' which was conducting me from the ' yellow leaf '
to the ground with all deliberate speed.   I am better in
health and morals.''

At Venice he wrote *Beppo, Mazeppa,* and the early
cantos of *Don Juan.*   The Venetians called him
'' the English fish,'' and declared that he '' dived for his
poetry ''!   They had good reason: one day he swam
from the Lido to the farther end of the grand canal,
being four hours and twenty minutes in the water without
touching bottom.   His income about this time amounted
to about £4,000 a year: he gave away a quarter of it in
charity.   Many who regularly received his benefactions
never knew from whom they came.   Though so cynical
— and with good reason — Byron was remarkably kind
to every one.   His servants adored him.

At a reception at the Countess Benzoni's in April,
1819, Byron was presented to the sixteen-year-old wife
of Count Guiccioli — a pretty blonde with fair skin and
yellow hair.   Her husband was about four times as old
as she, and very rich.

Byron became her *cicisbeo* or legalized lover.   This
curious state of things was peculiar to Italy: the *marriage
de convenance* demanded a correction in some acknowledgment of human nature.   The lady with a husband whom
she did not love had a *cavalier servente* whom she did
love.

Byron wrote to Mr. Murray : —

'' Their system has its rules and its fitnesses and its
decorums, so as to be reduced to a kind of discipline or
game at hearts, which admits few deviations, unless
you wish to lose it. . . . They transfer marriage to adul-

tery and strike the *not* out of that commandment. The reason is that they marry for their parents and love for themselves."

Byron prefaced this explanation by declaring that the Englishman could not appreciate such an order of things. "Their moral is not your moral, their life is not your life ; you would not understand it." Byron himself at first found it hard to understand it. The count came to call upon him and took him out to drive in his coach and six. He showed no jealousy when the countess accompanied Byron on an excursion that lasted several days. He tried to borrow money of him. He even lodged him at his palace at Ravenna, and made him pay dear for the privilege. Byron was warned that the count might cause him to be assassinated, and for some time he went armed.

After a sudden fit of propriety, in which the husband demanded that there should be no more communication between the lady and her lover, the lady fell ill. Then even her father begged Byron to hasten to her side; the count became complaisant again and remained so till July, 1820, when the Pope, at the solicitation of herself and friends, pronounced a separation beween the husband and wife.

Byron had made the count's house a headquarters for the revolutionary movement. When the Carbonari insurrection was supressed, several of the countess's family were involved. The Gambas were banished from the Romagna, and took refuge first in Florence, then in Pisa.

Byron joined them there in November, 1882. Shelley wrote about this time :—

"He has completely recovered his health, and lives a life totally the reverse of that which he led in Venice. . . . Poor fellow! he is completely immersed in politics and literature . . . is greatly improved in every respect, in genius, in temper, in moral views, in health and happiness. His connection with La Guiccioli has been an inestimable benefit to him."

With all respect to Shelley, we may doubt if his judgment on such a point be accepted as correct. Still the countess doubtless caused him to modify *Don Juan* for the better. It was during these months that he wrote his dramatic works.

Byron had found an object in life. Disappointed in not having succeeded in home politics, he knew that he was meant for public affairs. He threw himself into the popular cause of Italy. He foresaw what it would be if freed and unified. But at that time it was still only a dream. The Austrian monster with its two heads still held the country in its gripe.

Byron spent almost a year in Pisa. While there he received a letter from an English clergyman informing him of a prayer for his conversion offered by his recently deceased wife. Byron replied: "I would not exchange the prayer of this pure and virtuous being in my behalf for the united glory of Homer, Cæsar, and Napoleon."

While there he also wrote the pathetic letter to his wife asking reconciliation on account of their daughter. It was never sent. The daughter Ada was growing up in utter ignorance of her father. Only a few weeks before her death in 1852, she read her father's poems and learned how she whom he had never seen had been the very idol of his heart. Then she asked to be buried near him. This seems the most touching thing in the whole sad story.

Leigh Hunt came to Pisa, and was Byron's pensioner, afterwards repaying his generosity by scurrilous abuse. He and Byron entered into a sort of literary partnership; they established the *Liberal*, to which Byron contributed *The Vision of Judgment* and a few other poems. It was not a successful venture.

During the summer of 1822 Shelley was drowned in the Gulf of Spezzia. Byron was present at the cremation of the body, and after it was over was seized with a strange delirious hilarity. He afterwards wrote that perhaps the world which had been ill-naturedly, ignorantly, and brutally mistaken about Shelley, would now, when it was too late, do him justice. This same summer his natural daughter Allegra, whom he was bringing up in the Roman Catholic faith, died.

In July the Gambas were exiled from Pisa, and Byron went with them to Genoa, where he wrote two of the last extant cantos of *Don Juan*. Cantos six to eleven were written at Pisa. At this time Lady Blessington, who saw much of him, thus described his appearance:—

"One of Byron's eyes was larger than the other; his nose was rather thick, so he was best seen in profile; his mouth was splendid, and his scornful expression was real, not affected, but a sweet smile often broke through his melancholy. He was at this time very pale and thin. His hair was dark brown, here and there turning to gray. His voice was harmonious, clear, and low."

The war of Greece against Turkey had been going on for two years. Byron's attention was drawn to it. He threw himself into the noble cause with the greatest ardor. He was perhaps tired of his shallow Italian mistress, with whom he had thought of emigrating to America. He longed for action. Newstead had been sold, and after paying Lady Byron her share (which she took without scruple), he had a small fortune remaining. In 1822 his mother-*at*-law (as he called his wife's mother) died, and he, without any scruple, added the Wentworth name of Noel to his own, and took his half of the estate. This gave him enough ready money to enable him to go to Greece in the guise of a general paymaster.

He hired the brig Hercules, and, accompanied by Trelawny, Count Pietro Gamba (La Guiccioli's brother, who had conceived a strong affection for him), and several servants, he embarked for Greece, July 14, 1822. On board he had two small cannon and other arms, five horses, medicines, and $50,000 in Spanish coin.

Coming in sight of the Morea, he remarked that it seemed to him as if the eleven long years of bitterness which he had just passed through were taken from his shoulders.

Byron's services in the Greek campaign were quickly cut short by his illness at Mesolonghi. But in the few weeks of his presence he displayed remarkable sagacity and wisdom in dealing with refractory elements. He saw that united action was necessary, and he bent all his energies to bringing about peace between rival factions.

He spent his money with liberality but with diplomacy. If he had lived to see the success of Greece, he would-not unlikely have been offered the throne.

He was made archistrategos of the turbulent Suliotes, whose favor he won by his skill with the pistol, and was about to undertake an expedition against Lepanto when he was seized with a fit. He had been living too abstemiously on toast, vegetables, and cheese. The doctors still further weakened him by bleeding.

Mesolonghi was situated on a malarial swamp. Byron was always subject to attacks of fever. He was now doomed. Before he could attend the Greek Congress as commissioner of the long-delayed but at last granted English loan, in April, 1824, he was on his death-bed.

He tried to intrust certain messages to Fletcher, his body servant, but his voice had failed. After many pathetic mutterings showing his love for his daughter, his last words were, " Now I shall go to sleep."

He died at quarter past six on the evening of April 19, 1824, during a terrific thunder-storm. Princely honors were paid him. The Greeks desired him to be buried in the temple of Theseus at Athens, but his friends wished him to be placed in Westminster Abbey.

This was not allowed by the dean; and Byron now rests in the church of his ancestors at Hucknall.

Such was the stormy life of Lord Byron, so magnificently ending, —

> " A man of many thoughts,
> And deeds of good and ill, extreme in both,
> Fatal and fated in his sufferings."

It is a tremendous lesson of the importance of character. Inheritance and education may handicap, but man's will can overcome. The ready words of censure are modified when one reads of the temptations, the environment, and the final outcome. The sin bore its own punishment. We may only look on and learn and at the last admire. Even his poems show his growth. So ill-educated that he thought Helicon was a spring and pronounced camelopard as though it were camel-leopard, that he could endure false rhymes and false quantities, still he wrote an enduring mass of noble verse which the world will always treasure.

"I am like the tiger," he wrote; "if I miss the first spring, I go grumbling back to my jungle again, but if I do hit, it is crushing."

His greatest failings were sensuality, which came by inheritance, selfishness uncorrected by his training, and vanity stimulated by the capricious treatment of him by the world. His generosity, tenderness of feeling, and public spirit were compensating virtues. He might have died a victim to his worse passions. It was ordained that he should perish a sacrifice to the land which he loved even better than his native land. Thus the blaze of his glory throws into shadow the sad mistakes which made his career so unenviable. Full of contradictions, the warring elements of his nature seem to personify the fabled eternal strife between Ormuzd and Ahriman.

It it a beautiful thought that here as always the highei at last is victorious over the lower, light over darkness.

NATHAN HASKELL DOLE.

CHRONOLOGICAL LIST OF BYRON'S POEMS.

Fugitive Pieces (suppressed), 1806.
Poems on Various Occasions, 1807.
Hours of Idleness, 1807.
English Bards and Scotch Reviewers, 1809.
Childe Harold's Pilgrimage,
      Cantos i., ii., 1812.
           iii., 1816.
           iv., 1818.
Curse of Minerva, 1812.
Waltz, 1813.
The Giaour, 1813.
The Bride of Abydos, 1813.
The Corsair, 1814.
Ode to Napoleon Buonaparte, 1814.
Lara, 1814.
Hebrew Melodies, 1815.
Siege of Corinth and Parisina, 1816.
Poems on his Domestic Circumstances, 1816.
The Prisoner of Chillon, 1816.
Monody on the Death of Sheridan, 1816.
Manfred, 1817.
The Lament of Tasso, 1817.

Beppo, 1818.

Mazeppa, 1819.

Don Juan, i. ii., 1819.

        iii., iv., v., 1821.

        vi., vii., viii., 1823.

        ix., x., xi., 1823.

        xii., xiii., xiv., 1823.

        xv., xvi., 1824.

Marino Faliero and Prophecy of Dante, 1821.

Sardanapalus; The Two Foscari; Cain, 1821.

Letter on the Rev. W. L. Bowles's Strictures on Pope, 1821.

The Vision of Judgment, 1822.

Morganti Maggiore, 1823.

Werner; The Age of Bronze, 1823.

The Island, 1824.

The Deformed Transformed; Parliamentary Speeches, 1824.

PREFACE.

WHEN at last I held in my hand the volume of poems which I had chosen from Wordsworth, and began to turn over its pages, there arose in me almost immediately the desire to see beside it, as a companion volume, a like collection of the best poetry of Byron. Alone amongst our poets of the earlier part of this century, Byron and Wordsworth not only furnish material enough for a volume of this kind, but, also, as it seems to me, they both of them gain considerably by being thus exhibited. There are poems of Coleridge and of Keats equal, if not superior, to anything of Byron or Wordsworth; but a dozen pages or two will contain them, and the remaining poetry is of a quality much inferior. Scott never, I think, rises as a poet to the level of Byron and Wordsworth at all. On the other hand, he never falls below his own usual level very far; and by a volume of selections from him, therefore, his effectiveness is not increased. As to Shelley there will be more question; and indeed Mr. Stopford Brooke, whose accomplishments, eloquence, and love of poetry we must all recognize and admire, has actually given us Shelley in such a volume. But for my own part I cannot think that Shelley's poetry, except by snatches and fragments, has the value of the good work of Wordsworth and Byron; or that it is possible for even Mr. Stopford Brooke to make up a volume of selections from him which, for real substance, power, and worth, can at all take rank with a like volume from Byron or Wordsworth.

Shelley knew quite well the difference between the achievement of such a poet as Byron and his own. He praises Byron too unreservedly, but he sincerely felt, and he was right in feeling, that Byron was a greater poetical power than himself. As a man, Shelley is at a number of points immeasurably Byron's superior; he is a beautiful and enchanting spirit, whose vision when we call it up, has far more loveliness, more charm for our soul, than the vision of Byron. But all the personal charm of Shelley cannot hinder us from at last discovering in his poetry the incurable want, in general, of a sound subject-matter, and the incurable fault, in consequence, of unsubstantiality. Those who extol him as the poet of clouds, the poet of sunsets, are only saying that he did not, in fact, lay hold upon the poet's right subject-matter; and in honest truth, with all his charm of soul and spirit, and with all his gift of musical diction and movement, he never or hardly ever, did. Except, as I have said, for a few short things and single stanzas, his original poetry is less satisfactory than his translations, for in these the subject-matter was found for him. Nay, I doubt whether his delightful Essays and Letters, which deserve to be far more read than they are now, will not resist the wear and tear of time better, and finally come to stand higher than his poetry.

There remain to be considered Byron and Wordsworth.

That Wordsworth affords good material for a volume of
selections, and that he gains by having his poetry thus
presented, is an old belief of mine which led me lately to
make up a volume of poems chosen out of Wordsworth,
and to bring it before the public.   By its kind reception
of the volume, the public seems to show itself a partaker
in my belief.   Now Byron, also, supplies plenty of
material for a like volume, and he too gains, I think, by
being so presented.   Mr. Swinburne urges, indeed, that
" Byron, who rarely wrote anything either worthless or
faultless, can only be judged or appreciated in the mass;
the greatest of his works was his whole work taken
together."   It is quite true that Byron rarely wrote anything either worthless or faultless; it is quite true, also,
that in the appreciation of Byron's power a sense of the
amount and variety of his work, defective though much
of his work is, enters justly into our estimate.   But
although there may be little in Byron's poetry which can
be pronounced either worthless or faultless, there are
portions of it which are far higher in worth and far more
free from fault than others.   And although, again, the
abundance and variety of his production is undoubtedly
a proof of his power, yet I question whether by reading
everything which he gives us we are so likely to acquire
an admiring sense even of his variety and abundance, as
by reading what he gives us at his happier moments.
Varied and abundant he amply proves himself even by
this taken alone.   Receive him absolutely without omis-
sion or compression, follow his whole outpouring stanza
by stanza and line by line from the very commencement
to the very end, and he is capable of being tiresome.

Byron has told us himself that the *Giaour* "is but a string of passages." He has made full confession of his own negligence. "No one," says he, "has done more through negligence to corrupt the language." This accusation brought by himself against his poems is not just; but when he goes on to say of them, that "their faults, whatever they may be, are those of negligence and not of labor," he says what is perfectly true. "*Lara*," he declares, "I wrote while undressing after coming home from balls and masquerades, in the year of revelry, 1814. The *Bride* was written in four, the *Corsair* in ten days." He calls this "a humiliating confession, as it proves my own want of judgment in publishing, and the public's in reading, things which cannot have stamina for permanence." Again he does his poems injustice; the producer of such poems could not but publish them, the public could not but read them. Nor could Byron have produced his work in any other fashion; his poetic work could not have first grown and matured in his own mind, and then come forth as an organic whole; Byron had not enough of the artist in him for this, nor enough of self-command. He wrote, as he truly tells us, to relieve himself, and he went on writing because he found the relief become indispensable. But it was inevitable that works so produced should be, in general, "a string of passages," poured out, as he describes them, with rapidity and excitement, and with new passages constantly suggesting themselves, and added while his work was going through the press. It is evident that we have here neither deliberate scientific construction, nor yet the instinctive artistic creation of poetic wholes; and that to take passages from work produced as Byron's was is a very different thing from taking passages out of the *Œdipus* or the *Tempest*, and deprives the poetry far less of its advantage.

Nay, it gives advantage to the poetry, instead of depriving it of any. Byron, I said, has not a great artist's profound and patient skill in combining an action or in developing a character, — a skill which we must watch and follow if we are to do justice to it. But he has a wonderful power of vividly conceiving a single incident, a single situation; of throwing himself upon it, grasping it as if it were real and he saw and felt it, and of making us see and feel it too. The *Giaour* is, as he truly called it, "a string of passages," not a work moving by a deep internal law of development to a necessary end; and our total impression from it cannot but receive from this, its inherent defect, a certain dimness and indistinctness. But the incidents of the journey and death of Hassan, in that poem, are conceived and presented with a vividness not to be surpassed; and our impression from them is correspondingly clear and powerful. In *Lara*, again, there is no adequate developement either of the character of the chief personage or of the action of the poem; our total impression from the work is a confused one. Yet such an incident as the disposal of the slain Ezzelin's body passes before our eyes as if we actually saw it. And in the same way as these bursts of incident, bursts of sentiment also, living and vigorous, often occur in the midst of poems which must be admitted to be weakly conceived and loosely combined wholes. Byron cannot but be a gainer by having attention concentrated upon what is vivid, powerful, effective in his work, and with-drawn from what is not so.

Byron, I say, cannot but be a gainer by this, just as Wordsworth is a gainer by a like proceeding. I esteem Wordsworth's poetry so highly, and the world, in my opinion, has done it such scant justice, that I could not rest satisfied until I had fulfilled, on Wordsworth's be-half, a long-cherished desire; — had disengaged, to the best of my power, his good work from the inferior work joined with it, and had placed before the public the body of his good work by itself. To the poetry of Byron the world has ardently paid homage; full justice from his contemporaries, perhaps even more than justice, his torrent of poetry received. His poetry was admired, adored, " with all its imperfections on its head," — in spite of negligence, in spite of diffuseness, in spite of repetitions, in spite of whatever faults it possessed. His name is still great and brilliant. Nevertheless the hour of irresistible vogue has passed away for him; even for Byron it could not but pass away. The time has come for him, as it comes for all poets, when he must take his real and permanent place, no longer depending upon the vogue of his own day and upon the enthusi-asm of his contemporaries. Whatever we may think of him, we shall not be subjugated by him as they were ; for, as he cannot be for us what he was for them, we cannot admire him so hotly and indiscriminately as they. His faults of negligence, of diffuseness, of repetition, his faults of whatever kind, we shall abundantly feel and unsparingly criticise ; the mere interval of time between us and him makes disillusion of this kind

inevitable. But how then will Byron stand, if we relieve him too, so far as we can, of the encumbrance of
his inferior and weakest work, and if we bring before us
his best and strongest work in one body together? That
is the question which I, who can even remember the
latter years of Byron's vogue, and have myself felt the
expiring wave of that mighty influence, but who certainly also regard him, and have long regarded him,
without illusion, cannot but ask myself, cannot but seek
to answer. The present volume is an attempt to pro-
vide adequate data for answering it.

Byron has been over-praised, no doubt. "Byron is
one of our French superstitions," says M. Edmond
Scherer; but where has Byron not been a superstition?
He pays now the penalty of this exaggerated worship.
"Alone among the English poets his contemporaries
Byron," said M. Taine, "*atteint à la cîme*, — gets to
the top of the poetic mountain." But the idol that M.
Taine had thus adored M. Scherer is almost for burning.
"In Byron," he declares, "there is a remarkable
inability ever to lift himself into the region of real
poetic art — art impersonal and disinterested — at all.
He has fecundity, eloquence, wit, but even these qualities themselves are confined within somewhat narrow
limits. He has treated hardly any subject but one, —
himself; now the man, in Byron, is of a nature even
less sincere than the poet. This beautiful and blighted
being is at bottom a coxcomb. He posed all his life
long."

Our poet could not well meet with more severe and
unsympathetic criticism. However, the praise often

given to Byron has been so exaggerated as to provoke, perhaps, a reaction in which he is unduly disparaged. "As various in composition as Shakspeare himself, Lord Byron has embraced," says Sir Walter Scott, "every topic of human life, and sounded every string on the divine harp, from its slightest to its most powerful and heart-astounding tones." It is not surprising that some one with a cool head should retaliate, on such provocation as this, by saying: "He has treated hardly any subject but one, *himself.*" "In the very grand and tremendous drama of *Cain,*" says Scott, "Lord Byron has certainly matched Milton on his own ground." And Lord Byron has done all this, Scott adds, "while managing his pen with the careless and negligent ease of a man of quality." Alas, "managing his pen with the careless and negligent ease of a man of quality," Byron wrote in his *Cain :*

> " Souls that dare look the Omnipotent tyrant in
> His everlasting face, and tell him that
> His evil is not good ; "

or he wrote:

> " . . . And *thou* would'st go on aspiring
> To the great double Mysteries ! the *two Principles !* "[1]

One has only to repeat to one's self a line from *Paradise Lost* in order to feel the difference.

Sainte-Beuve, speaking of that exquisite master of language, the Italian poet Leopardi, remarks how often we see the alliance, singular though it may at first sight

---

[1] The italics are in the original.

appear, of the poetical genius with the genius for scholar-
ship and philology.   Dante and Milton are instances
which will occur to every one's mind.   Byron is so negligent in his poetical style, he is often, to say the truth,
so slovenly, slipshod, and infelicitous, he is so little
haunted by the true artist's fine passion for the correct
use and consummate management of words, that he
may be described as having for this artistic gift the
insensibility of the barbarian;—which is perhaps only
another and a less flattering way of saying, with Scott,
that he "manages his pen with the careless and negligent ease of a man of quality."   Just of a piece with
the rhythm of

> " Dare you await the event of a few minutes'
>   Deliberation ? "

or of

> " All shall be void —
>   Destroy'd ! "

is the diction of

> " Which now is painful to these eyes,
>   Which have not seen the sun to rise ; "

or of

> ".   .   .   .   there let him lay ! "

or of the famous passage beginning

> " He who hath bent him o'er the dead ; "

with those trailing relatives, that crying grammatical
solecism, that inextricable anacolouthon !   To class the

work of the author of such things with the work of the
authors of such verse as

> " In the dark backward and abysm of time " —

or as

> " Presenting Thebes, or Pelops' line,
> Or the tale of Troy divine " —

is ridiculous. Shakspeare and Milton, with their
secret of consummate felicity in diction and movement,
are of another and an altogether higher order from
Byron, nay, for that matter, from Wordsworth also;
from the author of such verse as

> " Sol hath dropt into his harbor " —

or (if Mr. Ruskin pleases) as

> " Parching summer hath no warrant " —

as from the author of

> " All shall be void —
> Destroy'd ! "

With a poetical gift and a poetical performance of the
very highest order, the slovenliness and tunelessness of
much of Byron's production, the pompousness and pon-
derousness of much of Wordsworth's, are incompatible.
Let us admit this to the full.

Moreover, while we are hearkening to M. Scherer, and
going along with him in his fault-finding, let us admit, it,
too, that the man in Byron is in many respects as unsat-
isfactory as the poet. And, putting aside all direct
moral criticism of him, — with which we need not concern ourselves here, — we shall find that he is unsatis-
factory in the same way. Some of Byron's most crying

faults as a man — his vulgarity, his affectation — are really akin to the faults of commonness, of want of art, in his workmanship as a poet. The ideal nature for the poet and artist is that of the finely touched and finely gifted man, the εὐφυής of the Greeks; now, Byron's nature was in substance not that of the εὐφυής at all, but rather, as I have said, of the barbarian. The want of fine perception which made it possible for him to formulate either the comparison between himself and Rousseau, or his reason for getting Lord Delawarr excused from a "licking" at Harrow, is exactly what made possible for him, also, his terrible dealings in, *An ye wool; I have redde thee; Sunburn me; Oons, and it is excellent well.* It is exactly, again, what made possible for him his precious dictum that Pope is a Greek temple, and a string of other criticisms of the like force; it is exactly, in fine, what deteriorated the quality of his poetic production. If we think of a good representative of that finely touched and exquisitely gifted nature which is the ideal nature for the poet and artist, — if we think of Raphael, for instance, who truly is εὐφυής just as Byron is not, — we shall bring into clearer light the connection in Byron between the faults of the man and the faults of the poet. With Raphael's character Byron's sins of vulgarity and false criticism would have been impossible, just as with Raphael's art Byron's sins of common and bad workmanship.

Yes, all this is true, but it is not the whole truth about Byron nevertheless; very far from it. The severe criticism of M. Scherer by no means gives us the whole truth about Byron, and we have not yet got it in what has

been added to that criticism here. The negative part of
the true criticism of him we perhaps have; the positive
part, by far the more important, we have not. Byron's
admirers appeal eagerly to foreign testimonies in his
favor. Some of these testimonies do not much move
me; but one testimony there is among them which will
always carry, with me at any rate, very great weight, —
the testimony of Goethe. Goethe's sayings about Byron
were uttered, it must however be remembered, at the
height of Byron's vogue, when that puissant and splendid personality was exercising its full power of attraction.
In Goethe's own household there was an atmosphere of
glowing Byron-worship; his daughter-in-law was a passionate admirer of Byron, nay, she enjoyed and prized
his poetry, as did Tieck and so many others in Germany
at that time, much above the poetry of Goethe himself.
Instead of being irritated and rendered jealous by this, a
nature like Goethe's was inevitably led by it to heighten,
not lower, the note of his praise. The Time-Spirit, or
Zeit-Geist, he would himself have said, was working just
then for Byron. This working of the *Zeit-Geist* in his
favor was an advantage added to Byron's other advan-
tages, an advantage of which he had a right to get the
benefit. This is what Goethe would have thought and
said to himself; and so he would have been led even to
heighten somewhat his estimate of Byron, and to accent-
uate the emphasis of praise. Goethe speaking of Byron
at that moment was not and could not be quite the same
cool critic as Goethe speaking of Dante, or Molière, or
Milton. This, I say, we ought to remember in reading
Goethe's judgments on Byron and his poetry. Still, if

we are careful to bear this in mind, and if we quote
Goethe's praise correctly, — which is not always done
by those who in this country quote it, — and if we add
to it that great and due qualification added to it by
Goethe himself, — which so far as I have seen has never
yet been done by his quoters in this country at all, —
then we shall have a judgment on Byron, which comes,
I think, very near to the truth, and which may well
command our adherence.

In his judicious and interesting Life of Byron, Professor Nichol quotes Goethe as saying that Byron "is undoubtedly to be regarded as the greatest genius of our
century." What Goethe did really say was "the greatest *talent*," not "the greatest *genius*." The difference
is important, because, while talent gives the notion of
power in a man's performance, genius gives rather the
notion of felicity and perfection in it; and this divine
gift of consummate felicity by no means, as we have
seen, belongs to Byron and to his poetry. Goethe said
that Byron "must unquestionably be regarded as the
greatest talent of the century."[1] He said of him moreover: "The English may think of Byron what they
please, but it is certain that they can point to no poet
who is his like. He is different from all the rest, and,
in the main, greater." Here, again, Professor Nichol
translates: "They can show no (living) poet who is to
be compared to him;" — inserting the word *living*, I
suppose, to prevent its being thought that Goethe would
have ranked Byron, as a poet, above Shakspeare and

[1] " Der ohne Frage als das grösste Talent des Jahrhunderts
anzusehen ist."

Milton. But Goethe did not use, or, I think, mean to imply, any limitation such as is added by Professor Nichol. Goethe said simply, and he meant to say, " *no* poet." Only the words which follow [1] ought not, I think, to be rendered, " who is to be compared to him," that is to say, " *who is his equal as a poet.*" They mean rather, " who may properly be compared with him," " *who is his parallel.*" And when Goethe said that Byron was " in the main greater " than all the rest of the English poets, he was not so much thinking of the strict rank, as poetry, of Byron's production; he was thinking of that wonderful personality of Byron which so enters into his poetry and which Goethe called " a personality such, for its eminence, as has never been yet, and such as is not likely to come again." He was thinking of that " daring, dash, and grandiosity," [2] of Byron, which are indeed so splendid; and which were, so Goethe maintained, of a character to do good, because " everything great is formative," and what is thus formative does us good.

The faults which went with this greatness, and which impaired Byron's poetical work, Goethe saw very well. He saw the constant state of warfare and combat, the " negative and polemical working," which makes Byron's poetry a poetry in which we can find so little rest ; he saw the *Hang zum Unbegrenzten,* the straining after the unlimited, which made it impossible for Byron to produce poetic wholes such as the *Tempest* or *Lear ;* he saw the

1 " Der ihm zu vergleichen wäre."

2 " Byron's Kühnheit, Keckheit und Grandiosität, ist das nicht alles bildend ? — Alles Grosse bildet, sobald wir es gewahr werden."

zu viel Empirie, the promiscuous adoption of all the
matter offered to the poet by life, just as it was offered,
without thought or patience for the mysterious transmu-
tation to be operated on this matter by poetic form.   But
in a sentence which I cannot, as I say, remember to have
yet seen quoted in any English criticism of Byron, Goethe
lays his finger on the cause of all these defects in Byron,
and on his real source of weakness both as a man and
as a poet.   "The moment he reflects, he is a child,"
says Goethe ; — "*sobald er reflectirt ist er ein Kind.*"

Now if we take the two parts of Goethe's criticism of
Byron, the favorable and the unfavorable, and put
them together, we shall have, I think, the truth.   On
the one hand a splendid and puissant personality, a personality "in eminence such as has never been yet, and
is not likely to come again ;" of which the like, therefore, is not to be found among the poets of our nation,
by which Byron "is different from all the rest, and, in
the main, greater."   Byron is, moreover, "the greatest
talent of our century."   On the other hand, this splendid
personality and unmatched talent, this unique Byron, "is
quite too much in the dark about himself ;" [1] nay, "the
moment he begins to reflect, he is a child."   There we
have, I think, Byron complete ; and in estimating him
and ranking him we have to strike a balance between
the gain which accrues to his poetry, as compared with
the productions of other poets, from his superiority, and
the loss which accrues to it from his defects.

A balance of this kind has to be struck in the case of
all poets except the few supreme masters in whom a

---

[1] "Gar zu dunkel über sich selbst."

profound criticism of life exhibits itself in indissoluble connection with the laws of poetic truth and beauty. I have seen it said that I allege poetry to have for its characteristic this : that it is a criticism of life ; and that I make it to be thereby distinguished from prose, which is something else. So far from it, that when I first used this expression, *a criticism of life*, now many years ago, it was to literature in general that I applied it, and not to poetry in especial. "The end and aim of all literature," I said, " is, if one considers it attentively, nothing but that : — *a criticism of life.*" And so it surely is ; the main end and aim of all our utterance, whether in prose or in verse, is surely a criticism of life. We are not brought much on our way, I admit, towards an adequate definition of poetry as distinguished from prose by that truth ; still a truth it is, and poetry can never prosper if it is forgotten. In poetry, however, the criticism of life has to be made conformably to the laws of poetic truth and poetic beauty. Truth and seriousness of substance and matter, felicity and perfection of diction and manner, as these are exhibited in the best poets, are what constitute a criticism of life made in conformity with the laws of poetic truth and poetic beauty ; and it is by knowing and feeling the work of those poets, that we learn to recognize the fulfilment and non-fulfilment of such conditions.

The moment, however, that we leave the small band of the very best poets, the true classics, and deal with poets of the next rank, we shall find that perfect truth and seriousness of matter, in close alliance with perfect truth and felicity of manner, is the rule no longer. We have now to take what we can get, to forego something here, to admit compensation for it there ; to strike a balance, and to see how our poets stand in respect to one another when that balance has been struck. Let us observe how this is so.

We will take three poets, among the most considererable of our century : Leopardi, Byron, Wordsworth. Giacomo Leopardi was ten years younger than Byron, and he died thirteen years after him ; both of them, therefore, died young, Byron at the age of thirty-six, Leopardi at the age of thirty-nine. Both of them were of noble birth, both of them suffered from physical defect, both of them were in revolt against the established facts and beliefs of their age ; but here the likeness between them ends. The stricken poet of Recanati had no country, for an Italy in his day did not exist ; he had no audience, no celebrity. The volume of his poems, published in the very year of Byron's death, hardly sold, I suppose, its tens, while the volumes of Byron's poetry were selling their tens of thousands. And yet Leopardi has the very qualities which we have found wanting to Byron ; he has the sense for form and style, the passion for just expression, the sure and firm touch of the true artist. Nay, more, he has a grave fulness of knowledge, an insight into the real bearings of the questions which as a sceptical poet he raises, a power of seizing the real point, a lucidity, with which the author of *Cain* has nothing to compare. I can hardly imagine Leopardi reading the

" . . . And *thou* would'st go on aspiring
To the great double Mysteries ! the *two Principles !* "

or following Byron in his theological controversy with

Dr. Kennedy, without having his features overspread by a calm and fine smile, and remarking of his brilliant contemporary, as Goethe did, that "the moment he begins to reflect, he is a child." But indeed whoever wishes to feel the full superiority of Leopardi over Byron in philosophic thought and in the expression of it, has only to read one paragraph of one poem, the paragraph of *La Ginestra,* beginning

> "Sovente in queste piagge,"

and ending

> "Non so se il riso o la pietà prevale."

In like manner, Leopardi is at many points the poetic superior of Wordsworth too. He has a far wider culture than Wordsworth, more mental lucidity, more freedom from illusions as to the real character of the established fact and of reigning conventions ; above all, this Italian, with his pure and sure touch, with his fineness of perception, is far more of the artist. Such a piece of pompous dulness as

> "O for the coming of that glorious time,"

and all the rest of it, or such lumbering verse as Mr. Ruskin's enemy,

> "Parching summer hath no warrant,"

would have been as impossible to Leopardi as to Dante. Where, then, is Wordsworth's superiority? for the worth of what he has given us in poetry I hold to be greater, on the whole, than the worth of what Leopardi has given us. It is in Wordsworth's sound and profound sense

"Of joy in widest commonalty spread;"

whereas Leopardi remains with his thoughts ever fixed upon the *essenza insanabile*, upon the *acerbo, indegno mistero delle cose*. It is in the power with which Wordsworth feels the resources of joy offered to us in nature, offered to us in the primary human affections and duties, and in the power with which in his moments of inspiration he renders this joy and makes us, too, feel it; a force greater than himself seeming to lift him and to prompt his tongue, so that he speaks in a style far above any style of which he has the constant command, and with a truth far beyond any philosophic truth of which he has the conscious and assured possession. Neither Leopardi nor Wordsworth is of the same order with the great poets who made such verse as

"Τλητὸν γὰρ Μοῖραι θυμὸν θέσαν ἀνθρώποισιν."

or as

"In la sua volontade e nostra pace;"

or as

"... Men must endure
Their going hence, even as their coming hither;
Ripeness is all."

But as compared with Leopardi, Wordsworth, though at many points less lucid, though far less a master of style, far less of an artist, gains so much by his criticism of life, being, in certain matters of profound importance, health-

ful and true, whereas Leopardi's pessimism is not, that
the value of Wordsworth's poetry, on the whole, stands
higher for us than that of Leopardi's, as it stands higher
for us, I think, than that of any modern poetry except
Goethe's.

Byron's poetic value is also greater, on the whole, than
Loepardi's; and his superiority turns, in the same way,
upon the surpassing worth of something which he had
and was, after all deduction has been made for his short-
comings.   We talk of Byron's *personality*, "a personality in eminence such as has never been yet, and is not
likely to come again; " and we say that by this personality Byron is " different from all the rest of English
poets, and, in the main, greater."   But can we not be a
litt'e more circumstantial, and name that in which the
wonderful power of this personality consisted?   We can;
with the instinct of a poet Mr. Swinburne has seized
upon it and named it for us.   The power of Byron's
personality lies in "the splendid and imperishable excellence which covers all his offences and outweighs all
his defects: *the excellence of sincerity and strength.*"

Byron found our nation, after its long and victorious
struggle with revolutionary France, fixed in a system of
established facts and dominant ideas which revolted him.
The mental bondage of the most powerful part of our
nation, of its strong middle class, to a narrow and false
system of this kind, is what we call British Philistinism.
That bondage is unbroken to this hour, but in Byron's
time it was even far more deep and dark than it is now.
Byron was an aristocrat, and it is not difficult for an
aristocrat to look on the prejudices and habits of the

British Philistine with scepticism and disdain. Plenty of young men of his own class Byron met at Almack's or at Lady Jersey's, who regarded the established facts and reigning beliefs of the England of that day with as little reverence as he did. But these men, disbelievers in British Philistinism in private, entered English public life, the most conventional in the world, and at once they saluted with respect the habits and ideas of British Philistinism as if they were a part of the order of creation, and as if in public no sane man would think of warring against them. With Byron it was different. What he called the *cant* of the great middle part of the English nation, what we call its Philistinism, revolted him; but the cant of his own class, deferring to this Philistinism and profiting by it, while they disbelieved in it, revolted him even more. "Come what may," are his own words, "I will never flatter the million's canting in any shape." His class in general, on the other hand, shrugged their shoulders at this cant, laughed at it, pandered to it, and ruled by it. The falsehood, cynicism, insolence, misgovernment, oppression, with their consequent unfailing crop of human misery, which were produced by this state of things, roused Byron to irreconcilable revolt and battle. They made him indignant, they infuriated him; they were so strong, so defiant, so maleficent, — and yet he felt that they were doomed. "You have seen every trampler down in turn," he comforts himself with saying, "from Buonaparte to the simplest individuals." The old order, as after 1815 it stood victorious, with its ignorance and misery below, its cant, selfishness, and cynicism above, was at home and abroad equally hateful to him

" I have simplified my politics," he writes, " into an utter detestation of all existing governments." And again: "Give me a republic. The king-times are fast finishing; there will be blood shed like water and tears like mist, but the peoples will conquer in the end. I shall not live to see it, but I foresee it."

Byron himself gave the preference, he tells us, to politicians and doers, far above writers and singers. But the politics of his own day and of his own class — even of the Liberals of his own class — were impossible for him. Nature had not formed him for a Liberal peer, proper to move the Address in the House of Lords, to pay compliments to the energy and self-reliance of British middle-class Liberalism, and to adapt his politics to suit it. Unfitted for such politics, he threw himself upon poetry as his organ; and in poetry his topics were not Queen Mab, and the Witch of Atlas, and the Sensitive Plant, they were the upholders of the old Order, George the Third and Lord Castlereagh and the Duke of Wellington and Southey, and they were the canters and tramplers of the great world, and they were his enemies and himself.

Such was Byron's personality, by which " he is different from all the rest of English poets, and, in the main, greater." But he posed all his life, says M. Scherer. Let us distinguish. There is the Byron who posed, there is the Byron with his affectations and silliness, the Byron whose weakness Lady Blessington, with a woman's acuteness, so admirably seized: " his great defect is flippancy and a total want of self-possession." But when this theatrical and easily criticised personage

betook himself to poetry, and when he had fairly warmed
to his work, then he became another man; then the
theatrical personage passed away; then a higher power
took possession of him and filled him; then at last came
forth into light that true and puissant personality, with
its direct strokes, its ever-welling force, its satire, its
energy, and its agony.   This is the real Byron; whoever
stops at the theatrical preludings, does not know him.
And this real Byron may well be superior to the stricken
Leopardi, he may well be declared "different from all
the rest of English poets, and, in the main, greater," in
so far as it is true of him, as M. Taine well says, that
"all other souls, in comparison with his, seem inert;"
in so far as it is true of him that with superb, exhaustless
energy he maintained, as Professor Nichol well says,
"the struggle that keeps alive, if it does not save, the
soul:" in so far, finally, as he deserves (and he does
deserve) the noble praise of him which I have already
quoted from Mr. Swinburne; the praise for "the splendid and imperishable excellence which covers all his
offences and outweighs all his defects: *the excellence of
sincerity and strength.*"

True, as a man, Byron could not manage himself,
could not guide his ways aright, but was all astray.
True, he has no light, cannot lead us from the past to
the future; "the moment he reflects, he is a child."
The way out of the false state of things which enraged
him he did not see,—the slow and laborious way up-
ward; he had not the patience, knowledge, self-disci-
pline, virtue, requisite for seeing it.   True, also, as a
poet, he has no fine and exact sense for word and

structure and rhythm; he has not the artist's nature and gifts. Yet a personality of Byron's force counts for so much in life, and a rhetorician of Byron's force counts for so much in literature. But it would be most unjust to label Byron, as M. Scherer is disposed to label him, as a rhetorician only. Along with his astounding power and passion, he had a strong and deep sense for what is beautiful in nature, and for what is beautiful in human action and suffering. When he warms to his work, when he is inspired, Nature herself seems to take the pen from him as she took it from Wordsworth, and to write for him as she wrote for Wordsworth, though in a different fashion, with her own penetrating simplicity. Goethe has well observed of Byron, that when he is at his happiest his representation of things is as easy and real as if he were improvising. It is so; and his verse then exhibits quite another and a higher quality from the rhetorical quality, — admirable as this also in its own kind of merit is, — of such verse as

" Minions of splendor shrinking from distress,"

and of so much more verse of Byron's of that stamp. Nature, I say, takes the pen for him; and then, assured master of a true poetic style though he is not, any more than Wordsworth, yet as from Wordsworth at his best there will come such verse as

" Will no one tell me what she sings ? "

so from Byron, too, at his best, there will come such verse as

" He heard it, but he heeded not ; his eyes
    Were with his heart, and that was far away."

Of verse of this high quality, Byron has much; of verse of a quality lower than this, of a quality rather rhetorical than truly poetic, yet still of extraordinary power and merit, he has still more. To separate, from the mass of poetry which Byron poured forth, all this higher portion, so superior to the mass, and still so considerable in quantity, and to present it in one body by itself, is to do a service, I believe, to Byron's reputation, and to the poetic glory of our country.

Such a service I have in the present volume attempted to perform. To Byron, after all the tributes which have been paid to him, here is yet one tribute more : —

"Among thy mightier offerings here are mine!"

not a tribute of boundless homage certainly, but sincere; a tribute which consists not in covering the poet with eloquent eulogy of our own, but in letting him, at his best and greatest, speak for himself. Surely the critic who does most for his author is the critic who gains readers for his author himself, not for any lucubrations on his author; — gains more readers for him, and enables those readers to read him with more admiration.

And in spite of his prodigious vogue, Byron has never yet, perhaps, had the serious admiration which he deserves. Society read him and talked about him, as it reads and talks about *Endymion* to-day; and with the same sort of result. It looked in Byron's glass as it looks in Lord Beaconsfield's, and sees, or fancies that it sees, its own face there; and then it goes its way, and straightway forgets what manner of man it saw. Even of his passionate admirers, how many never got beyond the theatrical Byron, from whom they caught the fashion of deranging their hair, or of knotting their neck-hand-kerchief, or of leaving their shirt-collar unbuttoned; how few profoundly felt his vital influence, the influence of his splendid and imperishable excellence of sincerity and strength!

His own aristocratic class, whose cynical make-believe drove him to fury; the great middle-class, on whose impregnable Philistinism he shattered himself to pieces, — how little have either of these felt Byron's vital influ-ence! As the inevitable break-up of the old order comes, as the English middle-class slowly awakens from its intellectual sleep of two centuries, as our actual present world, to which this sleep has condemned us, shows itself more clearly, — our world of an aristocracy materialized and null, a middle-class purblind and hid-eous, a lower class crude and brutal, — we shall turn our eyes again, and to more purpose, upon this passionate and dauntless soldier of a forlorn hope, who, ignorant of the future and unconsoled by its promises, neverthe-less waged against the conservation of the old impossible world so fiery battle; waged it till he fell, — waged it with such splendid and imperishable excellence of sin-cerity and strength.

Wordsworth's value is of another kind. Wordsworth has an insight into permanent sources of joy and conso-lation for mankind which Byron has not; his poetry gives us more which we may rest upon than Byron's — more which we can rest upon now, and which men may rest upon always. I place Wordsworth's poetry, therefore, above Byron's on the whole, although in some points he

was greatly Byron's inferior, and although Byron's poetry
will always, probably, find more readers than Wordsworth's, and will give pleasure more easily. But these
two, Wordsworth and Byron, stand, it seems to me, first
and pre-eminent in actual performance, a glorious pair,
among the English poets of this century. Keats had
probably, indeed, a more consummate poetic gift than
either of them; but he died having produced too little
and being as yet too immature to rival them. I for my
part can never even think of equalling with them any
other of their contemporaries; — either Coleridge, poet
and philosopher wrecked in a mist of opium; or Shelley,
beautiful and ineffectual angel, beating in the void his
luminous wings in vain. Wordsworth and Byron stand
out by themselves. When the year 1900 is turned, and
our nation comes to recount her poetic glories in the
century which has then just ended, the first names with
her will be these.

MATTHEW ARNOLD.

CONTENTS.

————

I. — PERSONAL, LYRIC, AND ELEGIAC.

II.—DESCRIPTIVE AND NARRATIVE.

III. — DRAMATIC.

IV. — SATIRIC.

I.

PERSONAL, LYRIC, AND ELEGIAC.

POETRY OF BYRON.

~~~~~~~~~

LOCH NA GARR.

AWAY, ye gay landscapes, ye gardens of roses!
　In you let the minions of luxury rove;
Restore me the rocks, where the snow-flake reposes,
　Though still they are sacred to freedom and love:
Yet, Caledonia, beloved are thy mountains,
　Round their white summits though elements war;
Though cataracts foam 'stead of smooth-flowing foun‑
　　tains,
　I sigh for the valley of dark Loch na Garr.

Ah! there my young footsteps in infancy wander'd;
　My cap was the bonnet, my cloak was the plaid;
On chieftains long perish'd my memory ponder'd,
　As daily I strode through the pine-cover'd glade:
I sought not my home till the day's dying glory
　Gave place to the rays of the bright polar star;
For fancy was cheer'd by traditional story,
　Disclosed by the natives of dark Loch na Garr.

"Shades of the dead! have I not heard your voices
　Rise on the night-rolling breath of the gale?"

Surely the soul of the hero rejoices,
   And rides on the wind o'er his own Highland vale.
Round Loch na Garr while the stormy mist gathers,
   Winter presides in his cold icy car:
Clouds there encircle the forms of my fathers;
   They dwell in the tempests of dark Loch na Garr.

"Illstarr'd, though brave, did no visions foreboding
   Tell you that fate had forsaken your cause?"
Ah! were you destined to die at Culloden,
   Victory crown'd not your fall with applause:
Still were you happy in death's earthy slumber,
   You rest with your clan in the caves of Braemar;
The pibroch resounds, to the piper's loud number,
   Your deeds on the echoes of dark Loch na Garr.

Years have roll'd on, Loch na Garr, since I left you,
   Years must elapse ere I tread you again:
Nature of verdure and flow'rs has bereft you,
   Yet still are you dearer than Albion's plain.
England! thy beauties are tame and domestic
   To one who has roved on the mountains afar:
Oh for the crags that are wild and majestic!
   The steep frowning glories of dark Loch na Garr!

——

WELL! THOU ART HAPPY.

WELL! thou art happy, and I feel
   That I should thus be happy too;
For still my heart regards thy weal
   Warmly, as it was wont to do.

Thy husband 's blest — and 't will impart
  Some pangs to view his happier lot:
But let them pass — Oh! how my heart
  Would hate him, if he loved thee not!

When late I saw thy favorite child,
  I thought my jealous heart would break;
But when the unconscious infant smiled,
  I kiss'd it for its mother's sake.

I kiss'd it, — and repressed my sighs
  Its father in its face to see;
But then it had its mother's eyes,
  And they were all to love and me.

Mary, adieu! I must away:
  While thou art blest I 'll not repine;
But near thee I can never stay;
  My heart would soon again be thine.

I deem'd that time, I deem'd that pride
  Had quench'd at length my boyish flame:
Nor knew, till seated by thy side,
  My heart in all, — save hope, — the same.

Yet was I calm: I knew the time
  My breast would thrill before thy look;
But now to tremble were a crime —
  We met, — and not a nerve was shook.

I saw thee gaze upon my face,
  Yet met with no confusion there:
One only feeling could'st thou trace;
  The sullen calmness of despair.

Away! away! my early dream
  Remembrance never must awake;
Oh! where is Lethe's fabled stream!
  My foolish heart be still, or break.

EPISTLE TO A FRIEND.

**IN ANSWER TO SOME LINES EXHORTING THE AUTHOR
TO BE CHEERFUL, AND TO " BANISH CARE."**

"OH! banish care" — such ever be
The motto of *thy* revelry!
Perchance of *mine*, when wassail nights
Renew those riotous delights,
Wherewith the Children of Despair
Lull the lone heart, and " banish care."
But not in morn's reflecting hour,
When present, past, and future lower,
When all I loved is changed or gone,
Mock with such taunts the woes of one,
Whose every thought — but let them pass —
Thou know'st I am not what I was.
But, above all, if thou would'st hold
Place in a heart that ne'er was cold,
By all the powers that men revere,
By all unto thy bosom dear,
Thy joys below, thy hopes above,
Speak — speak of anything but love.

  'T were long to tell, and vain to hear,
The tale of one who scorns a tear;

And there is little in that tale
Which better bosoms would bewail.
But mine has suffer'd more than well
'T would suit philosophy to tell.
I 've seen my bride another's bride, —
Have seen her seated by his side, —
Have seen the infant, which she bore,
Wear the sweet smile the mother wore,
When she and I in youth have smiled,
As fond and faultless as her child; —
Have seen her eyes in cold disdain,
Ask if I felt no secret pain;
And *I* have acted well my part
And made my cheek belie my heart,
Return'd the freezing glance she gave,
Yet felt the while *that* woman's slave; —
Have kiss'd, as if without design,
The babe which ought to have been mine,
And show'd, alas! in each caress,
Time had not made me love the less.

But let this pass — I 'll whine no more,
Nor seek again an eastern shore;
The world befits a busy brain, —
I 'll hie me to its haunts again.
But if, in some succeeding year,
When Britain's " May is in the sere,"
Thou hear'st of one, whose deepening crimes
Suit with the sablest of the times,
Of one, whom love nor pity sways,
Nor hope of fame, nor good men's praise,

One, who in stern ambition's pride,
Perchance not blood shall turn aside,
One rank'd in some recording page
With the worst anarchs of the age,
Him wilt thou *know* — and *knowing* pause,
Nor with the *effect* forget the cause.

TO THOMAS MOORE.

My boat is on the shore,
   And my bark is on the sea;
But, before I go, Tom Moore,
   Here 's a double health to thee!

Here 's a sigh to those who love me,
   And a smile to those who hate;
And, whatever sky 's above me,
   Here 's a heart for every fate.

Though the ocean roar around me,
   Yet it still shall bear me on:
Though a desert should surround me,
   It hath springs that may be won.

Were 't the last drop in the well,
   As I gasp'd upon the brink,
Ere my fainting spirit fell,
   'T is to thee that I would drink.

With that water, as this wine,
   The libation I would pour
Should be — peace with thine and mine,
   And a health to thee, Tom Moore.

CHILDE HAROLD'S DEPARTURE.

(CHILDE HAROLD, Canto i. Stanzas 4–11.)

CHILDE HAROLD bask'd him in the noontide sun,
Disporting there like any other fly;
Nor deem'd before his little day was done
One blast might chill him into misery.
But long ere scarce a third of his pass'd by,
Worse than adversity the Childe befell;
He felt the fulness of satiety:
Then loathed he in his native land to dwell,
Which seemed to him more lone than Eremite's sad cell.

For he through Sin's long labyrinth had run,
Nor made atonement when he did amiss,
Had sigh'd to many though he loved but one,
And that loved one, alas! could ne'er be his.
Ah, happy she! to 'scape from him whose kiss
Had been pollution unto aught so chaste;
Who soon had left her charms for vulgar bliss,
And spoil'd her goodly lands to gild his waste,
Nor calm domestic peace had ever deign'd to taste.

And now Childe Harold was sore sick at heart,
And from his fellow bacchanals would flee;
'T is said, at times the sullen tear would start,
But Pride congeal'd the drop within his ee:
Apart he stalk'd in joyless reverie,
And from his native land resolved to go,
And visit scorching climes beyond the sea;
With pleasure drugg'd, he almost long'd for woe,
And e'en for change of scene would seek the shades below.

The Childe departed from his father's hall:
It was a vast and venerable pile;
So old, it seemed only not to fall,
Yet strength was pillar'd in each massy aisle.
Monastic dome! condemn'd to uses vile!
Where Superstition once had made her den
Now Paphian girls were known to sing and smile;
And monks might deem their time was come agen,
If ancient tales say true, nor wrong these holy men.

Yet oft-times in his maddest mirthful mood
Strange pangs would flash along Childe Harold's brow,
As if the memory of some deadly feud
Or disappointed passion lurk'd below:
But this none knew, nor haply cared to know;
For his was not that open, artless soul
That feels relief by bidding sorrow flow,
Nor sought he friend to counsel or condole,
Whate'er this grief mote be, which he could not control.

And none did love him — though to hall and bower
He gather'd revellers from far and near,
He knew them flatt'rers of the festal hour;
The heartless parasites of present cheer.
Yea! none did love him — nor his lemans dear —
But pomp and power alone are woman's care,
And where these are light Eros finds a feere;
Maidens, like moths, are ever caught by glare,
And Mammon wins his ways where Seraphs might despair.

Childe Harold had a mother — not forgot,
Though parting from that mother he did shun;

A sister whom he loved, but saw her not
Before his weary pilgrimage begun:
If friends he had, he bade adieu to none.
Yet deem not thence his breast a breast of steel:
Ye, who have known what 't is to dote upon
A few dear objects, will in sadness feel
Such partings break the heart they fondly hope to heal.

His house, his home, his heritage, his lands,
The laughing dames in whom he did delight,
Whose large blue eyes, fair locks, and snowy hands,
Might shake the saintship of an anchorite,
And long had fed his youthful appetite;
His goblets brimm'd with every costly wine,
And all that mote to luxury invite,
Without a sigh he left, to cross the brine,
And traverse Paynim shores, and pass Earth's central
    line.

———

STANZAS

COMPOSED DURING A THUNDERSTORM.

CHILL and mirk is the nightly blast,
  Where Pindus' mountains rise,
And angry clouds are pouring fast
  The vengeance of the skies.

Our guides are gone, our hope is lost,
  And lightnings, as they play,
But show where rocks our path have crost,
  Or gild the torrent's spray.

Is yon a cot I saw, though low?
  When lightning broke the gloom —
How welcome were its shade! — ah, no!
  'T is but a Turkish tomb.

Through sounds of foaming waterfalls,
  I hear a voice exclaim —
My way-worn countryman, who calls
  On distant England's name.

A shot is fired — by foe or friend?
  Another — 't is to tell
The mountain-peasants to descend,
  And lead us where they dwell.

Oh! who in such a night will dare
  To tempt the wilderness?
And who 'mid thunder peals can hear
  Our signal of distress?

And who that heard our shouts would rise
  To try the dubious road?
Nor rather deem from nightly cries
  That outlaws were abroad.

Clouds burst, skies flash, oh, dreadful hour!
  More fiercely pours the storm!
Yet here one thought has still the power
  To keep my bosom warm.

While wand'ring through each broken path,
  O'er brake and craggy brow;
While elements exhaust their wrath,
  Sweet Florence, where art thou?

Not on the sea, not on the sea!
   Thy bark hath long been gone:
Oh, may the storm that pours on me,
   Bow down my head alone!

Full swiftly blew the swift Siroc,
   When last I press'd thy lip;
And long ere now, with foaming shock,
   Impell'd thy gallant ship.

Now thou art safe; nay, long ere now
   Hast trod the shore of Spain;
'T were hard if aught so fair as thou
   Should linger on the main.

And since I now remember thee
   In darkness and in dread,
As in those hours of revelry
   Which mirth and music sped;

Do thou, amid the fair white walls,
   If Cadiz yet be free,
At times from out her latticed halls
   Look o'er the dark blue sea;

Then think upon Calypso's isles,
   Endear'd by days gone by;
To others give a thousand smiles,
   To me a single sigh.

And when the admiring circle mark
   The paleness of thy face,
A half-form'd tear, a transient spark
   Of melancholy grace,

Again thou 'lt smile, and blushing shun
   Some coxcomb's raillery;
Nor own for once thou thought'st of one
   Who ever thinks on thee.

Though smile and sigh alike are vain,
   When sever'd hearts repine,
My spirit flies o'er mount and main,
   And mourns in search of thine.

———

" *MAID OF ATHENS.*"

Ζώη μοῦ, σάς ἀγαπῶ.

MAID of Athens, ere we part,
Give, oh, give me back my heart!
Or, since that has left my breast,
Keep it now, and take the rest!
Hear my vow before I go,
   Ζώη μοῦ, σάς ἀγαπῶ.

By those tresses unconfined,
Woo'd by each Ægean wind;
By those lids whose jetty fringe
Kiss thy soft cheeks' blooming tinge;
By those wild eyes like the roe,
   Ζώη μοῦ, σάς ἀγαπῶ.

By that lip I long to taste;
By that zone-encircled waist;
By all the token-flowers that tell
What words can never speak so well;

By love's alternate joy and woe,
Ζώη μοῦ, σάς ἀγαπῶ.

Maid of Athens! I am gone;
Think of me, sweet! when alone.
Though I fly to Istambol,
Athens holds my heart and soul:
Can I cease to love thee?   No!
Ζώη μοῦ, σάς ἀγαπῶ.

TO INEZ.

NAY, smile not at my sullen brows;
  Alas! I cannot smile again:
Yet Heaven avert that ever thou
  Shouldst weep, and haply weep in vain.

And dost thou ask, what secret woe
  I bear, corroding joy and youth?
And wilt thou vainly seek to know
  A pang ev'n thou must fail to soothe?

It is not love, it is not hate,
  Nor low Ambition's honors lost,
That bids me loathe my present state,
  And fly from all I prized the most:

It is that weariness which springs
  From all I meet, or hear, or see:
To me no pleasure beauty brings;
  Thine eyes have scarce a charm for me.

It is that settled, ceaseless gloom
 The fabled Hebrew wanderer bore;
That will not look beyond the tomb,
 But cannot hope for rest before.

What Exile from himself can flee?
 To zones, though more and more remote,
Still, still pursues, where'er I be,
 The blight of life — the demon thought.

Yet others wrapt in pleasure seem,
 And taste of all that I forsake;
Oh! may they still of transport dream,
 And ne'er, at least like me, awake!

Through many a clime 't is mine to go,
 With many a retrospection curst;
And all my solace is to know,
 Whate'er betides, I 've known the worst.

What is that worst? Nay do not ask —
 In pity from the search forbear;
Smile on — nor venture to unmask
 Man's heart, and view the Hell that 's there.

———

"ONE STRUGGLE MORE."

"One struggle more," and I am free
 From pangs that rend my heart in twain;
One last long sigh to love and thee,
 Then back to busy life again.

It suits me well to mingle now
   With things that never pleased before:
Though every joy is fled below,
   What future grief can touch me more?

Then bring me wine, the banquet bring;
   Man was not form'd to live alone:
I 'll be that light, unmeaning thing
   That smiles with all, and weeps with none.
It was not thus in days more dear,
   It never would have been, but thou
Hast fled, and left me lonely here;
   Thou 'rt nothing, — all are nothing now.

In vain my lyre would lightly breathe!
   The smile that sorrow fain would wear
But mocks the woe that lurks beneath,
   Like roses o'er a sepulchre.
Though gay companions o'er the bowl
   Dispel awhile the sense of ill;
Though pleasure fires the maddening soul,
   The heart — the heart is lonely still!

On many a lone and lovely night
   It sooth'd to gaze upon the sky;
For then I deem'd the heavenly light
   Shone sweetly on thy pensive eye:
And oft I thought at Cynthia's noon,
   When sailing o'er the Ægean wave,
"Now Thyrza gazes on that moon — "
   Alas, it gleam'd upon her grave!

When stretch'd on fever's sleepless bed,
  And sickness shrunk my throbbing veins,
" 'T is comfort still," I faintly said,
  " That Thyrza cannot know my pains: "
Like freedom to the time-worn slave,
  A boon 't is idle then to give,
Relenting Nature vainly gave
  My life, when Thyrza ceased to live!

My Thyrza's pledge in better days,
  When love and life alike were new!
How different now thou meet'st my gaze!
  How tinged by time with sorrow's hue!
The heart that gave itself with thee
  Is silent — ah, were mine as still!
Though cold as e'en the dead can be,
  It feels, it sickens with the chill.

Thou bitter pledge! thou mournful token!
  Though painful, welcome to my breast!
Still, still, preserve that love unbroken,
  Or break the heart to which thou 'rt press'd!
Time tempers love, but not removes,
  More hallow'd when its hope is fled:
Oh! what are thousand living loves
  To that which cannot quit the dead?

EUTHANASIA.

WHEN Time, or soon or late, shall bring
  The dreamless sleep that lulls the dead,
Oblivion ! may thy languid wing
  Wave gently o'er my dying bed !

No band of friends or heirs be there,
  To weep, or wish, the coming blow :
No maiden, with dishevell'd hair,
  To feel, or feign, decorous woe.

But silent let me sink to earth,
  With no officious mourners near :
I would not mar one hour of mirth,
  Nor startle friendship with a fear.

Yet Love, if Love in such an hour
  Could nobly check its useless sighs,
Might then exert its latest power
  In her who lives and him who dies.

'T were sweet, my Psyche ! to the last
  Thy features still serene to see :
Forgetful of its struggles past,
  E'en Pain itself should smile on thee.

But vain the wish — for Beauty still
  Will shrink, as shrinks the ebbing breath ;
And woman's tears, produced at will,
  Deceive in life, unman in death.

Then lonely be my latest hour,
　　Without regret, without a groan;
For thousands Death hath ceased to lower,
　　And pain been transient or unknown.

" Ay, but to die, and go," alas !
　　Where all have gone, and all must go !
To be the nothing that I was
　　Ere born to life and living woe ! —

Count o'er the joys thine hours have seen,
　　Count o'er thy days from anguish free,
And know, whatever thou hast been,
　　'T is something better not to be.

AND THOU ART DEAD.

" Heu, quanto minus est cum reliquis versari quam tui meminisse !"

AND thou art dead, as young and fair
　　As aught of mortal birth;
And form so soft, and charms so rare,
　　Too soon return'd to Earth !
Though earth received them in her bed,
And o'er the spot the crowd may tread
　　In carelessness or mirth,
There is an eye which could not brook
A moment on that grave to look.

I will not ask where thou liest low,
　　Nor gaze upon the spot;

There flowers or weeds at will may grow,
  So I behold them not:
It is enough for me to prove
That what I loved, and long must love,
  Like common earth can rot;
To me there needs no stone to tell,
'T is Nothing that I loved so well.

Yet did I love thee to the last
  As fervently as thou,
Who didst not change through all the past,
  And canst not alter now.
The love where Death has set his seal,
Nor age can chill, nor rival steal,
  Nor falsehood disavow:
And, what were worse, thou canst not see
Or wrong, or change, or fault in me.

The better days of life were ours;
  The worst can be but mine:
The sun that cheers, the storm that lowers,
  Shall never more be thine.
The silence of that dreamless sleep
I envy now too much to weep;
  Nor need I to repine
That all those charms have pass'd away,
I might have watch'd through long decay.

The flower in ripen'd bloom unmatch'd
  Must fall the earliest prey;
Though by no hand untimely snatch'd,
  The leaves must drop away:

And yet it were a greater grief
To watch it withering, leaf by leaf,
  Than see it pluck'd to-day;
Since earthly eye but ill can bear
To trace the change to foul from **fair.**

I know not if I could have borne
  To see thy beauties fade;
The night that follow'd such a morn
  Had worn a deeper shade.
The day without a cloud hath pass'd,
And thou wert lovely to the last;
  Extinguish'd, not decay'd;
As stars that shoot along the sky
Shine brightest as they fall from high.

As once I wept, if I could weep,
  My tears might well be shed,
To think I was not near to keep
  One vigil o'er thy bed;
To gaze, how fondly! on thy face,
To fold thee in a faint embrace,
  Uphold thy drooping head;
And show that love, however vain,
Nor thou nor I can feel again.

Yet how much less it were to gain,
  Though thou hast left me free
The loveliest things that still remain
  Than thus remember thee!
The all of thine that cannot die

Through dark and dread Eternity
　　Returns again to me,
And more thy buried love endears
Than aught, except its living years.

WHEN WE TWO PARTED.

WHEN we two parted
　　In silence and tears,
Half broken-hearted
　　To sever for years,
Pale grew thy cheek and cold,
　　Colder thy kiss;
Truly that hour foretold
　　Sorrow to this.

The dew of the morning
　　Sunk chill on my brow —
It felt like the warning
　　Of what I feel now.
Thy vows are all broken,
　　And light is thy fame;
I hear thy name spoken,
　　And share in its shame.

They name thee before me,
　　A knell to mine ear;
A shudder comes o'er me —
　　Why wert thou so dear?
They know not I knew thee,
　　Who knew thee too well: —

Long, long shall I rue thee,
　Too deeply to tell.

In secret we met —
　In silence I grieve,
That thy heart could forget,
　Thy spirit deceive.
If I should meet thee
　After long years,
How should I greet thee? —
　With silence and tears.

STANZAS FOR MUSIC.

" O Lachrymarum fons, tenero sacros
　Ducentium ortus ex animo : quater
　Felix! in imo qui scatentem
　Pectore te, pia Nympha, seusit."
　　　　　　　　GRAY'S *Poemata.*

THERE 'S not a joy the world can give like that it takes
　away,
When the glow of early thought declines in feeling's dull
　decay;
'T is not on youth's smooth cheek the blush alone, which
　fades so fast,
But the tender bloom of heart is gone, ere youth itself be
　past.

Then the few whose spirits float above the wreck of
　happiness
Are driven o'er the shoals of guilt or ocean of excess:

The magnet of their course is gone, or only points in
vain

The shore to which their shiver'd sail shall never stretch
again.

Then the mortal coldness of the soul like death itself
comes down;

It cannot feel for others' woes, it dare not dream its
own;

That heavy chill has frozen o'er the fountain of our
tears,

And though the eye may sparkle still, 't is where the ice
appears.

Though wit may flash from fluent lips, and mirth distract
the breast,

Through midnight hours that yield no more their former
hope of rest;

'T is but as ivy-leaves around the ruin'd turret wreath,

All green and wildly fresh without, but worn and gray
beneath.

Oh could I feel as I have felt, — or be what I have been,

Or weep as I could once have wept, o'er many a vanish'd
scene;

As springs in deserts found seem sweet, all brackish
though they be,

So, midst the wither'd waste of life, those tears would
flow to me.

STANZAS FOR AUGUSTA.

THOUGH the day of my destiny 's over,
  And the star of my fate hath declined,
Thy soft heart refused to discover
  The faults which so many could find;
Though thy soul with my grief was acquainted,
  It shrunk not to share it with me,
And the love which my spirit hath painted
  It never hath found but in *thee*.

Then when nature around me is smiling,
  The last smile which answers to mine,
I do not believe it beguiling,
  Because it reminds me of thine;
And when winds are at war with the ocean,
  As the breasts I believed in with me,
If their billows excite an emotion,
  It is that they bear me from *thee*.

Though the rock of my last hope is shiver'd,
  And its fragments are sunk in the wave,
Though I feel that my soul is deliver'd
  To pain — it shall not be its slave.
There is many a pang to pursue me:
  They may crush, but they shall not contemn —
They may torture, but shall not subdue me —
  'T is of *thee* that I think — not of them.

Though human, thou didst not deceive me,
  Though woman, thou didst not forsake,
Though loved, thou forborest to grieve me,
  Though slander'd, thou never could'st shake, —

Though trusted, thou didst not disclaim me,
  Though parted, it was not to fly,
Though watchful, 't was not to defame me,
  Nor, mute, that the world might belie.

Yet I blame not the world, nor despise it,
  Nor the war of the many with one —
If my soul was not fitted to prize it,
  'T was folly not sooner to shun:
And if dearly that error hath cost me,
  And more than I once could foresee,
I have found that, whatever it lost me,
  It could not deprive me of *thee*.

From the wreck of the past, which hath perish'd,
  Thus much I at least may recall,
It hath taught me that what I most cherish'd
  Deserved to be dearest of all:
In the desert a fountain is springing,
  In the wide waste there still is a tree,
And a bird in the solitude singing,
  Which speaks to my spirit of *thee*.

SOLITUDE.

(CHILDE HAROLD, Canto ii. Stanzas 25, 26.)

To sit on rocks, to muse o'er flood and fell,
To slowly trace the forest's shady scene,
Where things that own not man's dominion dwell,
And mortal foot hath ne'er or rarely been;

To climb the trackless mountain all unseen,
With the wild flock that never needs a fold:
Alone o'er steeps and foaming falls to lean;
This is not solitude; 't is but to hold
Converse with Nature's charms, and view her stores un-
    roll'd.

But midst the crowd, the hum, the shock of men,
To hear, to see, to feel, and to possess,
And roam along, the world's tired denizen,
With none who bless us, none whom we can bless;
Minions of splendor shrinking from distress!
None that, with kindred consciousness endued,
If we were not, would seem to smile the less
Of all that flatter'd, follow'd, sought, and sued;
This is to be alone; this, this is solitude.

NATURE THE CONSOLER.

(CHILDE HAROLD, Canto iii. Stanzas 13–15.)

WHERE rose the mountains, there to him were friends;
Where roll'd the ocean, thereon was his home;
Where a blue sky, and glowing clime, extends,
He had the passion and the power to roam;
The desert, forest, cavern, breaker's foam,
Were unto him companionship; they spake
A mutual language, clearer than the tome
Of his land's tongue, which he would oft forsake
For Nature's pages glass'd by sunbeams on the lake.

Like the Chaldean, he could watch the stars,
Till he had peopled them with beings bright
As their own beams; and earth, and earth-born jars,
And human frailties, were forgotten quite:
Could he have kept his spirit to that flight
He had been happy; but this clay will sink
Its spark immortal, envying it the light
To which it mounts, as if to break the link
That keeps us from yon heaven which woos us to its
      brink.

But in Man's dwellings he became a thing
Restless and worn, and stern and wearisome,
Droop'd as a wild-born falcon with clipt wing,
To whom the boundless air alone were home:
Then came his fit again, which to o'ercome,
As eagerly the barr'd-up bird will beat
His breast and beak against his wiry dome
Till the blood tinge his plumage, so the heat
Of his impeded soul would through his bosom eat.

THE SAME.

(CHILDE HAROLD, Canto iii. Stanzas 71-75.)

Is it not better, then, to be alone,
And love Earth only for its earthly sake?
By the blue rushing of the arrowy Rhone,
Or the pure bosom of its nursing lake,
Which feeds it as a mother who doth make

A fair but froward infant her own care,
Kissing its cries away as these awake; —
Is it not better thus our lives to wear,
Than join the crushing crowd, doom'd to inflict or bear?

I live not in myself, but I become
Portion of that around me; and to me
High mountains are a feeling, but the hum
Of human cities torture: I can see
Nothing to loathe in nature, save to be
A link reluctant in a fleshly chain,
Class'd among creatures, when the soul can flee,
And with the sky, the peak, the heaving plain
Of ocean, or the stars, mingle, and not in vain.

And thus I am absorb'd, and this is life;
I look upon the peopled desert past,
As on a place of agony and strife,
Where, for some sin, to sorrow I was cast,
To act and suffer, but remount at last
With a fresh pinion; which I feel to spring,
Though young, yet waxing vigorous, as the blast
Which it would cope with, on delighted wing,
Spurning the clay-cold bonds which round our being
        cling.

And when, at length, the mind shall be all free
From what it hates in this degraded form,
Reft of its carnal life, save what shall be
Existent happier in the fly and worm, —
When elements to elements conform,

And dust is as it should be, shall I not
Feel all I see, less dazzling, but more warm?
The bodiless thought? the Spirit of each spot?
Of which, even now, I share at times the immortal lot?

Are not the mountains, waves, and skies, a part
Of me and of my soul, as I of them?
Is not the love of these deep in my heart
With a pure passion? should I not contemn
All objects, if compared with these? and stem
A tide of suffering, rather than forego
Such feelings for the hard and worldly phlegm
Of those whose eyes are only turn'd below,
Gazing upon the ground, with thoughts which dare not
    glow?

———

THE POET AND THE WORLD.

(CHILDE HAROLD, Canto iii. Stanzas 113, 114.)

I HAVE not loved the world, nor the world me;
I have not flatter'd its rank breath, nor bow'd
To its idolatries a patient knee, —
Nor coin'd my cheek to smiles, — nor cried aloud
In worship of an echo; in the crowd
They could not deem me one of such; I stood
Among them, but not of them; in a shroud
Of thoughts which were not their thoughts, and still
    could,
Had I not filed my mind, which thus itself subdued.

I have not loved the world, nor the world me, —
But let us part fair foes; I do believe,
Though I have found them not, that there may be
Words v hich are things, — hopes which will not de
        ceive,
And virtues which are merciful, nor weave
Snares for the failing: I would also deem
O'er others' griefs that some sincerely grieve;
That two, or one, are almost what they seem, —
That goodness is no name, and happiness no dream.

BEREAVEMENT.

(CHILDE HAROLD, Canto ii. Stanza 98.)

WHAT is the worst of woes that wait on age?
What stamps the wrinkle deeper on the brow?
To view each loved one blotted from life's page,
And be alone on earth, as I am now.
Before the Chastener humbly let me bow,
O'er hearts divided and o'er hopes destroy'd:
Roll on, vain days! full reckless may ye flow,
Since Time hath reft whate'er my soul enjoy'd,
And with the ills of Eld mine earlier years alloy'd.

LAST LEAVING ENGLAND.

(CHILDE HAROLD, Canto iii. Stanzas 1, 2.)

Is thy face like thy mother's, my fair child!
ADA! sole daughter of my house and heart?
When last I saw thy young blu eyes they smiled,

And then we parted, — not as now we part,
But with a hope. —

              Awaking with a start,
The waters heave around me; and on high
The winds lift up their voices: I depart,
Whither I know not; but the hour 's gone by,
When Albion's lessening shores could grieve or glad
      mine eye.

Once more upon the waters! yet once more!
And the waves bound beneath me as a steed
That knows his rider. Welcome to the roar!
Swift be their guidance, wheresoe'er it lead!
Though the strain'd mast should quiver as a reed,
And the rent canvas fluttering strew the gale,
Still must I on; for I am as a weed,
Flung from the rock, on Ocean's foam, to sail
Where'er the surge may sweep, the tempest's breath
      prevail.

———

ENGLAND.

(CHILDE HAROLD, Canto iv. Stanzas 8–10.)

I 've taught me other tongues — and in strange eyes
Have made me not a stranger; to the mind
Which is itself, no changes bring surprise;
Nor is it harsh to make, nor hard to find
A country with — ay, or without mankind;
Yet was I born where men are proud to be,
Not without cause; and should I leave behind

The inviolate island of the sage and free,
And seek me out a home by a remoter sea,

Perhaps I loved it well; and should I lay
My ashes in a soil which is not mine,
My spirit shall resume it — if we may
Unbodied choose a sanctuary.   I twine
My hopes of being remember'd in my line
With my land's language: if too fond and far
These aspirations in their scope incline, —
If my fame should be, as my fortunes are,
Of hasty growth and blight, and dull Oblivion bar

My name from out the temple where the dead
Are honor'd by the nations — let it be —
And light the laurels on a loftier head!
And be the Spartan's epitaph on me —
" Sparta hath many a worthier son than he."
Meantime I seek no sympathies, nor need;
The thorns which I have reap'd are of the tree
I planted, — they have torn me, — and I bleed:
I should have known what fruit would spring from such
    a seed.

––––––

RUINS TO RUINS.

(Childe Harold, Canto iv. Stanzas 130, 131.)

Oh Time! the beautifier of the dead,
Adorner of the ruin, comforter
And only healer when the heart hath bled —
Time! the corrector where our judgments err,

The test of truth, love, — sole philosopher,
For all beside are sophists, from thy thrift,
Which never loses though it doth defer —
Time, the avenger! unto thee I lift
My hands, and eyes, and heart, and crave of thee a gift:

Amidst this wreck, where thou hast made a shrine
And temple more divinely desolate,
Among thy mightier offerings here are mine,
Ruins of years — though few, yet full of fate: —
If thou hast ever seen me too elate,
Hear me not; but if calmly I have borne
Good, and reserved my pride against the hate
Which shall not whelm me, let me not have worn
This iron in my soul in vain — shall *they* not mourn?

THE DREAM.

I SAW two beings in the hues of youth
Standing upon a hill, a gentle hill,
Green and of mild declivity, the last
As 't were the cape of a long ridge of such,
Save that there was no sea to lave its base,
But a most living landscape, and the wave
Of woods and cornfields, and the abodes of men
Scatter'd at intervals, and wreathing smoke
Arising from such rustic roofs; the hill
Was crown'd with a peculiar diadem
Of trees, in circular array, so fix'd,
Not by the sport of nature, but of man:

These two, a maiden and a youth, were there
Gazing — the one on all that was beneath
Fair as herself — but the boy gazed on her;
And both were young, and one was beautiful:
And both were young — yet not alike in youth.
As the sweet moon on the horizon's verge,
The maid was on the eve of womanhood;
The boy had fewer summers, but his heart
Had far outgrown his years, and to his eye
There was but one belovèd face on earth,
And that was shining on him; he had look'd
Upon it till it could not pass away;
He had no breath, no being, but in hers;
She was his voice; he did not speak to her,
But trembled on her words; she was his sight,
For his eye follow'd hers, and saw with hers,
Which color'd all his objects: — he had ceased
To live within himself; she was his life,
The ocean to the river of his thoughts,
Which terminated all: upon a tone,
A touch of hers, his blood would ebb and flow,
And his cheek change tempestuously — his heart
Unknowing of its cause of agony.
But she in these fond feelings had no share:
Her sighs were not for him; to her he was
Even as a brother — but no more; 't was much,
For brotherless she was, save in the name
Her infant friendship had bestow'd on him;
Herself the solitary scion left
Of a time-honor'd race. — It was a name
Which pleased him, and yet pleased him not — and why?

Time taught him a deep answer — when she loved
Another; even *now* she loved another,
And on the summit of that hill she stood
Looking afar if yet her lover's steed
Kept pace with her expectancy and flew.

A change came o'er the spirit of my dream.
There was an ancient mansion, and before
Its walls there was a steed caparison'd:
Within an antique Oratory stood
The Boy of whom I spake; — he was alone,
And pale, and pacing to and fro: anon
He sate him down, and seized a pen, and traced
Words which I could not guess of; then he lean'd
His bow'd head on his hands, and shook as 't were
With a convulsion — then arose again,
And with his teeth and quivering hands did tear
What he had written, but he shed no tears.
And he did calm himself, and fix his brow
Into a kind of quiet: as he paused,
The Lady of his love re-enter'd there;
She was serene and smiling then, and yet
She knew she was by him beloved, — she knew,
For quickly comes such knowledge, that his heart
Was darken'd with her shadow, and she saw
That he was wretched, but she saw not all.
He rose, and with a cold and gentle grasp
He took her hand; a moment o'er his face
A tablet of unutterable thoughts
Was traced, and then it faded, as it came;
He dropp'd the hand he held, and with slow steps

Retired, but not as bidding her adieu,
For they did part with mutual smiles; he pass'd
From out the massy gate of that old Hall,
And mounting on his steed he went his way;
And ne'er repass'd that hoary threshold more.

A change came o'er the spirit of my dream.
The Boy was sprung to manhood: in the wilds
Of fiery climes he made himself a home,
And his Soul drank their sunbeams: he was girt
With strange and dusky aspects; he was not
Himself like what he had been; on the sea
And on the shore he was a wanderer;
There was a mass of many images
Crowded like waves upon me, but he was
A part of all; and in the last he lay
Reposing from the noontide sultriness,
Couch'd among fallen columns, in the shade
Of ruin'd walls that had survived the names
Of those who rear'd them; by his sleeping side
Stood camels grazing, and some goodly steeds
Were fasten'd near a fountain; and a man
Clad in a flowing garb did watch the while,
While many of his tribe slumber'd around:
And they were canopied by the blue sky,
So cloudless, clear, and purely beautiful,
That God alone was to be seen in Heaven.

A change came o'er the spirit of my dream.
The Lady of his love was wed with One
Who did not love her better: — in her home,

A thousand leagues from his, — her native home,
She dwelt, begirt with growing Infancy,
Daughters and sons of Beauty, — but behold!
Upon her face there was the tint of grief,
The settled shadow of an inward strife,
And an unquiet drooping of the eye
As if its lid were charged with unshed tears.
What could her grief be? — she had all she loved,
And he who had so loved her was not there
To trouble with bad hopes, or evil wish,
Or ill-repress'd affliction, her pure thoughts.
What could her grief be? — she had loved him not,
Nor given him cause to deem himself beloved,
Nor could he be a part of that which prey'd
Upon her mind — a spectre of the past.

A change came o'er the spirit of my dream,
The Wanderer was return'd. — I saw him stand
Before an Altar — with a gentle bride;
Her face was fair, but was not that which made
The Starlight of his Boyhood; — as he stood
Even at the altar, o'er his brow there came
The self-same aspect, and the quivering shock
That in the antique Oratory shook
His bosom in its solitude; and then —
As in that hour — a moment o'er his face
The tablet of unutterable thoughts
Was traced, — and then it faded as it came,
And he stood calm and quiet, and he spoke
The fitting vows, but heard not his own words,
And all things reel'd around him; he could see

Not that which was, nor that which should have been —
But the old mansion, and the accustom'd hall,
And the remember'd chambers, and the place,
The day, the hour, the sunshine, and the shade,
All things pertaining to that place and hour,
And her who was his destiny, came back
And thrust themselves between him and the light:
What business had they there at such a time?

A change came o'er the spirit of my dream.
The Lady of his love; — Oh! she was changed
As by the sickness of the soul; her mind
Had wander'd from its dwelling, and her eyes
They had not their own lustre, but the look
Which is not of the earth; she was become
The queen of a fantastic realm; her thoughts
Were combinations of disjointed things;
And forms impalpable and unperceived
Of others' sight, familiar were to hers.
And this the world calls frenzy; but the wise
Have a far deeper madness, and the glance
Of melancholy is a fearful gift;
What is it but the telescope of truth?
Which strips the distance of its fantasies,
And brings life near in utter nakedness,
Making the cold reality too real!

A change came o'er the spirit of my dream.
The Wanderer was alone as heretofore,
The beings which surrounded him were gone,
Or were at war with him; he was a mark

For blight and desolation, compass'd round
With Hatred and Contention; Pain was mix'd
In all which was served up to him, until,
Like to the Pontic monarch of old days,
He fed on poisons, and they had no power,
But were a kind of nutriment; he lived
Through that which had been death to many men,
And made him friends of mountains: with the stars
And the quick Spirit of the Universe
He held his dialogues; and they did teach
To him the magic of their mysteries;
To him the book of Night was open'd wide,
And voices from the deep abyss reveal'd
A marvel and a secret — Be it so.

My dream was past; it had no further change.
It was of a strange order, that the doom
Of these two creatures should be thus traced out
Almost like a reality — the one
To end in madness — both in misery.

THE POET'S CURSE.

(CHILDE HAROLD, Canto iv. Stanzas 134-137.)

AND if my voice break forth, 't is not that now
I shrink from what is suffer'd: let him speak
Who hath beheld decline upon my brow,
Or seen my mind's convulsion leave it weak;
But in this page a record will I seek.

Not in the air shall these my words disperse,
Though I be ashes; a far hour shall wreak
The deep prophetic fulness of this verse,
And pile on human heads the mountain of my curse!

That curse shall be Forgiveness. — Have I not —
Hear me, my mother Earth! behold it, Heaven! —
Have I not had to wrestle with my lot?
Have I not suffer'd things to be forgiven?
Have I not had my brain sear'd, my heart riven,
Hopes sapp'd, name blighted, Life's life lied away?
And only not to desperation driven,
Because not altogether of such clay
As rots into the souls of those whom I survey.

From mighty wrongs to petty perfidy
Have I not seen what human things could do?
From the loud roar of foaming calumny
To the small whisper of the as paltry few,
And subtler venom of the reptile crew,
The Janus glance of whose significant eye,
Learning to lie with silence, would *seem* true,
And without utterance, save the shrug or sigh,
Deal round to happy fools its speechless obloquy.

But I have lived, and have not lived in vain:
My mind may lose its force, my blood its fire,
And my frame perish even in conquering pain;
But there is that within me which shall tire
Torture and Time, and breathe when I expire;
Something unearthly, which they deem not of,
Like the remember'd tone of a mute lyre,
Shall on their soften'd spirits sink, and move
In hearts all rocky now the late remorse of love.

NATURE TO THE LAST.

(CHILDE HAROLD, Canto iv. Stanzas 175–184.)

MY Pilgrim's shrine is won,
And he and I must part, — so let it be !
His task and mine alike are nearly done;
Yet once more let us look upon the sea.
The midland ocean breaks on him and me,
And from the Alban Mount we now behold
Our friend of youth, that ocean, which when we
Beheld it last by Calpe's rock unfold
Those waves, we follow'd on till the dark Euxine roll'd

Upon the blue Symplegades; long years —
Long, though not very many, since have done
Their work on both; some suffering and some tears
Have left us nearly where we had begun:
Yet not in vain our mortal race hath run,
We have had our reward — and it is here;
That we can yet feel gladden'd by the sun,
And reap from earth, sea, joy almost as dear
As if there were no man to trouble what is clear.

Oh! that the Desert were my dwelling-place,
With one fair Spirit for my minister,
That I might all forget the human race,
And, hating no one, love but only her !
Ye Elements ! — in whose ennobling stir
I feel myself exalted — Can ye not
Accord me such a being? Do I err
In deeming such inhabit many a spot?
Though with them to converse can rarely be our lot.

There is a pleasure in the pathless woods,
There is a rapture on the lonely shore,
There is society, where none intrudes,
By the deep Sea, and music in its roar.
I love not man the less, but Nature more,
From these our interviews, in which I steal
From all I may be, or have been before,
To mingle with the Universe, and feel
What I can ne'er express, yet cannot all conceal.

Roll on, thou deep and dark blue Ocean — roll!
Ten thousand fleets sweep over thee in vain;
Man marks the earth with ruin — his control
Stops with the shore; — upon the watery plain
The wrecks are all thy deed, nor doth remain
A shadow of man's ravage, save his own,
When, for a moment, like a drop of rain,
He sinks into thy depths with bubbling groan,
Without a grave, unknell'd, uncoffin'd, and unknown.

His steps are not upon thy paths, — thy fields
Are not a spoil for him, — thou dost arise
And shake him from thee; the vile strength he wields
For earth's destruction thou dost all despise,
Spurning him from thy bosom to the skies,
And send'st him, shivering in thy playful spray
And howling, to his Gods, where haply lies
His petty hope in some near port or bay,
And dashest him again to earth: — there let him lay.

The armaments which thunderstrike the walls
Of rock-built cities, bidding nations quake,

And monarchs tremble in their capitals,
The oak leviathans, whose huge ribs make
Their clay creator the vain title take
Of lord of thee, and arbiter of war;
These are thy toys, and, as the snowy flake,
They melt into thy yeast of waves, which mar
Alike the Armada's pride, or spoils of Trafalgar.

Thy shores are empires, changed in all save thee —
Assyria, Greece, Rome, Carthage, what are they?
Thy waters wasted them while they were free,
And many a tyrant since; their shores obey
The stranger, slave, or savage; their decay
Has dried up realms to deserts: — not so thou,
Unchangeable save to thy wild waves' play —
Time writes no wrinkle on thine azure brow —
Such as creation's dawn beheld, thou rollest now.

Thou glorious mirror, where the Almighty's form
Glasses itself in tempests; in all time,
Calm or convulsed — in breeze, or gale, or storm,
Icing the pole, or in the torrid clime
Dark-heaving; — boundless, endless, and sublime —
The image of Eternity — the throne
Of the Invisible; even from out thy slime
The monsters of the deep are made; each zone
Obeys thee; thou goest forth, dread, fathomless, alone.

And I have loved thee, Ocean! and my joy
Of youthful sports was on thy breast to be
Borne, like thy bubbles, onward: from a boy
I wanton'd with thy breakers — they to me

Were a delight; and if the freshening sea
Made them a terror — 't was a pleasing fear,
For I was as it were a child of thee,
And trusted to thy billows far and near,
And laid my hand upon thy mane — as I do here.

———

"*SHE WALKS IN BEAUTY.*"

SHE walks in beauty, like the night
  Of cloudless climes and starry skies;
And all that 's best of dark and bright
  Meet in her aspect and her eyes:
Thus mellow'd to that tender light
  Which heaven to gaudy day denies.

One shade the more, one ray the less,
  Had half impair'd the nameless grace
Which waves in every raven tress,
  Or softly lightens o'er her face;
Where thoughts serenely sweet express
  How pure, how dear their dwelling-place.

And on that cheek, and o'er that brow,
  So soft, so calm, yet eloquent,
The smiles that win, the tints that glow,
  But tell of days in goodness spent,
A mind at peace with all below,
  A heart whose love is innocent!

"OH! SNATCH'D AWAY."

Oн! snatch'd away in beauty's bloom,
On thee shall press no ponderous tomb;
   But on thy turf shall roses rear
   Their leaves, the earliest of the year;
And the wild cypress wave in tender gloom:

And oft by yon blue gushing stream
   Shall Sorrow lean her drooping head,
And feed deep thought with many a dream,
   And lingering pause and lightly tread;
   Fond wretch! as if her step disturb'd the dead.

Away! we know that tears are vain,
   That death nor heeds nor hears distress:
Will this unteach us to complain?
   Or make one mourner weep the less?
And thou—who tell'st me to forget,
Thy looks are wan, thine eyes are wet.

SONG OF SAUL.

Warriors and chiefs! should the shaft or the sword
Pierce me in leading the host of the Lord,
Heed not the corse, though a king's, in your path:
Bury your steel in the bosoms of Gath!

Thou who art bearing my buckler and bow,
Should the soldiers of Saul look away from the foe,
Stretch me that moment in blood at thy feet!
Mine be the doom which they dared not to meet.

Farewell to others, but never we part,
Heir to my royalty, son of my heart!
Bright is the diadem, boundless the sway,
Or kingly the death, which awaits us to-day!

————

VISION OF BELSHAZZAR.

THE King was on his throne,
  The Satraps throng'd the hall;
A thousand bright lamps shone
  O'er that high festival.
A thousand cups of gold,
  In Judah deem'd divine —
Jehovah's vessels hold
  The godless Heathen's wine!

In that same hour and hall,
  The fingers of a hand
Came forth against the wall,
  And wrote as if on sand:
The fingers of a man; —
  A solitary hand
Along the letters ran,
  And traced them like a wand.

The monarch saw, and shook,
  And bade no more rejoice;
All bloodless wax'd his look,
  And tremulous his voice.

" Let the men of lore appear,
   The wisest of the earth
And expound the words of fear
   Which mar our royal mirth."

Chaldea's seers are good,
   But here they have no skill;
And the unknown letters stood
   Untold and awful still.
And Babel's men of age
   Are wise and deep in lore;
But now they were not sage,
   They saw — but knew no more.

A captive in the land,
   A stranger and a youth,
He heard the king's command,
   He saw that writing's truth.
The lamps around were bright,
   The prophecy in view;
He read it on that night, —
   The morrow proved it true.

" Belshazzar's grave is made,
   His kingdom pass'd away,
He, in the balance weigh'd,
   Is light and worthless clay.
The shroud, his robe of state,
   His canopy the stone;
The Mede is at his gate!
   The Persian on his throne!"

DESTRUCTION OF SENNACHERIB.

THE Assyrian came down like the wolf on the fold,
And his cohorts were gleaming in purple and gold;
And the sheen of their spears were like stars on the sea,
When the blue wave rolls nightly on deep Galilee.

Like the leaves of the forest when Summer is green,
That host with their banners at sunset were seen;
Like the leaves of the forest when Autumn hath blown,
That host on the morrow lay wither'd and strown.

For the Angel of Death spread his wings on the blast,
And breathed in the face of the foe as he pass'd;
And the eyes of the sleepers wax'd deadly and chill,
And their hearts but once heaved, and forever grew still!

And there lay the steed with his nostril all wide,
But through it there roll'd not the breath of his pride;
And the foam of his gasping lay white on the turf,
And cold as the spray of the rock-beating surf.

And there lay the rider distorted and pale,
With the dew on his brow, and the rust on his mail;
And the tents were all silent, the banners alone,
The lances unlifted, the trumpet unblown.

And the widows of Ashur are loud in their wail,
And the idols are broke in the temple of Baal;
And the might of the Gentile, unsmote by the sword,
Hath melted like snow in the glance of the Lord!

ODE TO NAPOLEON BUONAPARTE.

'T is done, — but yesterday a King!
  And arm'd with Kings to strive —
And now thou art a nameless thing:
  So abject — yet alive!
Is this the man of thousand thrones,
Who strew'd our earth with hostile bones,
  And can he thus survive? —
Since he, miscall'd the Morning Star,
Nor man nor fiend hath fallen so far.

Ill-minded man! why scourge thy kind
  Who bow'd so low the knee?
By gazing on thyself grown blind,
  Thou taught'st the rest to see.
With might unquestion'd, — power to save, —
Thine only gift hath been the grave
  To those that worshipp'd thee;
Nor till thy fall could mortals guess
Ambition's less than littleness!

Thanks for that lesson — it will teach
  To after-warriors more
Than high Philosophy can preach,
  And vainly preach'd before.
That spell upon the minds of men
Breaks never to unite again,
  That led them to adore
Those Pagod things of sabre sway,
With fronts of brass, and feet of clay.

The triumph, and the vanity,
　The rapture of the strife —
The earthquake voice of Victory,
　To thee the breath of life;
The sword, the sceptre, and that sway
Which man seem'd made but to obey,
　Wherewith renown was rife —
All quell'd ! — Dark Spirit ! what must be
The madness of thy memory !

The Desolater desolate?
　The Victor overthrown !
The Arbiter of others' fate
　A Suppliant for his own !
Is it some yet imperial hope
That with such change can calmly cope?
　Or dread of death alone?
To die a prince — or live a slave —
Thy choice is most ignobly brave !

He who of old would rend the oak,
　Dream'd not of the rebound;
Chain'd by the trunk he vainly broke —
　Alone — how look'd he round?
Thou in the sternness of thy strength
An equal deed hast done at length,
　And darker fate hast found;
He fell, the forest prowlers' prey;
But thou must eat thy heart away !

The Roman when his burning heart
　Was slaked with blood of Rome,

Threw down the dagger — dared depart,
  In savage grandeur, home. —
He dared depart in utter scorn
Of men that such a yoke had borne,
  Yet left him such a doom!
His only glory was that hour
Of self-upheld abandon'd power.

The Spaniard, when the lust of sway
  Had lost its quickening spell,
Cast crowns for rosaries away,
  An empire for a cell;
A strict accountant of his beads,
A subtle disputant on creeds,
  His dotage trifled well:
Yet better had he never known
A bigot's shrine, nor despot's throne.

But thou — from thy reluctant hand
  The thunderbolt is wrung —
Too late thou leav'st the high command
  To which thy weakness clung;
All Evil Spirit as thou art,
It is enough to grieve the heart
  To see thine own unstrung;
To think that God's fair world hath been
The footstool of a thing so mean;

And Earth hath spilt her blood for him,
  Who thus can hoard his own!
And Monarchs bow'd the trembling limb,
  And thank'd him for a throne!

Fair Freedom! we may hold thee dear,
When thus thy mightiest foes their fear
 In humblest guise have shown.
Oh! ne'er may tyrant leave behind
A brighter name to lure mankind!

Thine evil deeds are writ in gore,
 Nor written thus in vain —
Thy triumphs tell of fame no more,
 Or deepen every stain:
If thou hadst died as honor dies,
Some new Napoleon might arise,
 To shame the world again —
But who would soar the solar height,
To set in such a starless night?

Weigh'd in the balance, hero dust
 Is vile as vulgar clay;
Thy scales, Mortality! are just
 To all that pass away:
But yet methought the living great
Some higher sparks should animate,
 To dazzle and dismay;
Nor deem'd Contempt could thus make mirth
Of these, the Conquerors of the earth.

And she, proud Austria's mournful flower,
 Thy still imperial bride;
How bears her breast the torturing hour?
 Still clings she to thy side?
Must she too bend, must she too share
Thy late repentance, long despair,
 Thou throneless Homicide?

If still she loves thee, hoard that gem,
'T is worth thy vanish'd diadem!

Then haste thee to thy sullen Isle,
　And gaze upon the sea;
That element may meet thy smile —
　It ne'er was ruled by thee!
Or trace with thine all idle hand
In loitering mood upon the sand
　That Earth is now as free!
That Corinth's pedagogue hath now
Transferr'd his by-word to thy brow.

Thou Timour! in his captive's cage
　What thoughts will there be thine.
While brooding in thy prison'd rage?
　But one — " The world *was* mine!"
Unless, like he of Babylon,
All sense is with thy sceptre gone,
　Life will not long confine
That spirit pour'd so widely forth —
So long obey'd — so little worth!

Or, like the thief of fire from heaven,
　Wilt thou withstand the shock?
And share with him, the unforgiven,
　His vulture and his rock!
Foredoom'd by God — by man accurst,
And that last act, though not thy worst,
　The very Fiend's arch mock;
He in his fall preserved his pride,
And, if a mortal, had as proudly died!

There was a day — there was an hour,
    While earth was Gaul's — Gaul thine —
When that immeasurable power
    Unsated to resign
Had been an act of purer fame
Than gathers round Marengo's name,
    And gilded thy decline
Through the long twilight of all time,
Despite some passing clouds of crime.

But thou forsooth must be a king,
    And don the purple vest, —
As if that foolish robe could wring
    Remembrance from thy breast.
Where is that faded garment? where
The gewgaws thou wert fond to wear,
    The star — the string — the crest?
Vain froward child of empire! say,
Are all thy playthings snatch'd away?

Where may the wearied eye repose
    When gazing on the Great;
Where neither guilty glory glows,
    Nor despicable state?
Yes — one — the first — the last — the best —
The Cincinnatus of the West,
    Whom envy dared not hate,
Bequeath'd the name of Washington,
To make man blush there was but one!

ODE ON WATERLOO.

WE do not curse thee, Waterloo!
Though Freedom's blood thy plain bedew;
There 't was shed, but is not sunk —
Rising from each gory trunk,
Like the water-spout from ocean,
With a strong and growing motion —
It soars, and mingles in the air,
With that of lost Labedoyère —
With that of him whose honor'd grave
Contains the "bravest of the brave."
A crimson cloud it spreads and glows,
But shall return to whence it rose;
When 't is full 't will burst asunder —
Never yet was heard such thunder
As then shall shake the world with wonder —
Never yet was seen such lightning
As o'er heaven shall then be bright'ning!
Like the Wormwood Star foretold
By the sainted Seer of old,
Show'ring down a fiery flood,
Turning rivers into blood.

The Chief has fallen, but not by you,
Vanquishers of Waterloo!
When the soldier citizen
Sway'd not o'er his fellow-men —
Save in deeds that led them on
Where Glory smiled on Freedom's son —

Who, of all the despots banded,
  With that youthful chief competed?
  Who could boast o'er France defeated,
Till lone Tyranny commanded?
Till, goaded by ambition's sting,
The Hero sunk into the King?
Then he fell: — so perish all,
Who would men by man enthrall!

And thou, too, of the snow-white plume!
Whose realm refused thee ev'n a tomb;
Better hadst thou still been leading
France o'er hosts of hirelings bleeding,
Than sold thyself to death and shame
For a meanly royal name;
Such as he of Naples wears,
Who thy blood-bought title bears.
Little didst thou deem, when dashing
  On thy war-horse through the ranks
  Like a stream which burst its banks,
While helmets cleft, and sabres clashing,
Shone and shiver'd fast around thee —
Of the fate at last which found thee:
Was that haughty plume laid low
By a slave's dishonest blow?
Once — as the Moon sways o'er the tide,
It roll'd in air, the warrior's guide;
Through the smoke-created night
Of the black and sulphurous fight,
The soldier raised his seeking eye
To catch that crest's ascendency, —

And, as it onward rolling rose,
So moved his heart upon our foes.
There, where death's brief pang was quickest,
And the battle's wreck lay thickest,
Strew'd beneath the advancing banner
   Of the eagle's burning crest —
(There with thunder-clouds to fan her,
   Who could then her wing arrest —
   Victory beaming from her breast?)
While the broken line enlarging
   Fell, or fled along the plain;
There be sure was Murat charging!
   There he ne'er shall charge again!

O'er glories gone the invaders march,
Weeps Triumph o'er each levell'd arch —
But let Freedom rejoice,
With her heart in her voice;
But, her hand on the sword,
Doubly shall she be adored;
France hath twice too well been taught
The " moral lesson " dearly bought —
Her safety sits not on a throne,
With Capet or Napoleon!
But in equal rights and laws,
Hearts and hands in one great cause —
Freedom, such as God hath given
Unto all beneath his heaven,
With their breath, and from their birth,
Though Guilt would sweep it from the earth—
With a fierce and lavish hand

Scattering nations' wealth like sand;
Pouring nations' blood like water,
In imperial seas of slaughter!

But the heart and the mind,
And the voice of mankind,
Shall arise in communion —
And who shall resist that proud union?
The time is past when swords subdued —
Man may die — the soul's renew'd:
Even in this low world of care
Freedom ne'er shall want an heir;
Millions breathe but to inherit
Her forever bounding spirit —
When once more her hosts assemble,
Tyrants shall believe and tremble —
Smile they at this idle threat?
Crimson tears will follow yet.

NAPOLEON'S FAREWELL.

FAREWELL to the Land, where the gloom of my Glory
Arose and o'ershadow'd the earth with her name —
She abandons me now — but the page of her story,
The brightest or blackest, is filled with my fame.
I have warr'd with a world which vanquish'd me only
When the meteor of conquest allured me too far;
I have coped with the nations which dread me thus lonely,
The last single Captive to millions in war.

Farewell to thee, France ! when thy diadem crown'd me,
I made thee the gem and the wonder of earth, —
But thy weakness decrees I should leave as I found thee,
Decay'd in thy glory, and sunk in thy worth.
Oh ! for the veteran hearts that were wasted
In strife with the storm, when their battles were won —
Then the Eagle, whose gaze in that moment was blasted,
Had still soar'd with eyes fix'd on victory's sun !

Farewell to thee, France ! — but when Liberty rallies
Once more in thy regions, remember me then.
The violet still grows in the depth of thy valleys;
Though wither'd, thy tear will unfold it again.
Yet, yet, I may baffle the hosts that surround us,
And yet may thy heart leap awake to my voice —
There are links which must break in the chain that has
    bound us,
Then turn thee and call on the Chief of thy choice !

LAMENT OF TASSO.

LONG years ! — It tries the thrilling frame to bear
And eagle-spirit of a Child of Song —
Long years of outrage, calumny, and wrong;
Imputed madness, prison'd solitude,
And the mind's canker in its savage mood,
When the impatient thirst of light and air
Parches the heart; and the abhorrèd grate,
Marring the sunbeams with its hideous shade,
Works through the throbbing eyeball to the brain

With a hot sense of heaviness and pain;
And bare, at once, Captivity display'd
Stands scoffing through the never-open'd gate,
Which nothing through its bars admits, save day,
And tasteless food, which I have eat alone
Till its unsocial bitterness is gone;
And I can banquet like a beast of prey,
Sullen and lonely, couching in the cave
Which is my lair, and — it may be — my grave.
All this hath somewhat worn me, and may wear,
But must be borne.   I stoop not to despair;
For I have battled with mine agony,
And made me wings wherewith to overfly
The narrow circus of my dungeon wall,
And freed the Holy Sepulchre from thrall;
And revell'd among men and things divine,
And pour'd my spirit over Palestine,
In honor of the sacred war for Him,
The God who was on earth and is in heaven,
For he hath strengthen'd me in heart and limb.
That through this sufferance I might be forgiven,
I have employ'd my penance to record
How Salem's shrine was won, and how adored.

But this is o'er — my pleasant task is done: —
My long-sustaining friend of many years!
If I do blot thy final page with tears,
Know, that my sorrows have wrung from me none.
But thou, my young creation! my soul's child!
Which ever playing round me came and smiled
And woo'd me from myself with that sweet sight,

Thou too art gone — and so is my delight:
And therefore do I weep and inly bleed
With this last bruise upon a broken reed.

———

DANTE IN EXILE.

(PROPHECY OF DANTE, Canto i.)

ALAS! with what a weight upon my brow
   The sense of earth and earthly things come back,
   Corrosive passions, feelings dull and low,
The heart's quick throb upon the mental rack,
   Long day, and dreary night; the retrospect
   Of half a century bloody and black,
And the frail few years I may yet expect
   Hoary and hopeless, but less hard to bear,
   For I have been too long and deeply wreck'd
On the lone rock of desolate Despair
   To lift my eyes more to the passing sail
   Which shuns that reef so horrible and bare;
Nor raise my voice — for who would heed my wail?
   I am not of this people, nor this age,
   And yet my harpings will unfold a tale
Which shall preserve these times when not a page
   Of their perturbèd annals could attract
   An eye to gaze upon their civil rage,
Did not my verse embalm full many an act
   Worthless as they who wrought it: 't is the doom
   Of spirits of my order to be rack'd

In life, to wear their hearts out, and consume
　　Their days in endless strife, and die alone;
　　Then future thousands crowd around their tomb,
And pilgrims come from climes where they have known
　　The name of him — who now is but a name,
　　And wasting homage o'er the sullen stone,
Spread his — by him unheard, unheeded — fame;
　　And mine at least hath cost me dear: to die
　　Is nothing; but to wither thus — to tame
My mind down from its own infinity —
　　To live in narrow ways with little men,
　　A common sight to every common eye,
A wanderer, while even wolves can find a den,
　　Ripp'd from all kindred, from all home, all things
　　That make communion sweet, and soften pain —
To feel me in the solitude of kings
　　Without the power that makes them bear a crown —
　　To envy every dove his nest and wings
Which waft him where the Apennine looks down
　　On Arno, till he perches, it may be,
　　Within my all inexorable town,
Where yet my boys are, and that fatal she,
　　Their mother, the cold partner who hath brought
　　Destruction for a dowry — this to see
And feel, and know without repair, hath taught
　　A bitter lesson; but it leaves me free:
　　I have not vilely found, nor basely sought,
They made an Exile — not a slave of me.

THE ISLES OF GREECE.

(SONG OF A GREEK.)

THE isles of Greece, the isles of Greece!
  Where burning Sappho loved and sung,
Where grew the arts of war and peace, —
  Where Delos rose, and Phœbus sprung!
Eternal summer gilds them yet,
But all, except their sun, is set.

The Scian and the Teian muse,
  The hero's harp, the lover's lute,
Have found the fame your shores refuse;
  Their place of birth alone is mute
To sounds which echo further west
Than your sires' "Islands of the Blest."

The mountains look on Marathon —
  And Marathon looks on the sea;
And musing there an hour alone,
  I dream'd that Greece might still be free;
For standing on the Persians' grave,
I could not deem myself a slave.

A king sate on the rocky brow
  Which looks o'er sea-born Salamis;
And ships, by thousands, lay below,
  And men in nations; — all were his!
He counted them at break of day —
And when the sun set where were they?

And where are they? and where art thou,
  My country?   On thy voiceless shore
The heroic lay is tuneless now —
  The heroic bosom beats no more!
And must thy lyre, so long divine,
Degenerate into hands like mine?

'T is something, in the dearth of fame,
  Though link'd among a fetter'd race,
To feel at least a patriot's shame,
  Even as I sing, suffuse my face;
For what is left the poet here?
For Greeks a blush — for Greece a tear.

Must *we* but weep o'er days more blest?
  Must *we* but blush? — Our fathers bled.
Earth! render back from out thy breast
  A remnant of our Spartan dead!
Of the three hundred grant but three,
To make a new Thermopylæ!

What, silent still? and silent all?
  Ah! no; — the voices of the dead
Sound like a distant torrent's fall,
  And answer, " Let one living head,
But one arise, — we come, we come! "
'T is but the living who are dumb.

In vain — in vain: strike other chords;
  Fill high the cup with Samian wine!

Leave battles to the Turkish hordes,
   And shed the blood of Scio's vine!
Hark! rising to the ignoble call —
How answers each bold Bacchanal!

You have the Pyrrhic dance as yet,
   Where is the Pyrrhic phalanx gone?
Of two such lessons, why forget
   The nobler and the manlier one?
You have the letters Cadmus gave —
Think ye he meant them for a slave?

Fill high the bowl with Samian wine!
   We will not think of themes like these!
It made Anacreon's song divine:
   He served — but served Polycrates —
A tyrant; but our masters then
Were still, at least, our countrymen.

The tyrant of the Chersonese
   Was freedom's best and bravest friend;
That tyrant was Miltiades!
   Oh! that the present hour would lend
Another despot of the kind!
Such chains as his were sure to bind.

Fill high the bowl with Samian wine!
   On Suli's rock, and Parga's shore,
Exists the remnant of a line
   Such as the Doric mothers bore;
And there, perhaps some seed is sown,
The Heracleidan blood might own.

Trust not for freedom to the Franks —
　　They have a king who buys and sells:
In native swords, and native ranks,
　　The only hope of courage dwells;
But Turkish force, and Latin fraud,
Would break your shield, however broad.

Fill high the bowl with Samian wine !
　　Our virgins dance beneath the shade —
I see their glorious black eyes shine;
　　But gazing on each glowing maid,
My own the burning tear-drop laves,
To think such breasts must suckle slaves.

Place me on Sunium's marbled steep,
　　Where nothing, save the waves and I,
May hear our mutual murmurs sweep;
　　There, swan-like, let me sing and die.
A land of slaves shall ne'er be mine —
Dash down yon cup of Samian wine !

LINES TO A LADY WEEPING.[1]

WEEP, daughter of a royal line,
　　A Sire's disgrace, a realm's decay;
Ah ! happy if each tear of thine
　　Could wash a father's fault away !

Weep — for thy tears are Virtue's tears —
　　Auspicious to these suffering isles;
And be each drop in future years
　　Repaid thee by thy people's smiles !

1 The Princess Charlotte.

DEATH OF THE PRINCESS CHAR-LOTTE.

(CHILDE HAROLD, Canto iv. Stanzas 167–172.)

HARK! forth from the abyss a voice proceeds,
A long low distant murmur of dread sound,
Such as arises when a nation bleeds
With some deep and immedicable wound;
Through storm and darkness yawns the rending ground,
The gulf is thick with phantoms, but the chief
Seems royal still, though with her head discrown'd,
And pale, but lovely, with maternal grief
She clasps a babe, to whom her breast yields no relief.

Scion of chiefs and monarchs, where art thou?
Fond hope of many nations, art thou dead?
Could not the grave forget thee, and lay low
Some less majestic, less belovèd head?
In the sad midnight, while thy heart still bled,
The mother of a moment, o'er thy boy,
Death hush'd that pang forever: with thee fled
The present happiness and promised joy
Which fill'd the imperial isles so full it seem'd to cloy.

Peasants bring forth in safety. —Can it be,
Oh thou that wert so happy, so adored!
Those who weep not for kings shall weep for thee,
And Freedom's heart, grown heavy, cease to hoard
Her many griefs for ONE; for she had pour'd

Her orisons for thee, and o'er thy head
Beheld her Iris. — Thou, too, lonely lord,
And desolate consort — vainly wert thou wed!
The husband of a year! the father of the dead!

Of sackcloth was thy wedding garment made;
Thy bridal's fruit is ashes: in the dust
The fair-hair'd Daughter of the Isles is laid,
The love of millions!   How did we intrust
Futurity to her! and, though it must
Darken above our bones, yet fondly deem'd
Our children should obey her child, and blest
Her and her hoped-for seed, whose promise seem'd
Like stars to shepherds' eyes: — 't was but a meteor
  beam'd.

Woe unto us, not her; for she sleeps well:
The fickle reek of popular breath, the tongue
Of hollow counsel, the false oracle,
Which from the birth of monarchy hath rung
Its knell in princely ears, till the o'erstung
Nations have arm'd in madness, the strange fate
Which tumbles mightiest sovereigns, and hath flung
Against their blind omnipotence a weight
Within the opposing scale, which crushes soon or late, —

These might have been her destiny; but no,
Our hearts deny it: and so young, so fair,
Good without effort, great without a foe,
But now a bride and mother — and now *there!*
How many ties did that stern moment tear!

From thy Sire's to his humblest subject's breast
Is link'd the electric chain of that despair,
Whose shock was as an earthquake's, and opprest
The land which loved thee so that none could love
    thee best.

————

IMMORTALITY.

(CHILDE HAROLD, Canto ii. Stanzas 7, 8.)

WELL didst thou speak, Athena's wisest son!
" All that we know is, nothing can be known."
Why should we shrink from what we cannot shun?
Each hath his pang, but feeble sufferers groan
With brain-born dreams of evil all their own.
Pursue what Chance or Fate proclaimeth best;
Peace waits us on the shores of Acheron:
There no forced banquet claims the sated guest,
But Silence spreads the couch of ever welcome rest.

Yet if, as holiest men have deem'd, there be
A land of souls beyond that sable shore,
To shame the doctrine of the Sadducee
And sophists, madly vain of dubious lore;
How sweet it were in concert to adore
With those who made our mortal labors light!
To hear each voice we fear'd to hear no more!
Behold each mighty shade reveal'd to sight,
The Bactrian, Samian sage, and all who taught the right!

"ON THIS DAY I COMPLETE MY THIRTY-SIXTH YEAR."

'T is time this heart should be unmoved,
    Since others it hath ceased to move;
Yet, though I cannot be beloved,
      Still let me love!

My days are in the yellow leaf;
    The flowers and fruits of love are gone;
The worm, the canker, and the grief
      Are mine alone!

The fire that on my bosom preys
    Is lone as some volcanic isle;
No torch is kindled at its blaze —
      A funeral pile!

The hope, the fear, the jealous care
    The exalted portion of the pain
And power of love, I cannot share,
      But wear the chain.

But 't is not *thus* — and 't is not *here* —
    Such thoughts should shake my soul, nor *now*,
Where glory decks the hero's bier,
      Or binds his brow.

The sword, the banner, and the field,
    Glory and Greece, around me see!
The Spartan, borne upon his shield,
      Was not more free.

Awake! (not Greece — she *is* awake!)
 Awake, my spirit!   Think through *whom*
Thy life-blood tracks its parent lake,
 And then strike home!

Tread those reviving passions down,
 Unworthy manhood! — unto thee
Indifferent should the smile or frown
 Of beauty be.

If thou regret'st thy youth, *why live?*
 The land of honorable death
Is here: — up to the field, and give
 Away thy breath!

Seek out — less often sought than found —
 A soldier's grave, for thee the best;
Then look around, and choose thy ground,
 And take thy rest.

———

LIFE.

(DON JUAN, Canto xv. Stanza 99.)

BETWEEN two worlds life hovers like a star,
 'Twixt night and morn, upon the horizon's verge.
How little do we know that which we are!
 How less what we may be!   The eternal surge
Of time and tide rolls on, and bears afar
 Our bubbles; as the old burst, new emerge,
Lash'd from the foam of ages; while the graves
Of empires heave but like some passing waves.

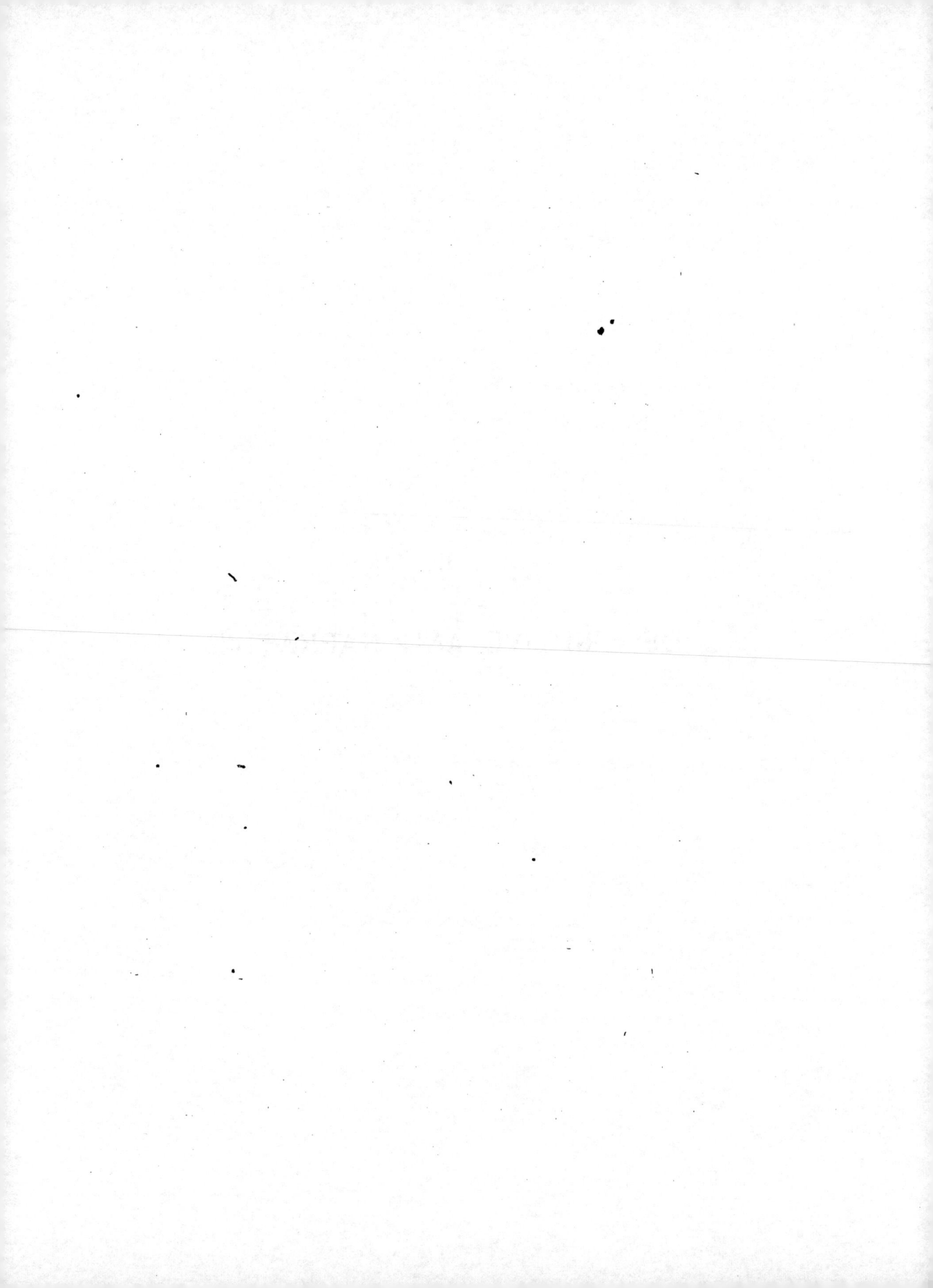

II.

DESCRIPTIVE AND NARRATIVE.

GREECE.

(THE CORSAIR, Canto iii.)

SLOW sinks, more lovely ere his race be run,
Along Morea's hills the setting sun;
Not, as in northern climes, obscurely bright,
But one unclouded blaze of living light;
O'er the hush'd deep the yellow beam he throws,
Gilds the green wave that trembles as it glows;
On old Ægina's rock and Hydra's isle
The god of gladness sheds his parting smile;
O'er his own regions lingering loves to shine,
Though there his altars are no more divine.
Descending fast, the mountain-shadows kiss
Thy glorious gulf, unconquer'd Salamis!
Their azure arches through the long expanse,
More deeply purpled, meet his mellowing glance,
And tenderest tints, along their summits driven,
Mark his gay course, and own the hues of heaven;
Till, darkly shaded from the land and deep,
Behind his Delphian rock he sinks to sleep.

On such an eve his palest beam he cast
When, Athens! here thy wisest look'd his last.
How watch'd thy better sons his farewell ray,
That closed their murder'd sage's latest day!
Not yet — not yet — Sol pauses on the hill,
The precious hour of parting lingers still;

But sad his light to agonizing eyes,
And dark the mountain's once delightful dyes;
Gloom o'er the lovely land he seem'd to pour,
The land where Phœbus never frown'd before;
But e'er he sunk below Citheron's head,
The cup of woe was quaff'd — the spirit fled;
The soul of him that scorn'd to fear or fly,
Who lived and died as none can live or die.

But, lo! from high Hymettus to the plain
The queen of night asserts her silent reign;
No murky vapor, herald of the storm,
Hides her fair face, or girds her glowing form.
With cornice glimmering as the moonbeams play,
There the white column greets her grateful ray,
And bright around, with quivering beams beset,
Her emblem sparkles o'er the minaret;
The groves of olive scatter'd dark and wide,
Where meek Cephisus sheds his scanty tide,
The cypress saddening by the sacred mosque,
The gleaming turret of the gay kiosk,
And sad and sombre mid the holy calm,
Near Theseus' fane, yon solitary palm;
All, tinged with varied hues, arrest the eye;
And dull were his that pass'd them heedless by.

Again the Ægean, heard no more afar,
Lulls his chafed breast from elemental war;
Again his waves in milder tints unfold
Their long expanse of sapphire and of gold,
Mix'd with the shades of many a distant isle,
That frown, where gentler ocean deigns to smile.

THE SAME.

(From The Giaour.)

FAIR clime! where every season smiles
Benignant o'er those blessed isles,
Which, seen from far Colonna's height,
Make glad the heart that hails the sight,
And lend to loneliness delight.
There mildly dimpling, Ocean's cheek
Reflects the tints of many a peak
Caught by the laughing tides that lave
These Edens of the eastern wave:
And if at times a transient breeze
Break the blue crystal of the seas,
Or sweep one blossom from the trees,
How welcome is each gentle air
That wakes and wafts the odors there!
For there — the Rose o'er crag or vale,
Sultana of the Nightingale,

   The maid for whom his melody,
   His thousand songs are heard on high,
Blooms blushing to her lover's tale:
His queen, the garden queen, his Rose,
Unbent by winds, unchill'd by snows,
Far from the winters of the west,
By every breeze and season blest,
Returns the sweets by nature given
In softest incense back to heaven;
And grateful yields that smiling sky
Her fairest hue and fragrant sigh.

And many a summer flower is there,
And many a shade that love might share,
And many a grotto, meant for rest,
That holds the pirate for a guest;
Whose bark in sheltering cove below
Lurks for the passing peaceful prow,
Till the gay mariner's guitar
Is heard, and seen the evening star;
Then stealing with the muffled oar
Far shaded by the rocky shore,
Rush the night-prowlers on the prey,
And turn to groans his roundelay.
Strange — that where Nature loved to trace,
As if for Gods, a dwelling place,
And every charm and grace hath mix't
Within the paradise she fix't,
There man, enamour'd of distress,
Should mar it into wilderness,
And trample, brute-like, o'er each flower
That tasks not one laborious hour;
Nor claims the culture of his hand
To bloom along the fairy land,
But springs as to preclude his care,
And sweetly woos him — but to spare !
Strange — that where all is peace beside,
There passion riots in her pride,
And lust and rapine wildly reign
To darken o'er the fair domain.
It is as though the fiends prevail'd
Against the seraphs they assail'd,
And, fix'd on heavenly thrones, should dwell

The free inheritors of hell;
So soft the scene, so form'd for joy,
So curst the tyrants that destroy!

He who hath bent him o'er the dead
Ere the first day of death is fled,
The first dark day of nothingness,
The last of danger and distress
(Before Decay's effacing fingers
Have swept the lines where beauty lingers,)
And mark'd the mild angelic air,
The rapture of repose that 's there,
The fix't yet tender traits that streak
The languor of the placid cheek,
And — but for that sad shrouded eye,
   That fires not, wins not, weeps not, now,
   And but for that chill, changeless brow,
Where cold Obstruction's apathy
Appals the gazing mourner's heart,
As if to him it could impart
The doom he dreads, yet dwells upon;
Yes, but for these and these alone,
Some moments, ay, one treacherous hour,
He still might doubt the tyrant's power;
So fair, so calm, so softly seal'd,
The first, last look by death reveal'd!
Such is the aspect of this shore;
'T is Greece, but living Greece no more!
So coldly sweet, so deadly fair,
We start, for soul is wanting there.
Hers is the loveliness in death,

That parts not quite with parting breath;
But beauty with that fearful bloom,
That hue which haunts it to the tomb,
Expression's last receding ray,
A gilded halo hovering round decay,
The farewell beam of Feeling past away!
Spark of that flame, perchance of heavenly birth,
Which gleams, but warms no more its cherish'd earth!

　　Clime of the unforgotten brave!
Whose land from plain to mountain-cave
Was Freedom's home or Glory's grave!
Shrine of the mighty! can it be,
That this is all remains of thee?
Approach, thou craven crouching slave:
　　Say, is not this Thermopylæ?
These waters blue that round you lave,
　　Oh servile offspring of the free —
Pronounce what sea, what shore is this?
The gulf, the rock of Salamis!
These scenes, their story not unknown,
Arise, and make again your own;
Snatch from the ashes of your sires
The embers of their former fires;
And he who in the strife expires
Will add to theirs a name of fear
That Tyranny shall quake to hear,
And leave his sons a hope, a fame,
They too will rather die than shame:
For Freedom's battle once begun,
Bequeath'd by bleeding Sire to Son,

Though baffled oft, is ever won.
Bear witness, Greece, thy living page,
Attest it many a deathless age !
While kings, in dusty darkness hid,
Have left a nameless pyramid,
Thy heroes, though the general doom
Hath swept the column from their tomb,
A mightier monument command,
The mountains of their native land !
There points thy Muse to stranger's eye
The graves of those that cannot die !
'T were long to tell and sad to trace,
Each step from splendor to disgrace;
Enough — no foreign foe could quell
Thy soul, till from itself it fell;
Yes ! Self-abasement paved the way
To villain bonds and despot sway.

THE SAME.

(CHILDE HAROLD, Canto ii. Stanzas 73-77.)

FAIR GREECE ! sad relic of departed worth !
Immortal, though no more; though fallen, great !
Who now shall lead thy scatter'd children forth,
And long accustom'd bondage uncreate?
Not such thy sons who whilome did await,
The hopeless warriors of a willing doom,
In bleak Thermopylæ's sepulchral strait —
Oh ! who that gallant spirit shall resume,
Leap from Eurotas' banks, and call thee from the tomb?

Spirit of freedom! when on Phyle's brow
Thou sat'st with Thrasybulus and his train,
Couldst thou forbode the dismal hour which now
Dims the green beauties of thine Attic plain?
Not thirty tyrants now enforce the chain,
But every carle can lord it o'er thy land;
Nor rise thy sons, but idly rail in vain,
Trembling beneath the scourge of Turkish hand,
From birth till death enslaved; in word, in deed,
    unmann'd.

In all save form alone, how changed! and who
That marks the fire still sparkling in each eye,
Who but would deem their bosoms burn'd anew
With thy unquenched beam, lost Liberty!
And many dream withal the hour is nigh
That gives them back their fathers' heritage:
For foreign arms and aid they fondly sigh,
Nor solely dare encounter hostile rage,
Or tear their name defiled from Slavery's mournful page.

Hereditary bondsmen! know ye not
Who would be free themselves must strike the blow?
By their right arms the conquest must be wrought?
Will Gaul or Muscovite redress ye? no!
True, they may lay your proud despoilers low,
But not for you will Freedom's altars flame.
Shades of the Helots! triumph o'er your foe!
Greece! change thy lords, thy state is still the same;
Thy glorious day is o'er, but not thine years of shame.

The city won for Allah from the Giaour,
The Giaour from Othman's race again may wrest;
And the Serai's impenetrable tower
Receive the fiery Frank, her former guest;
Or Wahab's rebel brood who dared divest
The prophet's tomb of all its pious spoil,
May wind their path of blood along the West;
But ne'er will freedom seek this fated soil,
But slave succeed to slave through years of endless toil.

THE SAME.

(CHILDE HAROLD, Canto ii. Stanzas 84–88.)

WHEN riseth Lacedæmon's hardihood,
When Thebes Epaminondas rears again,
When Athens' children are with hearts endued,
When Grecian mothers shall give birth to men,
Then may'st thou be restored; but not till then!
A thousand years scarce serve to form a state;
An hour may lay it in the dust: and when
Can man its shatter'd splendor renovate,
Recall its virtues back, and vanquish Time and Fate?

And yet how lovely in thine age of woe,
Land of lost gods and godlike men! art thou!
Thy vales of evergreen, thy hills of snow,
Proclaim thee Nature's varied favorite now;
Thy fanes, thy temples to thy surface bow,
Commingling slowly with heroic earth,
Broke by the share of every rustic plough:

So perish monuments of mortal birth,
So perish all in turn, save well-recorded Worth;

Save where some solitary column mourns
Above its prostrate brethren of the cave;
Save where Tritonia's airy shrine adorns
Colonna's cliff, and gleams along the wave;
Save o'er some warrior's half-forgotten grave,
Where the gray stones and unmolested grass
Ages, but not oblivion, feebly brave,
While strangers only not regardless pass,
Lingering like me, perchance, to gaze, and sigh " Alas ! "

Yet are thy skies as blue, thy crags as wild;
Sweet are thy groves, and verdant are thy fields,
Thine olive ripe as when Minerva smiled,
And still his honied wealth Hymettus yields;
There the blithe bee his fragrant fortress builds,
The freeborn wanderer of thy mountain-air;
Apollo still thy long, long summer gilds,
Still in his beam Mendeli's marbles glare;
Art, Glory, Freedom fail, but Nature still is fair.

Where'er we tread 't is haunted, holy ground,
No earth of thine is lost in vulgar mould,
But one vast realm of wonder spreads around,
And all the Muse's tales seem truly told,
Till the sense aches with gazing to behold
The scenes our earliest dreams have dwelt upon:
Each hill and dale, each deepening glen and wold
Defies the power which crush'd thy temples gone:
Age shakes Athena's tower, but spares gray Marathon.

HELLESPONT.

(THE BRIDE OF ABYDOS, Canto ii.)

THE winds are high on Helle's wave,
    As on that night of stormy water
When Love, who sent, forgot to save
The young, the beautiful, the brave,
    The lonely hope of Sestos' daughter.
Oh! when alone along the sky
Her turret-torch was blazing high,
Though rising gale, and breaking foam,
And shrieking sea-birds warn'd him home;
And clouds aloft and tides below,
With signs and sounds, forbade to go,
He could not see, he would not hear,
Or sound or sign foreboding fear;
His eye but saw that light of love,
The only star it hail'd above;
His ear but rang with Hero's song,
"Ye waves, divide not lovers long!" —
That tale is old, but love anew
May nerve young hearts to prove as true.

The winds are high, and Helle's tide
    Rolls darkly heaving to the main;
And Night's descending shadows hide
    That field with blood bedew'd in vain,
The desert of old Priam's pride;
    The tombs, sole relics of his reign,
All — save immortal dreams that could beguile
The blind old man of Scio's rocky isle!

TROY.

(DON JUAN, Canto iv. Stanzas 76–78.)

THERE, on the green and village-cotted hill, is
  (Flank'd by the Hellespont, and by the sea)
Entomb'd the bravest of the brave, Achilles;
  They say so — (Bryant says the contrary);
And further downward, tall and towering still, is
  The tumulus — of whom? Heaven knows; 't may be
Patroclus, Ajax, or Protesilaus;
All heroes, who, if living still, would slay us.

High barrows, without marble, or a name,
  A vast, untill'd, and mountain-skirted plain,
And Ida in the distance, still the same,
  And old Scamander (if 't is he), remain;
The situation seems still form'd for fame —
  A hundred thousand men might fight again
With ease; but where I sought for Ilion's walls,
The quiet sheep feeds, and the tortoise crawls;

Troops of untended horses; here and there
  Some little hamlets, with new names uncouth;
Some shepherds (unlike Paris) led to stare
  A moment at the European youth
Whom to the spot their school-boy feelings bear;
  A Turk, with beads in hand, and pipe in mouth,
Extremely taken with his own religion,
Are what I found there — but the devil a Phrygian.

THE DRACHENFELS.

(CHILDE HAROLD, Canto iii.)

THE castled crag of Drachenfels
Frowns o'er the wide and winding Rhine,
Whose breast of waters broadly swells
Between the banks which bear the vine,
And hills all rich with blossom'd trees,
And fields which promise corn and wine,
And scatter'd cities crowning these,
Whose far white walls along them shine,
Have strew'd a scene, which I should see
With double joy wert *thou* with me.

And peasant girls, with deep blue eyes,
And hands which offer early flowers,
Walk smiling o'er this paradise;
Above, the frequent feudal towers
Through green leaves lift their walls of gray,
And many a rock which steeply lowers,
And noble arch in proud decay,
Look o'er this vale of vintage-bowers;
But one thing want these banks of Rhine, —
Thy gentle hand to clasp in mine!

I send the lilies given to me;
Though long before thy hand they touch,
I know that they must wither'd be,
But yet reject them not as such;
For I have cherish'd them as dear,
Because they yet may meet thine eye,

And guide thy soul to mine even here,
When thou behold'st them drooping nigh,
And know'st them gather'd by the Rhine,
And offer'd from my heart to thine!

The river nobly foams and flows,
The charm of this enchanted ground,
And all its thousand turns disclose
Some fresher beauty varying round:
The haughtiest breast its wish might bound;
Through life to dwell delighted here;
Nor could on earth a spot be found
To nature and to me so dear,
Could thy dear eyes in following mine
Still sweeten more these banks of Rhine!

———

WATERLOO.

(CHILDE HAROLD, Canto iii. Stanzas 21–30.)

THERE was a sound of revelry by night,
And Belgium's capital had gather'd then
Her Beauty and her Chivalry, and bright
The lamps shone o'er fair women and brave men;
A thousand hearts beat happily; and when
Music arose with its voluptuous swell,
Soft eyes look'd love to eyes which spake again,
And all went merry as a marriage-bell;
But hush! hark! a deep sound strikes like a rising knell!

Did ye not hear it? — No; 't was but the wind,
Or the car rattling o'er the stony street;
On with the dance! let joy be unconfined;
No sleep till morn, when Youth and Pleasure meet
To chase the glowing hours with flying feet —
But, hark! — that heavy sound breaks in once more,
As if the clouds its echo would repeat;
And nearer, clearer, deadlier than before!
Arm! Arm! it is — it is — the cannon's opening roar!

Within a window'd niche of that high hall
Sate Brunswick's fated chieftain; he did hear
That sound the first amidst the festival,
And caught its tone with Death's prophetic ear;
And when they smiled because he deem'd it near,
His heart more truly knew that peal too well
Which stretch'd his father on a bloody bier,
And roused the vengeance blood alone could quell:
He rush'd into the field, and, foremost fighting, fell.

Ah! then and there was hurrying to and fro,
And gathering tears, and tremblings of distress,
And cheeks all pale, which but an hour ago
Blush'd at the praise of their own loveliness;
And there were sudden partings, such as press
The life from out young hearts, and choking sighs
Which ne'er might be repeated; who could guess
If ever more should meet those mutual eyes,
Since upon night so sweet such awful morn could rise!

And there was mounting in hot haste: the steed,
The mustering squadron, and the clattering car,

Went pouring forward with impetuous speed,
And swiftly forming in the ranks of war;
And the deep thunder peal on peal afar;
And near, the beat of the alarming drum
Roused up the soldier ere the morning star;
While throng'd the citizens with terror dumb,
Or whispering, with white lips — "The foe! They
      come! they come!"

And wild and high the "Cameron's gathering" rose!
The war-note of Lochiel, which Albyn's hills
Have heard, and heard, too, have her Saxon foes: —
How in the noon of night that pibroch thrills,
Savage and shrill!   But with the breath which fills
Their mountain-pipe, so fill the mountaineers
With the fierce native daring which instils
The stirring memory of a thousand years,
And Evan's, Donald's fame rings in each clansman's
      ears!

And Ardennes waves above them her green leaves,
Dewy with nature's tear-drops, as they pass,
Grieving, if aught inanimate e'er grieves,
Over the unreturning brave, — alas!
Ere evening to be trodden like the grass
Which now beneath them, but above shall grow
In its next verdure, when this fiery mass
Of living valor, rolling on the foe
And burning with high hope, shall moulder cold and low.

Last noon beheld them full of lusty life,
Last eve in Beauty's circle proudly gay,

The midnight brought the signal-sound of strife,
The morn the marshalling in arms, — the day
Battle's magnificently-stern array!
The thunder-clouds close o'er it, which when rent
The earth is cover'd thick with other clay,
Which her own clay shall cover, heap'd and pent,
Rider and horse, — friend, foe, — in one red burial
     blent!

Their praise is hymn'd by loftier harps than mine;
Yet one I would select from that proud throng,
Partly because they blend me with his line,
And partly that I did his sire some wrong,
And partly that bright names will hallow song;
And his was of the bravest, and when shower'd
The death-bolts deadliest the thinn'd files along,
Even where the thickest of war's tempest lower'd,
They reach'd no nobler breast than thine, young, gallant
     Howard!

There have been tears and breaking hearts for thee,
And mine were nothing, had I such to give;
But when I stood beneath the fresh green tree,
Which living waves where thou didst cease to live,
And saw around me the wide field revive
With fruits and fertile promise, and the Spring
Come forth her work of gladness to contrive,
With all her reckless birds upon the wing,
I turn'd from all she brought to those she could not
     bring.

LAKE OF GENEVA. — CALM.

(CHILDE HAROLD, Canto iii. Stanzas 85–87.)

CLEAR, placid Leman! thy contrasted lake,
With the wild world I dwelt in, is a thing
Which warns me, with its stillness, to forsake
Earth's troubled waters for a purer spring.
This quiet sail is as a noiseless wing
To waft me from distraction; once I loved
Torn ocean's roar, but thy soft murmuring
Sounds sweet as if a Sister's voice reproved,
That I with stern delights should e'er have been so
    moved.

It is the hush of night, and all between
Thy margin and the mountains, dusk, yet clear,
Mellow'd and mingling, yet distinctly seen,
Save darken'd Jura, whose capt heights appear
Precipitously steep; and drawing near,
There breathes a living fragrance from the shore,
Of flowers yet fresh with childhood; on the ear
Drops the light drip of the suspended oar,
Or chirps the grasshopper one good-night carol more;

He is an evening reveller, who makes
His life an infancy, and sings his fill;
At intervals, some bird from out the brakes
Starts into voice a moment, then is still.
There seems a floating whisper on the hill,

But that is fancy, for the starlight dews
All silently their tears of love instil,
Weeping themselves away, till they infuse
Deep into Nature's breast the spirit of her hues.

LAKE OF GENEVA.—STORM.

(CHILDE HAROLD, Canto iii. Stanzas 92–96.)

THY sky is changed!—and such a change! Oh night,
And storm, and darkness, ye are wondrous strong,
Yet lovely in your strength, as is the light
Of a dark eye in woman! Far along,
From peak to peak, the rattling crags among
Leaps the live thunder! Not from one lone cloud,
But every mountain now hath found a tongue,
And Jura answers, through her misty shroud,
Back to the joyous Alps, who call to her aloud!

And this is in the night:—Most glorious night!
Thou wert not sent for slumber! let me be
A sharer in thy fierce and far delight,
A portion of the tempest and of thee!
How the lit lake shines, a phosphoric sea,
And the big rain comes dancing to the earth!
And now again 't is black,—and now, the glee
Of the loud hills shakes with its mountain-mirth,
As if they did rejoice o'er a young earthquake's birth.

Now, where the swift Rhone cleaves his way between
Heights which appear as lovers who have parted

In hate, whose mining depths so intervene,
That they can meet no more, though broken-hearted!
Though in their souls, which thus each other thwarted,
Love was the very root of the fond rage
Which blighted their life's bloom, and then departed:
Itself expired, but leaving them an age
Of years all winters, — war within themselves to wage.

Now, where the quick Rhone thus hath cleft his way,
The mightiest of the storms hath ta'en his stand:
For here, not one, but many make their play,
And fling their thunder-bolts from hand to hand,
Flashing and cast around: of all the band,
The brightest through these parted hills hath fork'd
His lightnings, — as if he did understand,
That in such gaps as desolation work'd,
There the hot shaft should blast whatever therein lurk'd.

Sky, mountains, river, winds, lake, lightnings! ye!
With night, and clouds, and thunder, and a soul
To make these felt and feeling, well may be
Things that have made me watchful; the far roll
Of your departing voices, is the knoll
Of what in me is sleepless, — if I rest.
But where of ye, oh tempests! is the goal?
Are ye like those within the human breast?
Or do ye find, at length, like eagles, some high nest?

CLARENS.

(CHILDE HAROLD, Canto iii. Stanzas 99–104.)

CLARENS! sweet Clarens, birthplace of deep love!
Thine air is the young breath of passionate thought;
Thy trees take root in Love; the snows above
The very Glaciers have his colors caught,
And sunset into rose-hues sees them wrought
By rays which sleep there lovingly: the rocks,
The permanent crags, tell here of Love, who sought
In them a refuge from the worldly shocks,
Which stir and sting the soul with hope that woos, then
    mocks.

Clarens! by heavenly feet thy paths are trod, —
Undying Love's, who here ascends a throne
To which the steps are mountains; where the god
Is a pervading life and light, — so shown
Not on those summits solely, nor alone
In the still cave and forest; o'er the flower
His eye is sparkling, and his breath hath blown,
His soft and summer breath, whose tender power
Passes the strength of storms in their most desolate hour.

All things are here of *him ;* from the black pines,
Which are his shade on high, and the loud roar
Of torrents, where he listeneth, to the vines
Which slope his green path downward to the shore,
Where the bow'd waters meet him, and adore,
Kissing his feet with murmurs; and the wood,
The covert of old trees, with trunks all hoar,

But light leaves, young as joy, stands where it stood,
Offering to him, and his, a populous solitude.

A populous solitude of bees and birds,
And fairy-form'd and many-color'd things,
Who worship him with notes more sweet than words,
And innocently open their glad wings,
Fearless and full of life: the gush of springs,
And fall of lofty fountains, and the bend
Of stirring branches, and the bud which brings
The swiftest thought of beauty, here extend,
Mingling, and made by Love, unto one mighty end.

He who hath loved not, here would learn that lore,
And make his heart a spirit; he who knows
That tender mystery, will love the more,
For this is Love's recess, where vain men's woes,
And the world's waste, have driven him far from those,
For 't is his nature to advance or die;
He stands not still, but or decays, or grows
Into a boundless blessing, which may vie
With the immortal lights, in its eternity.

'T was not for fiction chose Rousseau this spot,
Peopling it with affections; but he found
It was the scene which passion must allot
To the mind's purified beings; 't was the ground
Where early Love his Psyche's zone unbound,
And hallow'd it with loveliness: 't is lone,
And wonderful, and deep, and hath a sound,
And sense, and sight of sweetness; here the Rhone
Hath spread himself a couch, the Alps have rear'd a
    throne.

ITALY.

(CHILDE HAROLD, Canto iv. Stanzas 42–47.)

ITALIA! oh Italia! thou who hast
The fatal gift of beauty, which became
A funeral dower of present woes and past,
On thy sweet brow is sorrow plough'd by shame,
And annals graved in characters of flame.
Oh, God! that thou wert in thy nakedness
Less lovely or more powerful, and couldst claim
Thy right, and awe the robbers back, who press
To shed thy blood, and drink the tears of thy distress;

Then might'st thou more appall; or, less desired,
Be homely and be peaceful, undeplored
For thy destructive charms; then, still untired,
Would not be seen the armed torrents poured
Down the deep Alps; nor would the hostile horde
Of many-nation'd spoilers from the Po
Quaff blood and water; nor the stranger's sword
Be thy sad weapon of defence, and so,
Victor or vanquish'd, thou the slave of friend or foe.

Wandering in youth, I traced the path of him,[1]
The Roman friend of Rome's least-mortal mind,
The friend of Tully: as my bark did skim
The bright blue waters with a fanning wind,
Came Megara before me, and behind

---

[1] Servius Sulpicius. See Middleton's *Cicero*, vol. ii. p. 371

Ægina lay, Piræus on the right,
And Corinth on the left; I lay reclined
Along the prow, and saw all these unite
In ruin, even as he had seen the desolate sight;

For Time hath not rebuilt them, but uprear'd
Barbaric dwellings on their shatter'd site,
Which only make more mourn'd and more endear'd
The few last rays of their far-scatter'd light,
And the crush'd relics of their vanish'd might.
The Roman saw these tombs in his own age,
These sepulchres of cities, which excite
Sad wonder, and his yet surviving page
The moral lesson bears, drawn from such pilgrimage.

That page is now before me, and on mine
His country's ruin added to the mass
Of perish'd states he mourn'd in their decline,
And I in desolation: all that *was*
Of then destruction *is;* and now, alas!
Rome — Rome imperial, bows her to the storm,
In the same dust and blackness, and we pass
The skeleton of her Titanic form,
Wrecks of another world, whose ashes still are warm.

Yet, Italy! through every other land
Thy wrongs should ring, and shall, from side to side;
Mother of Arts! as once of arms; thy hand
Was then our guardian, and is still our guide;
Parent of our Religion! whom the wide
Nations have knelt to for the keys of heaven!

Europe, repentant of her parricide,
  Shall yet redeem thee, and, all backward driven,
Roll the barbarian tide, and sue to be forgiven.

VENICE.

(CHILDE HAROLD, Canto iv. Stanzas 1–4.)

I STOOD in Venice, on the Bridge of Sighs;
A palace and a prison on each hand:
I saw from out the wave her structures rise
As from the stroke of the enchanter's wand:
A thousand years their cloudy wings expand
Around me, and a dying Glory smiles
O'er the far times, when many a subject land
Look'd to the winged Lion's marble piles,
Where Venice sate in state, throned on her hundred isles!

She looks a sea Cybele, fresh from ocean,
Rising with her tiara of proud towers
At airy distance, with majestic motion,
A ruler of the waters and their powers:
And such she was; — her daughters had their dowers
From spoils of nations, and the exhaustless East
Pour'd in her lap all gems in sparkling showers.
In purple was she robed, and of her feast
Monarchs partook, and deem'd their dignity increased.

In Venice Tasso's echoes are no more,
And silent rows the songless gondolier;

Her palaces are crumbling to the shore,
And music meets not always now the ear:
Those days are gone — but Beauty still is here.
States fall, arts fade — but Nature doth not die,
Nor yet forget how Venice once was dear,
The pleasant place of all festivity,
The revel of the earth, the masque of Italy!

But unto us she hath a spell beyond
Her name in story, and her long array
Of mighty shadows, whose dim forms despond
Above the dogeless city's vanish'd sway;
Ours is a trophy which will not decay
With the Rialto; Shylock and the Moor,
And Pierre, cannot be swept or worn away —
The keystones of the arch! though all were o'er
For us repeopled were the solitary shore.

VENICE IN DECAY.

(CHILDE HAROLD, Canto iv. Stanzas 11–13.)

THE spouseless Adriatic mourns her lord;
And, annual marriage, now no more renew'd,
The Bucentaur lies rotting unrestored,
Neglected garment of her widowhood!
St. Mark yet sees his lion where he stood,
Stand, but in mockery of his wither'd power,
Over the proud Place where an Emperor sued,
And monarchs gazed and envied in the hour
When Venice was a queen with an unequall'd dower.

The Suabian sued, and now the Austrian reigns —
An Emperor tramples where an Emperor knelt;
Kingdoms are shrunk to provinces, and chains
Clank over sceptred cities; nations melt
From power's high pinnacle, when they have felt
The sunshine for awhile, and downward go
Like lauwine loosen'd from the mountain's belt;
Oh for one hour of blind old Dandolo!
Th' octogenarian chief, Byzantium's conquering foe.

Before St. Mark still glow his steeds of brass,
Their gilded collars glittering in the sun;
But is not Doria's menace come to pass?
Are they not *bridled?* — Venice, lost and won,
Her thirteen hundred years of freedom done,
Sinks, like a sea-weed, into whence she rose!
Better be whelm'd beneath the waves, and shun,
Even in destruction's depth, her foreign foes,
From whom submission wrings an infamous repose.

THE SAME.

(CHILDE HAROLD, Canto iv. Stanza 18.)

I LOVED her from my boyhood — she to me
Was as a fairy city of the heart,
Rising like water-columns from the sea,
Of joy the sojourn, and of wealth the mart;
And Otway, Radcliffe, Schiller, Shakspeare's art,
Had stamp'd her image in me, and even so,
Although I found her thus, we did not part,
Perchance even dearer in her day of woe,
Than when she was a boast, a marvel, and a show.

AN AUGUST EVENING IN ITALY.

(CHILDE HAROLD, Canto iv. Stanzas 27-29.)

THE moon is up, and yet it is not night —
Sunset divides the sky with her — a sea
Of glory streams along the Alpine height
Of blue Friuli's mountains; Heaven is free
From clouds, but of all colors seems to be
Melted to one vast Iris of the West,
Where the Day joins the past Eternity;
While, on the other hand, meek Dian's crest
Floats through the azure air — an island of the blest !

A single star is at her side, and reigns
With her o'er half the lovely heaven; but still
Yon sunny sea heaves brightly, and remains
Roll'd o'er the peak of the far Rhætian hill,
As day and Night contending were, until
Nature reclaim'd her order: — gently flows
The deep-dyed Brenta, wheie their hues instil
The odorous purple of a new-born rose,
Which streams upon her stream, and glass'd within it
        glows,

Fill'd with the face of heaven, which, from afar,
Comes down upon the waters; all its hues,
From the rich sunset to the rising star,
Their magical variety diffuse:
And now they change; a paler shadow strews

Its mantle o'er the mountains; parting day
Dies like the dolphin, whom each pang imbues
With a new color as it gasps away,
The last still loveliest, till — 't is gone — and all is gray.

THE AVE MARIA.

(Don Juan, Canto iii. Stanzas 102–109.)

Ave Maria! blessed be the hour!
  The time, the clime, the spot, where I so oft
Have felt that moment in its fullest power
  Sink o'er the earth so beautiful and soft,
While swung the deep bell in the distant tower,
  Or the faint dying day-hymn stole aloft,
And not a breath crept through the rosy air,
And yet the forest leaves seem'd stirr'd with prayer.

Ave Maria! 't is the hour of prayer!
  Ave Maria! 't is the hour of love!
Ave Maria! may our spirits dare
  Look up to thine and to thy Son's above!
Ave Maria! oh, that face so fair!
  Those downcast eyes beneath the Almighty dove —
What though 't is but a pictured image? — strike —
That painting is no idol — 't is too like.

Sweet hour of twilight! — in the solitude
  Of the pine forest, and the silent shore
Which bounds Ravenna's immemorial wood,
  Rooted where once the Adrian wave flowed o'er,

To where the last Cæsarean fortress stood,
　Evergreen forest! which Boccaccio's lore
And Dryden's lay made haunted ground to me,
How have I loved the twilight hour and thee!

The shrill cicalas, people of the pine,
　Making their summer lives one ceaseless song,
Were the sole echoes, save my steed's and mine,
　And vesper bell's that rose the boughs along;
The spectre huntsman of Onesti's line,
　His hell-dogs, and their chase, and the fair throng
Which learn'd from this example not to fly
From a true lover,—shadow'd my mind's eye.

Oh, Hesperus! thou bringest all good things —
　Home to the weary, to the hungry cheer,
To the young bird the parent's brooding wings,
　The welcome stall to the o'erlabor'd steer;
Whate'er of peace about our hearthstone clings,
　Whate'er our household gods protect of dear,
Are gather'd round us by thy look of rest;
Thou bring'st the child, too, to the mother's breast.

Soft hour! which wakes the wish and melts the heart
　Of those who sail the seas, on the first day
When they from their sweet friends are torn apart;
　Or fills with love the pilgrim on his way
As the far bell of vesper makes him start,
　Seeming to weep the dying day's decay;
Is this a fancy which our reason scorns?
Ah! surely nothing dies but something mourns!

When Nero perish'd by the justest doom
  Which ever the destroyer yet destroy'd,
Amidst the roar of liberated Rome,
  Of nations freed, and the world overjoy'd,
Some hand unseen strew'd flowers upon his tomb:
  Perhaps the weakness of a heart not void
Of feeling for some kindness done, when power
Had left the wretch an uncorrupted hour.

ARQUA.

(CHILDE HAROLD, Canto iv. Stanzas 30–32.)

THERE is a tomb in Arqua; — rear'd in air,
Pillar'd in their sarcophagus, repose
The bones of Laura's lover; here repair
Many familiar with his well-sung woes,
The pilgrims of his genius.   He arose
To raise a language, and his land reclaim
From the dull yoke of her barbaric foes:
Watering the tree which bears his lady's name
With his melodious tears, he gave himself to fame.

They keep his dust in Arqua, where he died;
The mountain-village where his latter days
Went down the vale of years; and 't is their pride —
An honest pride — and let it be their praise,
To offer to the passing stranger's gaze
His mansion and his sepulchre; both plain
And venerably simple, such as raise
A feeling more accordant with his strain
Than if a pyramid form'd his monumental fane.

And the soft quiet hamlet where he dwelt
Is one of that complexion which seems made
For those who their mortality have felt,
And sought a refuge from their hopes decay'd
In the deep umbrage of a green hill's shade,
Which shows a distant prospect far away
Of busy cities, now in vain display'd,
For they can lure no further; and the ray
Of a bright sun can make sufficient holiday.

CLITUMNUS.

(CHILDE HAROLD, Canto iv. Stanzas 66, 67.)

BUT thou, Clitumnus! in thy sweetest wave
Of the most living crystal that was e'er
The haunt of river nymph, to gaze and lave
Her limbs where nothing hid them, thou dost rear
Thy grassy banks whereon the milk-white steer
Grazes; the purest god of gentle waters!
And most serene of aspect, and most clear;
Surely that stream was unprofaned by slaughters —
A mirror and a bath for Beauty's youngest daughters!

And on thy happy shore a Temple still,
Of small and delicate proportion, keeps,
Upon a mild declivity of hill,
Its memory of thee; beneath it sweeps
Thy current's calmness; oft from out it leaps
The finny darter with the glittering scales,
Who dwells and revels in thy glassy deeps;

While, chance, some scatter'd water-lily sails
Down where the shallower wave still tells its bubbling
 tales.

———

TERNI.

(CHILDE HAROLD, Canto iv. Stanzas 69-72.)

THE roar of waters! — from the headlong height
Velino cleaves the wave-worn precipice;
The fall of waters! rapid as the light
The flashing mass foams shaking the abyss;
The hell of waters! where they howl and hiss,
And boil in endless torture; while the sweat
Of their great agony, wrung out from this
Their Phlegethon, curls round the rocks of jet
That gird the gulf around, in pitiless horror set,

And mounts in spray the skies, and thence again
Returns in an unceasing shower, which round,
With its unemptied cloud of gentle rain,
Is an eternal April to the ground,
Making it all one emerald: — how profound
The gulf! and how the giant element
From rock to rock leaps with delirious bound,
Crushing the cliffs, which, downward worn and rent
With his fierce footsteps, yield in chasms a fearful vent

To the broad column which rolls on, and shows
More like the fountain of an infant sea
Torn from the womb of mountains by the throes
Of a new world, than only thus to be

Parent of rivers, which flow gushingly,
With many windings, through the vale: — Look back!
Lo! where it comes like an eternity,
As if to sweep down all things in its track,
Charming the eye with dread, a matchless cataract,

Horribly beautiful! but on the verge,
From side to side, beneath the glittering morn,
An Iris sits, amidst the infernal surge,
Like Hope upon a death-bed, and, unworn
Its steady dyes, while all around is torn
By the distracted waters, bears serene
Its brilliant hues with all their beams unshorn:
Resembling, 'mid the torture of the scene,
Love watching Madness with unalterable mien.

———

ROME.

(CHILDE HAROLD, Canto iv. Stanzas 78, 79.)

OH Rome! my country! city of the soul!
The orphans of the heart must turn to thee,
Lone mother of dead empires! and control
In their shut breasts their petty misery.
What are our woes and sufferance?   Come and see
The cypress, hear the owl, and plod your way
O'er steps of broken thrones and temples, Ye!
Whose agonies are evils of a day —
A world is at our feet as fragile as our clay.

The Niobe of nations! there she stands,
Childless and crownless, in her voiceless woe;

An empty urn within her wither'd hands,
Whose holy dust was scatter'd long ago;
The Scipios' tomb contains no ashes now;
The very sepulchres lie tenantless
Of their heroic dwellers: dost thou flow,
Old Tiber! through a marble wilderness?
Rise, with thy yellow waves, and mantle her distress

THE COLISEUM.

(CHILDE HAROLD, Canto iv. Stanzas 139–145.)

AND here the buzz of eager nations ran,
In murmur'd pity, or loud-roar'd applause,
As man was slaughter'd by his fellow-man.
And wherefore slaughter'd? wherefore, but because
Such were the bloody Circus' genial laws,
And the imperial pleasure. — Wherefore not?
What matters where we fall to fill the maws
Of worms — on battle-plains or listed spot?
Both are but theatres where the chief actors rot.

I see before me the Gladiator lie:
He leans upon his hand — his manly brow
Consents to death, but conquers agony,
And his droop'd head sinks gradually low —
And through his side the last drops, ebbing slow
From the red gash, fall heavy, one by one,
Like the first of a thunder-shower; and now
The arena swims around him — he is gone,
Ere ceased the inhuman shout which hail'd the wretch
    who won.

He heard it, but he heeded not — his eyes
Were with his heart, and that was far away:
He reck'd not of the life he lost nor prize,
But where his rude hut by the Danube lay,
There were his young barbarians all at play,
There was their Dacian mother — he, their sire,
Butcher'd to make a Roman holiday —
All this rush'd with his blood — Shall he expire
And unavenged? — Arise! ye Goths, and glut your ire!

But here, where Murder breathed her bloody steam;
And here, where buzzing nations choked the ways,
And roar'd or murmur'd like a mountain stream
Dashing or winding as its torrent strays;
Here, where the Roman millions' blame or praise
Was death or life, the playthings of a crowd,
My voice sounds much — and fall the stars' faint rays
On the arena void — seats crush'd — walls bow'd —
And galleries, where my steps seem echoes strangely
    loud.

A ruin — yet what ruin! from its mass
Walls, palaces, half-cities, have been rear'd;
Yet oft the enormous skeleton ye pass,
And marvel where the spoil could have appear'd.
Hath it indeed been plunder'd, or but clear'd?
Alas! developed, opens the decay,
When the colossal fabric's form is near'd:
It will not bear the brightness of the day,
Which streams too much on all years, man, have reft
    away.

But when the rising moon begins to climb
Its topmost arch, and gently pauses there;
When the stars twinkle through the loops of time,
And the low night-breeze waves along the air
The garland forest, which the gray walls wear,
Like laurels on the bald first Cæsar's head;
When the light shines serene but doth not glare,
Then in this magic circle raise the dead:
Heroes have trod this spot — 't is on their dust ye tread.

"While stands the Coliseum, Rome shall stand;
When falls the Coliseum, Rome shall fall;
And when Rome falls — the World." From our
own land
Thus spake the pilgrims o'er this mighty wall
In Saxon times, which we are wont to call
Ancient; and these three mortal things are still
On their foundations, and unalter'd all;
Rome and her Ruin past Redemption's skill,
The World, the same wide den — of thieves, or what ye
will.

TOMB OF CECILIA METELLA.

(CHILDE HAROLD, Canto iv. Stanzas 99–103.)

THERE is a stern round tower of other days
Firm as a fortress, with its fence of stone,
Such as an army's baffled strength delays,
Standing with half its battlements alone,
And with two thousand years of ivy grown,
The garland of eternity, where wave

The green leaves over all by time o'erthrown; —
What was this tower of strength? within its cave
What treasure lay so lock'd, so hid? — A woman's grave.

But who was she, the lady of the dead,
Tomb'd in a palace?   Was she chaste and fair?
Worthy a king's — or more — a Roman's bed?
What race of chiefs and heroes did she bear?
What daughter of her beauties was the heir?
How lived — how loved — how died she?   Was she
    not
So honor'd — and conspicuously there,
Where meaner relics must not dare to rot,
Placed to commemorate a more than mortal lot?

Was she as those who love their lords, or they
Who love the lords of others? such have been
Even in the olden time, Rome's annals say.
Was she a matron of Cornelia's mien,
Or the light air of Egypt's graceful queen,
Profuse of joy — or 'gainst it did she war,
Inveterate in virtue?   Did she lean
To the soft side of the heart, or wisely bar
Love from amongst her griefs? — for such the affections
    are.

Perchance she died in youth: it may be, bow'd
With woes far heavier than the ponderous tomb
That weigh'd upon her gentle dust, a cloud
Might gather o'er her beauty, and a gloom
In her dark eye, prophetic of the doom

Heaven gives its favorites — early death; yet shed
A sunset charm around her, and illume
With hectic light, the Hesperus of the dead,
Of her consuming cheek the autumnal leaf-like red.

Perchance she died in age — surviving all,
Charms, kindred, children — with the silver gray
On her long tresses, which might yet recall,
It may be, still a something of the day
When they were braided, and her proud array
And lovely form were envied, praised, and eyed
By Rome — but whither would Conjecture stray?
Thus much alone we know — Metella died,
The wealthiest Roman's wife: Behold his love or pride!

GROTTO OF EGERIA.

(CHILDE HAROLD, Canto iv. Stanzas 115–124.)

EGERIA! sweet creation of some heart
Which found no mortal resting-place so fair
As thine ideal breast; whate'er thou art
Or wert, — a young Aurora of the air,
The nympholepsy of some fond despair;
Or, it might be, a beauty of the earth,
Who found a more than common votary there
Too much adoring; whatsoe'er thy birth,
Thou wert a beautiful thought, and softly bodied forth.

The mosses of thy fountain still are sprinkled
With thine Elysian water-drops; the face

Of thy cave-guarded spring, with years unwrinkled,
Reflects the meek-eyed genius of the place,
Whose green, wild margin now no more erase
Art's works, nor must the delicate waters sleep,
Prison'd in marble; bubbling from the base
Of the cleft statue, with a gentle leap
The rill runs o'er, and round, fern, flowers, and ivy
    creep

Fantastically tangled; the green hills
Are clothed with early blossoms, through the grass
The quick-eyed lizard rustles, and the bills
Of summer-birds sing welcome as ye pass;
Flowers fresh in hue, and many in their class,
Implore the pausing step, and with their dyes
Dance in the soft breeze in a fairy mass;
The sweetness of the violet's deep blue eyes,
Kiss'd by the breath of heaven, seems colored by its
    skies.

Here didst thou dwell, in this enchanted cover,
Egeria! thy all heavenly bosom beating
For the far footsteps of thy mortal lover;
The purple Midnight veiled that mystic meeting
With her most starry canopy, and seating
Thyself by thine adorer, what befell?
This cave was surely shaped out for the greeting
Of an enamoured Goddess, and the cell
Haunted by holy Love — the earliest oracle!

And didst thou not, thy breast to his replying,
Blend a celestial with a human heart;

And Love, which dies as it was born, in sighing,
Share with immortal transports? could thine art
Make them indeed immortal, and impart
The purity of heaven to earthly joys,
Expel the venom and not blunt the dart —
The dull satiety which all destroys —
And root from out the soul the deadly weed which cloys?

Alas! our young affections run to waste,
Or water but the desert; whence arise
But weeds of dark luxuriance, tares of haste,
Rank at the core, though tempting to the eyes,
Flowers whose wild odors breathe but agonies,
And trees whose gums are poison; such the plants,
Which spring beneath her steps as Passion flies
O'er the world's wilderness, and vainly pants
For some celestial fruit forbidden to our wants.

Oh Love! no habitant of earth thou art —
An unseen seraph, we believe in thee,
A faith whose martyrs are the broken heart,
But never yet hath seen, nor e'er shall see
The naked eye, thy form, as it should be;
The mind hath made thee, as it peopled heaven,
Even with its own desiring phantasy,
And to a thought such shape and image given,
As haunts the unquench'd soul — parch'd — wearied —
    wrung — and riven.

Of its own beauty is the mind diseased,
And fevers into false creation; — where,

Where are the forms the sculptor's soul hath seized?
In him alone.   Can Nature show so fair?
Where are the charms and virtues which we dare
Conceive in boyhood and pursue as men,
The unreach'd Paradise of our despair,
Which o'er-informs the pencil and the pen,
And overpowers the page where it would bloom again?

Who loves, raves — 't is youth's frenzy — but the cure
Is bitterer still: as charm by charm unwinds
Which robed our idols, and we see too sure
Nor worth nor beauty dwells from out the mind's
Ideal shape of such; yet still it binds
The fatal spell, and still it draws us on,
Reaping the whirlwind from the oft-sown winds;
The stubborn heart, its alchemy begun,
Seems ever near the prize — wealthiest when most
        undone.

We wither from our youth, we gasp away —
Sick — sick; unfound the boon — unslaked the thirst,
Though to the last, in verge of our decay,
Some phantom lures, such as we sought at first —
But all too late, — so are we doubly curst.
Love, fame, ambition, avarice — 't is the same,
Each idle — and all ill — and none the worst —
For all are meteors with a different name,
And Death the sable smoke where vanishes the flame.

SONNET ON CHILLON.

ETERNAL Spirit of the chainless Mind!
  Brightest in dungeons, Liberty! thou art,
  For there thy habitation is the heart—
The heart which love of thee alone can bind;
And when thy sons to fetters are consign'd—
  To fetters, and the damp vault's dayless gloom,
  Their country conquers with their martyrdom,
And Freedom's fame finds wings on every wind.
Chillon! thy prison is a holy place,
  And thy sad floor an altar—for 't was trod,
Until his very steps have left a trace
  Worn, as if thy cold pavement were a sod,
By Bonnivard!—May none those marks efface!
  For they appeal from tyranny to God.

BONNIVARD AND HIS BROTHERS.

(PRISONER OF CHILLON, Stanzas 6–8.)

LAKE Leman lies by Chillon's walls:
A thousand feet in depth below
Its massy waters meet and flow;
Thus much the fathom-line was sent
From Chillon's snow-white battlement,
  Which round about the wave inthralls:
A double dungeon wall and wave
Have made—and like a living grave.

Below the surface of the lake
The dark vault lies wherein we lay,
We heard it ripple night and day;
    Sounding o'er our heads it knock'd;
And I have felt the winter's spray
Wash through the bars when winds were high.
And wanton in the happy sky;
    And then the very rock hath rock'd,
    And I have felt it shake, unshock'd,
Because I could have smiled to see
The death that would have set me free.

I said my nearer brother pined,
I said his mighty heart declined,
He loathed and put away his food;
It was not that 't was coarse and rude,
For we were used to hunter's fare,
And for the like had little care:
The milk drawn from the mountain goat
Was changed for water from the moat,
Our bread was such as captives' tears
Have moisten'd many a thousand years,
Since man first pent his fellow-men
Like brutes within an iron den;
But what were these to us or him?
These wasted not his heart or limb;
My brother's soul was of that mould
Which in a palace had grown cold,
Had his free breathing been denied
The range of the steep mountain's side;
But why delay the truth? — he died.

I saw, and could not hold his head,
Nor reach his dying hand — nor dead, —
Though hard I strove, but strove in vain,
To rend and gnash my bonds in twain.
He died — and they unlock'd his chain,
And scoop'd for him a shallow grave
Even from the cold earth of our cave.
I begg'd them, as a boon, to lay
His corse in dust whereon the day
Might shine — it was a foolish thought,
But then within my brain it wrought,
That even in death his freeborn breast
In such a dungeon could not rest.
I might have spared my idle prayer —
They coldly laugh'd — and laid him there:
The flat and turfless earth above
The being we so much did love;
His empty chain above it leant,
Such murder's fitting monument!

But he, the favorite and the flower,
Most cherish'd since his natal hour,
His mother's image in fair face,
The infant love of all his race,
His martyr'd father's dearest thought,
My latest care, for whom I sought
To hoard my life, that his might be
Less wretched now, and one day free;
He, too, who yet had held untired
A spirit natural or inspired —
He, too, was struck, and day by day

Was wither'd on the stalk away.
Oh, God ! it is a fearful thing
To see the human soul take wing
In any shape, in any mood : —
I've seen it rushing forth in blood,
I've seen it on the breaking ocean
Strive with a swoln convulsive motion,
I've seen the sick and ghastly bed
Of Sin delirious with its dread;
But these were horrors — this was woe
Unmix'd with such — but sure and slow:
He faded, and so calm and meek,
So softly worn, so sweetly weak,
So tearless, yet so tender — kind,
And grieved for those he left behind !
With all the while a cheek whose bloom
Was as a mockery of the tomb,
Whose tints as gently sunk away
As a departing rainbow's ray —
An eye of most transparent light,
That almost made the dungeon bright,
And not a word of murmur — not
A groan o'er his untimely lot, —
A little talk of better days,
A little hope my own to raise,
For I was sunk in silence — lost
In this last loss, of all the most;
And then the sighs he would suppress
Of fainting nature's feebleness,
More slowly drawn, grew less and less:
I listen'd, but I could not hear —

I call'd, for I was wild with fear;
I knew 't was hopeless, but my dread
Would not be thus admonishèd;
I call'd, and thought I heard a sound —
I burst my chain with one strong bound,
And rush'd to him: — I found him not,
I only stirr'd in this black spot,
I only lived — *I* only drew
The accursed breath of dungeon-dew;
The last — the sole — the dearest link
Between me and the eternal brink,
Which bound me to my failing race,
Was broken in this fatal place.

BONNIVARD ALONE.

(PRISONER OF CHILLON, Stanzas 9–14.)

WHAT next befell me then and there
I know not well — I never knew —
First came the loss of light, and air,
And then of darkness too:
I had no thought, no feeling — none —
Among the stones I stood a stone,
And was, scarce conscious what I wist,
As shrubless crags within the mist;
For all was blank, and bleak, and gray,
It was not night — it was not day,
It was not even the dungeon-light,
So hateful to my heavy sight,

But vacancy absorbing space,
And fixedness — without a place;
There were no stars — no earth — no time —
No check — no change — no good — no crime —
But silence, and a stirless breath
Which neither was of life nor death;
A sea of stagnant idleness,
Blind, boundless, mute, and motionless!

A light broke in upon my brain, —
    It was the carol of a bird;
It ceased, and then it came again,
    The sweetest song ear ever heard,
And mine was thankful till my eyes
Ran over with the glad surprise,
And they that moment could not see
I was the mate of misery;
But then by dull degrees came back
My senses to their wonted track,
I saw the dungeon walls and floor
Close slowly round me as before,
I saw the glimmer of the sun
Creeping as it before had done,
But through the crevice where it came
That bird was perch'd, as fond and tame,
    And tamer than upon the tree;
A lovely bird, with azure wings,
And song that said a thousand things,
    And seem'd to say them all for me!
I never saw its like before,
I ne'er shall see its likeness more:

It seem'd like me to want a mate,
But was not half so desolate,
And it was come to love me when
None lived to love me so again,
And cheering from my dungeon's brink,
Had brought me back to feel and think.
I know not if it late were free,
   Or broke its cage to perch on mine,
But knowing well captivity,
   Sweet bird! I could not wish for thine!
Or if it were, in wingèd guise,
A visitant from Paradise;
For — Heaven forgive that thought! the while
Which made me both to weep and smile —
I sometimes deem'd that it might be
My brother's soul come down to me;
But then at last away it flew,
And then 't was mortal — well I knew;
For he would never thus have flown,
And left me twice so doubly lone —
Lone — as the corse within its shroud,
Lone — as a solitary cloud,
   A single cloud on a sunny day,
While all the rest of heaven is clear,
A frown upon the atmosphere,
That hath no business to appear
   When skies are blue, and earth is gay.

A kind of change came in my fate,
My keepers grew compassionate;
I know not what had made them so,

They were inured to sights of woe,
But so it was: — my broken chain
With links unfasten'd did remain,
And it was liberty to stride
Along my cell from side to side,
And up and down, and then athwart,
And tread it over every part;
And round the pillars one by one,
Returning where my walk begun,
Avoiding only, as I trod,
My brothers' graves without a sod;
For if I thought with heedless tread
My step profaned their lowly bed,
My breath came gaspingly and thick,
And my crush'd heart fell blind and sick.

I made a footing in the wall,
    It was not therefrom to escape,
For I had buried one and all
    Who loved me in a human shape;
And the whole earth would henceforth be
A wider prison unto me:
No child — no sire — no kin had I,
No partner in my misery;
I thought of this, and I was glad,
For thought of them had made me mad;
But I was curious to ascend
To my barr'd windows, and to bend
Once more, upon the mountains high,
The quiet of a loving eye.

I saw them — and they were the same,
They were not changed like me in frame;
I saw their thousand years of snow
On high — their wide long lake below,
And the blue Rhone in fullest flow;
I heard the torrents leap and gush
O'er channell'd rock and broken bush;
I saw the white-wall'd distant town,
And whiter sails go skimming down;
And then there was a little isle,
Which in my very face did smile.
     The only one in view;
A small green isle, it seem'd no more,
Scarce broader than my dungeon floor,
But in it there were three tall trees,
And o'er it blew the mountain breeze,
And by it there were waters flowing,
And on it there were young flowers growing,
     Of gentle breath and hue.
The fish swam by the castle wall,
And they seem'd joyous each and all;
The eagle rode the rising blast,
Methought he never flew so fast
As then to me he seem'd to fly,
And then new tears came in my eye.
And I felt troubled — and would fain
I had not left my recent chain;
And when I did descend again,
The darkness of my dim abode
Fell on me as a heavy load;
It was as is a new-dug grave,

Closing o'er one we sought to save, —
And yet my glance, too much opprest,
Had almost need of such a rest.

It might be months, or years, or days,
   I kept no count, I took no note,
I had no hope my eyes to raise,
   And clear them of their dreary mote;
At last men came to set me free,
   I ask'd not why, and reck'd not where,
It was at length the same to me
Fetter'd or fetterless to be,
   I learn'd to love despair.
And thus when they appear'd at last,
And all my bonds aside were cast,
These heavy walls to me had grown
A hermitage — and all my own!
And half I felt as they were come
To tear me from a second home:
With spiders I had friendship made,
And watch'd them in their sullen trade,
Had seen the mice by moonlight play,
And why should I feel less than they?
We were all inmates of one place,
And I, the monarch of each race,
Had power to kill — yet, strange to tell!
In quiet we had learn'd to dwell.
My very chains and I grew friends,
So much a long communion tends
To make us what we are; — even I
Regain'd my freedom with a sigh.

THE EAST.

(BRIDE OF ABYDOS, Canto i. Stanza 1.)

KNOW ye the land where the cypress and myrtle
  Are emblems of deeds that are done in their clime,
Where the rage of the vulture, the love of the turtle,
  Now melt into sorrow, now madden to crime?
Know ye the land of the cedar and vine,
Where the flowers ever blossom, the beams ever shine;
Where the light wings of Zephyr, opprest with per-
    fume,
Wax faint o'er the Gardens of Gúl in her bloom;
Where the citron and olive are fairest of fruit,
And the voice of the nightingale never is mute:
Where the tints of the earth, and the hues of the sky,
In color though varied, in beauty may vie,
And the purple of Ocean is deepest in dye;
Where the virgins are soft as the roses they twine,
And all, save the spirit of man, is divine?
'T is the clime of the East; 't is the land of the Sun —
Can he smile on such deeds as his children have done?
Oh! wild as the accents of lovers' farewell
Are the hearts which they bear, and the tales which they
    tell.

JOURNEY AND DEATH OF HASSAN.

(From THE GIAOUR.)

STERN Hassan hath a journey ta'en
With twenty vassals in his train,

Each arm'd, as best becomes a man,
With arquebus and ataghan;
The chief before, as deck'd for war,
Bears in his belt the scimitar
Stain'd with the best of Arnaut blood,
When in the pass the rebels stood,
And few return'd to tell the tale
Of what befell in Parne's vale.
The pistols which his girdle bore
Were those that once a pacha wore,
Which still, though gemm'd and boss'd with gold
Even robbers tremble to behold.
'T is said he goes to woo a bride
More true than her who left his side;
The faithless slave that broke her bower,
And, worse than faithless, for a Giaour!

    *   *   *   *   *

  The sun's last rays are on the hill,
And sparkle in the fountain rill,
Whose welcome waters, cool and clear,
Draw blessings from the mountaineer:
Here may the loitering merchant Greek
Find that repose 't were vain to seek
In cities lodged too near his lord,
And trembling for his secret hoard —
Here may he rest where none can see,
In crowds a slave, in deserts free;
And with forbidden wine may stain
The bowl a Moslem must not drain.

    *   *   *   *   *

  The foremost Tartar's in the gap,
Conspicuous by his yellow cap;

The rest in lengthening line the while
Wind slowly through the long defile:
Above, the mountain rears a peak,
Where vultures whet the thirsty beak,
And theirs may be a feast to-night,
Shall tempt them down ere morrow's light;
Beneath, a river's wintry stream
Has shrunk before the summer beam,
And left a channel bleak and bare,
Save shrubs that spring to perish there:
Each side the midway path there lay
Small broken crags of granite gray,
By time, or mountain lightning, riven
From summits clad in mists of heaven;
For where is he that hath beheld
The peak of Liakura unveil'd?

     *   *   *   *   *

   They reach the grove of pine at last:
"Bismillah! now the peril's past;
For yonder view the opening plain,
And there we'll prick our steeds amain:"
The Chiaus spake, and as he said,
A bullet whistled o'er his head;
The foremost Tartar bites the ground!
   Scarce had they time to check the rein,
Swift from their steeds the riders bound;
   But three shall never mount again:
Unseen the foes that gave the wound,
   The dying ask revenge in vain.
With steel unsheath'd, and carbine bent,
Some o'er their courser's harness leant,

Half shelter'd by the steed;
Some fly behind the nearest rock,
And there await the coming shock,
    Nor tamely stand to bleed
Beneath the shaft of foes unseen,
Who dare not quit their craggy screen.
Stern Hassan only from his horse
Disdains to light, and keeps his course,
Till fiery flashes in the van
Proclaim too sure the robber-clan
Have well secured the only way
Could now avail the promised prey;
Then curl'd his very beard with ire,
And glared his eye with fiercer fire:
"Though far and near the bullets hiss,
I 've 'scaped a bloodier hour than this."
And now the foe their covert quit,
And call his vassals to submit;
But Hassan's frown and furious word
Are dreaded more than hostile sword,
Nor of his little band a man
Resign'd carbine or ataghan,
Nor raised the craven cry, Amaun![1]
In fuller sight, more near and near,
The lately ambush'd foes appear,
And, issuing from the grove, advance
Some who on battle-charger prance.
Who leads them on with foreign brand,
Far flashing in his red right hand?
" 'T is he! 't is he! I know him now;

[1] Quarter, pardon.

I know him by his pallid brow;
I know him by the evil eye
That aids his envious treachery;
I know him by his jet-black barb:
Though now array'd in Arnaut garb,
Apostate from his own vile faith,
It shall not save him from the death:
'T is he! well met in any hour,
Lost Leila's love, accursed Giaour!"

    *   *   *   *   *

With sabre shiver'd to the hilt,
Yet dripping with the blood he spilt;
Yet strain'd within the sever'd hand
Which quivers round that faithless brand;
His turban far behind him roll'd,
And cleft in twain its firmest fold;
His flowing robe by falchion torn,
And crimson as those clouds of morn
That, streak'd with dusky red, portend
The day shall have a stormy end;
A stain on every bush that bore
A fragment of his palampore,[1]
His breast with wounds unnumber'd riven,
His back to earth, his face to heaven,
Fall'n Hassan lies — his unclosed eye
Yet lowering on his enemy,
As if the hour that seal'd his fate
Surviving left his quenchless hate;
And o'er him bends that foe with brow
As dark as his that bled below.

[1] The flowered shawl generally worn by persons of rank.

HASSAN'S MOTHER.

(From THE GIAOUR.)

THE browsing camels' bells are tinkling:
His Mother look'd from her lattice high,
She saw the dews of eve besprinkling
The pasture green beneath her eye,
She saw the planets faintly twinkling:
" 'T is twilight — sure his train is nigh."
She could not rest in the garden-bower,
But gazed through the grate of his steepest tower:
" Why comes he not? his steeds are fleet,
Nor shrink they from the summer heat;
Why sends not the Bridegroom his promised gift:
Is his heart more cold, or his barb less swift?
Oh, false reproach! yon Tartar now
Has gain'd our nearest mountain's brow,
And warily the steep descends,
And now within the valley bends;
And he bears the gift at his saddle bow —
How could I deem his courser slow?
Right well my largess shall repay
His welcome speed, and weary way."

The Tartar lighted at the gate,
But scarce upheld his fainting weight:
His swarthy visage spake distress,
But this might be from weariness;
His garb with sanguine spots was dyed,
But these might be from his courser's side;
He drew the token from his vest —

Angel of death! 't is Hassan's cloven crest!
His calpac [1] rent — his caftan red —
" Lady, a fearful bride thy Son hath wed:
Me, not from mercy, did they spare,
But this impurpled pledge to bear.
Peace to the brave! whose blood is spilt;
Woe to the Giaour! for his the guilt.''

THE GIAOUR'S LOVE.

(From THE GIAOUR.)

THE cold in clime are cold in blood,
   Their love can scarce deserve the name;
But mine was like the lava flood
   That boils in Ætna's breast of flame.
I cannot prate in puling strain
Of ladye-love, and beauty's chain:
If changing cheek, and scorching vein,
Lips taught to writhe, but not complain,
If bursting heart, and madd'ning brain,
And daring deed, and vengeful steel,
And all that I have felt, and feel,
Betoken love — that love was mine,
And shown by many a bitter sign.
'T is true, I could not whine nor sigh,
I knew but to obtain or die.

[1] The solid cap or centre of the head-dress; the shawl is wound
round it and forms the turban.

I die — but first I have possess'd,
And come what may, I *have been* blest.
Shall I the doom I sought upbraid?
No — reft of all, yet undismay'd
But for the thought of Leila slain,
Give me the pleasure with the pain,
So would I live and love again.
I grieve, but not, my holy guide!
For him who dies, but her who died:
She sleeps beneath the wandering wave —
Ah! had she but an earthly grave,
This breaking heart and throbbing head
Should seek and share her narrow bed.
She was a form of life and light,
That, seen, became a part of sight;
And rose, where'er I turn'd mine eye,
The Morning-star of Memory!

DEATH OF SELIM.

(BRIDE OF ABYDOS, Canto ii. Stanzas 22–26.)

ZULEIKA, mute and motionless,
Stood·like that statue of distress,
When, her last hope forever gone,
The mother harden'd into stone;
All in the maid that eye could see
Was but a younger Niobe.
But ere her lip, or even her eye,
Essay'd to speak, or look reply,

Beneath the garden's wicket porch
Far flash'd on high a blazing torch !
Another — and another — and another, —
" Oh ! fly — no more — yet now my more than brother ! "
Far, wide, through every thicket spread,
The fearful lights are gleaming red ;
Nor these alone — for each right hand
Is ready with a sheathless brand.
They part, pursue, return, and wheel
With searching flambeau, shining steel ;
And last of all, his sabre waving,
Stern Giaffir in his fury raving :
And now almost they touch the cave —
Oh ! must that grot be Selim's grave?

Dauntless he stood — " 'T is come — soon past—
One kiss, Zuleika — 't is my last :
    But yet my band not far from shore
May hear this signal, see the flash ;
Yet now too few — the attempt were rash :
    No matter — yet one effort more."
Forth to the cavern mouth he stept ;
    His pistol's echo rang on high,
Zuleika started not, nor wept,
    Despair benumb'd her breast and eye ! —
" They hear me not, or if they ply
Their oars, 't is but to see me die ;
That sound hath drawn my foes more nigh.
Then forth my father's scimitar,
Thou ne'er hast seen less equal war !
Farewell, Zuleika ! — Sweet ! retire :

Yet stay within — here linger safe,
At thee his rage will only chafe.
Stir not — lest even to thee perchance
Some erring blade or ball should glance.
Fear'st thou for him? — may I expire
If in this strife I seek thy sire!
No — though by him that poison pour'd:
No — though again he call me coward!
But tamely shall I meet their steel?
No — as each crest save *his* may feel!"
One bound he made, and gain'd the sand:
  Already at his feet hath sunk
The foremost of the prying band,
  A gasping head, a quivering trunk:
Another falls — but round him close
A swarming circle of his foes;
From right to left his path he cleft,
  And almost met the meeting wave:
  His boat appears — not five oars' length —
His comrades strain with desperate strength —
  Oh! are they yet in time to save?
  His feet the foremost breakers lave;
His band are plunging in the bay,
Their sabres glitter through the spray;
Wet — wild — unwearied to the strand
They struggle — now they touch the land!
They come — 't is but to add to slaughter —
His heart's best blood is on the water.

Escaped from shot, unharm'd by steel,
Or scarcely grazed its force to feel,

Had Selim won, betray'd, beset,
To where the strand and billows met ;
There as his last step left the land,
And the last death-blow dealt his hand —
Ah ! wherefore did he turn to look
  For her his eye but sought in vain ?
That pause, that fatal gaze he took,
  Hath doom'd his death, or fix'd his chain.
Sad proof, in peril and in pain,
How late will Lover's hope remain !
His back was to the dashing spray ;
Behind, but close, his comrades lay,
When at the instant, hiss'd the ball —
" So may the foes of Giaffir fall ! "
Whose voice is heard ? whose carbine rang ?
Whose bullet through the night-air sang,
Too nearly, deadly aim'd to err ?
'Tis thine — Abdallah's Murderer !
The father slowly rued thy hate,
The son hath found a quicker fate :
Fast from his breast the blood is bubbling,
The whiteness of the sea-foam troubling —
If aught his lips essay'd to groan,
The rushing billows choked the tone !

Morn slowly rolls the clouds away ;
  Few trophies of the fight are there :
The shouts that shook the midnight-bay
Are silent ; but some signs of fray
  That strand of strife may bear,
And fragments of each shiver'd brand ;

Steps stamp'd ; and dash'd into the sand
The print of many a struggling hand
   May there be mark'd ; nor far remote
   A broken torch, an oarless boat ;
And, tangled on the weeds that heap
The beach where shelving to the deep,
   There lies a white capote !
'T is rent in twain — one dark-red stain
The wave yet ripples o'er in vain :
     But where is he who wore ?
Ye ! who would o'er his relics weep,
Go, seek them where the surges sweep
Their burthen round Sigæum's steep
     And cast on Lemnos' shore :
The sea-birds shriek above the prey,
O'er which their hungry beaks delay,
As shaken on his restless pillow,
 His head heaves with the heaving billow;
That hand, whose motion is not life,
Yet feebly seems to menace strife,
Flung by the tossing tide on high,
   Then levell'd with the wave —
What recks it, though that corse shall lie
   Within a living grave ?
The bird that tears that prostrate form
Hath only robb'd the meaner worm;
The only heart, the only eye
Had bled or wept to see him die,
Had seen those scatter'd limbs composed,
   And mourn'd above his turban-stone,
That heart hath burst — that eye was closed —
   Yea — closed before his own !

CORSAIR LIFE.

(Corsair, Canto i. Stanza 1.)

O'er the glad waters of the dark blue sea,
Our thoughts are boundless, and our souls as free,
Far as the breeze can bear, the billows foam,
Survey our empire, and behold our home!
These are our realms, no limits to their sway —
Our flag the sceptre all who meet obey.
Ours the wild life in tumult still to range
From toil to rest, and joy in every change.
Oh, who can tell? not thou, luxurious slave!
Whose soul would sicken o'er the heaving wave;
Not thou, vain lord of wantonness and ease!
Whom slumber soothes not — pleasure cannot please —
Oh, who can tell, save he whose heart hath tried,
And danced in triumph o'er the waters wide,
The exulting sense — the pulse's maddening play,
That thrills the wanderer of that trackless way?
That for itself can woo the approaching fight,
And turn what some deem danger to delight;
That seeks what cravens shun with more than zeal,
And where the feebler faint — can only feel —
Feel — to the rising bosom's inmost core,
Its hope awaken and its spirit soar?
No dread of death — if with us die our foes —
Save that it seems even duller than repose:
Come when it will — we snatch the life of life —
When lost — what recks it — by disease or strife?
Let him who crawls enamour'd of decay

Cling to his couch, and sicken years away;
Heave his thick breath, and shake his palsied head;
Ours — the fresh turf, and not the feverish bed.
While gasp by gasp he falters forth his soul,
Ours with one pang — one bound — escapes control.
His corse may boast its urn and narrow cave,
And they who loath'd his life may gild his grave:
Ours are the tears, though few, sincerely shed,
When Ocean shrouds and sepulchres our dead.
For us. even banquets fond regret supply
In the red cup that crowns our memory;
And the brief epitaph in danger's day,
When those who win at length divide the prey,
And cry, remembrance saddening o'er each brow
How had the brave who fell exulted *now!*

PARTING OF CONRAD AND MEDORA.

(CORSAIR, Canto i. Stanzas 14, 15.)

SHE rose — she sprung — she clung to his embrace
Till his heart heaved beneath her hidden face.
He dared not raise to his that deep-blue eye.
Which downcast droop'd in tearless agony.
Her long fair hair lay floating o'er his arms.
In all the wildness of dishevell'd charms;
Scarce beat that bosom where his image dwelt
So full — *that* feeling seem'd almost unfelt!
Hark — peals the thunder of the signal-gun!
It told 't was sunset — and he cursed that sun.

Again — again — that form he madly press'd,
Which mutely clasp'd, imploringly caress'd!
And tottering to the couch his bride he bore,
One moment gazed — as if to gaze no more;
Felt — that for him earth held but her alone,
Kiss'd her cold forehead — turn'd — is Conrad gone?

" And is he gone? " — on sudden solitude
How oft that fearful question will intrude!
" 'T was but an instant past — and here he stood!
And now " — without the portal's porch she rush'd,
And then at length her tears in freedom gush'd;
Big — bright — and fast, unknown to her they fell;
But still her lips refused to send — " Farewell!"
For in that word — that fatal word — howe'er
We promise — hope — believe — there breathes despair.
O'er every feature of that still, pale face,
Had sorrow fix'd what time can ne'er erase:
The tender blue of that large loving eye
Grew frozen with its gaze on vacancy,
Till — Oh, how far! — it caught a glimpse of him,
And then it flow'd — and frenzied seem'd to swim
Through those long, dark, and glistening lashes dew'd
With drops of sadness oft to be renew'd.
" He 's gone!" — against her heart that hand is driven,
Convulsed and quick — then gently raised to heaven;
She look'd and saw the heaving of the main;
The white sail set — she dared not look again;
But turn'd with sickening soul within the gate —
" It is no dream — and I am desolate!"

CONRAD'S RETURN.

(CORSAIR, Canto iii. Stanzas 19–21.)

THE lights are high on beacon and from bower,
And 'midst them Conrad seeks Medora's tower:
He looks in vain — 't is strange — and all remark,
Amid so many, hers alone is dark.
'T is strange — of yore its welcome never fail'd,
Nor now, perchance, extinguish'd, only veil'd.
With the first boat descends he for the shore,
And looks impatient on the lingering oar.
Oh! for a wing beyond the falcon's flight,
To bear him like an arrow to that height!
With the first pause the resting rowers gave,
He waits not — looks not — leaps into the wave,
Strives through the surge, bestrides the beach, and high
Ascends the path familiar to his eye.

He reach'd his turret door — he paused — no sound
Broke from within; and all was night around.
He knock'd, and loudly — footstep nor reply
Announced that any heard or deem'd him nigh;
He knock'd — but faintly — for his trembling hand
Refused to aid his heavy heart's demand.
The portal opens — 't is a well-known face —
But not the form he panted to embrace.
Its lips are silent — twice his own essay'd,
And fail'd to frame the question they delay'd;
He snatch'd the lamp — its light will answer all —
It quits his grasp, expiring in the fall.

He would not wait for that reviving ray —
As soon could he have linger'd there for day;
But, glimmering through the dusky corridor,
Another checkers o'er the shadow'd floor;
His steps the chamber gain — his eyes behold
All that his heart believed not — yet foretold!

He turn'd not — spoke not — sunk not — fix'd his look,
And set the anxious frame that lately shook:
He gazed — how long we gaze despite of pain,
And know, but dare not own, we gaze in vain!
In life itself she was so still and fair,
That death with gentler aspect wither'd there;
And the cold flowers her colder hand contain'd,
In that last grasp as tenderly were strain'd
As if she scarcely felt, but feign'd a sleep,
And made it almost mockery yet to weep:
The long dark lashes fringed her lids of snow,
And veil'd — thought shrinks from all that lurk'd below —
Oh! o'er the eye Death most exerts his might,
And hurls the spirit from her throne of light!
Sinks those blue orbs in that long last eclipse,
But spares, as yet, the charm around her lips —
Yet, yet they seem as they forbore to smile,
And wish'd repose — but only for a while;
But the white shroud, and each extended tress,
Long — fair — but spread in utter lifelessness,
Which, late the sport of every summer wind,
Escaped the baffled wreath that strove to bind;
These — and the pale pure cheek, became the bier —
But she is nothing — wherefore is he here?

He ask'd no question — all were answer'd now
By the first glance on that still — marble brow.
It was enough — she died — what reck'd it how?

———

ALP AND FRANCESCA.

(SIEGE OF CORINTH, Stanzas 16–21.)

STILL by the shore Alp mutely mused,
And woo'd the freshness Night diffused.
There shrinks no ebb in that tideless sea,
Which changeless rolls eternally;
So that wildest of waves, in their angriest mood,
Scarce break on the bounds of the land for a rood;
And the powerless moon beholds them flow,
Heedless if she come or go:
Calm or high, in main or bay,
On their course she hath no sway.
The rock unworn its base doth bare,
And looks o'er the surf, but it comes not there;
And the fringe of the foam may be seen below,
On the line that it left long ages ago:
A smooth short space of yellow sand
Between it and the greener land.

He wander'd on, along the beach,
Till within the range of a carbine's reach
Of the leaguer'd wall; but they saw him not,
Or how could he 'scape from the hostile shot?
Did traitors lurk in the Christians' hold?

Were their hands grown stiff, or their hearts wax'd cold?
I know not, in sooth; but from yonder wall
There flash'd no fire, and there hiss'd no ball,
Though he stood beneath the bastion's frown,
That flank'd the seaward gate of the town;
Though he heard the sound, and could almost tell
The sullen words of the sentinel,
As his measured step on the stone below
Clank'd as he paced it to and fro;
And he saw the lean dogs beneath the wall
Hold o'er the dead their carnival,
Gorging and growling o'er carcass and limb;
They were too busy to bark at him!
From a Tartar's skull they had stripp'd the flesh,
As ye peel the fig when its fruit is fresh;
And their white tusks crunch'd o'er the whiter skull,
As it slipp'd through their jaws, when their edge grew
    dull,
As they lazily mumbled the bones of the dead,
When they scarce could rise from the spot where they fed;
So well had they broken a lingering fast
With those who had fallen for that night's repast.
And Alp knew, by the turbans that roll'd on the sand,
The foremost of these were the best of his band:
Crimson and green were the shawls of their wear,
And each scalp had a single long tuft of hair,
All the rest was shaven and bare.
The scalps were in the wild dog's maw,
The hair was tangled round his jaw.
But close by the shore, on the edge of the gulf,
There sate a vulture flapping a wolf.

Who had stolen from the hills, but kept away,
Scared by the dogs, from the human prey;
But he seized on his share of a steed that lay,
Pick'd by the birds, on the sands of the bay.

Alp turn'd him from the sickening sight:
Never had shaken his nerves in fight;
But he better could brook to behold the dying,
Deep in the tide of their warm blood lying,
Scorch'd with the death-thirst, and writhing in vain,
Than the perishing dead who are past all pain.
There is something of pride in the perilous hour,
Whate'er be the shape in which death may lower;
For Fame is there to say who bleeds,
And Honor's eye on daring deeds!
But when all is past, it is humbling to tread
O'er the weltering field of the tombless dead,
And see worms of the earth, and fowls of the air,
Beasts of the forest, all gathering there;
All regarding man as their prey,
All rejoicing in his decay.

There is a temple in ruin stands,
Fashion'd by long forgotten hands;
Two or three columns, and many a stone,
Marble and granite, with grass o'ergrown!
Out upon Time! it will leave no more
Of the things to come than the things before!
Out upon Time! who forever will leave
But enough of the past for the future to grieve
O'er that which hath been, and o'er that which must be:

What we have seen, our sons shall see;
Remnants of things that have past away,
Fragments of stone, rear'd by creatures of clay!

He sate him down at a pillar's base,
And past his hand athwart his face;
Like one in dreary musing mood,
Declining was his attitude;
His head was drooping on his breast,
Fever'd, throbbing, and opprest;
And o'er his brow, so downward bent,
Oft his beating fingers went,
Hurriedly, as you may see
Your own run over the ivory key,
Ere the measured tone is taken
By the chords you would awaken.
There he sate all heavily,
As he heard the night-wind sigh.
Was it the wind, through some hollow stone,
Sent that soft and tender moan?
He lifted his head, and he look'd on the sea,
But it was unrippled as glass may be;
He look'd on the long grass — it waved not a blade;
How was that gentle sound convey'd?
He look'd to the banners — each flag lay still,
So did the leaves on Cithæron's hill,
And he felt not a breath come over his cheek;
What did that sudden sound bespeak?
He turn'd to the left — is he sure of sight?
There sate a lady, youthful and bright!

He started up with more of fear
Than if an armed foe were near.
"God of my fathers! what is here?
Who art thou, and wherefore sent
So near a hostile armament?"
His trembling hands refused to sign
The cross he deem'd no more divine:
He had resumed it in that hour,
But conscience wrung away the power.
He gazed, he saw: he knew the face
Of beauty, and the form of grace;
It was Francesca by his side,
The maid who might have been his bride!
The rose was yet upon her cheek,
But mellow'd with a tenderer streak:
Where was the play of her soft lips fled?
Gone was the smile that enliven'd their red.
The ocean's calm within their view,
Beside her eye had less of blue;
But like that cold wave it stood still,
And its glance, though clear, was chill.
Around her form a thin robe twining,
Naught conceal'd her bosom shining;
Through the parting of her hair,
Floating darkly downward there,
Her rounded arm show'd white and bare:
And ere yet she made reply,
Once she raised her hand on high;
It was so wan, and transparent of hue,
You might have seen the moon shine through.

" I come from my rest to him I love best,
That I may be happy, and he may be blest.
I have pass'd the guards, the gate, the wall;
Sought thee in safety through foes and all.
'T is said the lion will turn and flee
From a maid in the pride of her purity;
And the Power on high, that can shield the good
Thus from the tyrant of the wood,
Hath extended its mercy to guard me as well
From the hands of the leaguering infidel.
I come — and if I come in vain,
Never, oh never, we meet again!
Thou hast done a fearful deed
In falling away from thy father's creed:
But dash that turban to earth, and sign
The sign of the cross, and forever be mine;
Wring the black drop from thy heart,
And to-morrow unites us no more to part."

" And where should our bridal couch be spread?
In the midst of the dying and the dead?
For to-morrow we give to the slaughter and flame
The sons and the shrines of the Christian name.
None, save thou and thine, I' ve sworn,
Shall be left upon the morn:
But thee will I bear to a lovely spot,
Where our hands shall be join'd, and our sorrow forgot.
There thou yet shalt be my bride,
When once again I' ve quelled the pride
Of Venice; and her hated race
Have felt the arm they would debase

Scourge with a whip of scorpions those
Whom vice and envy made my foes.''

Upon his hand she laid her own —
Light was the touch, but it thrill'd to the bone,
And shot a chillness to his heart,
Which fix'd him beyond the power to start.
Though slight, was that grasp so mortal cold,
He could not loose him from its hold;
But never did clasp of one so dear
Strike on the pulse with such feeling of fear,
As those thin fingers, long and white,
Froze through his blood by their touch that night.
The feverish glow of his brow was gone,
And his heart sank so still that it felt like stone,
As he look'd on the face, and beheld its hue,
So deeply changed from what he knew:
Fair but faint — without the ray
Of mind, that made each feature play
Like sparkling waves on a sunny day;
And her motionless lips lay still as death,
And her words came forth without her breath,
And there rose not a heave o'er her bosom's swell,
And there seem'd not a pulse in her veins to dwell.
Though her eye shone out, yet the lids were fixt,
And the glance that it gave was wild and unmixt
With aught of change, as the eyes may seem,
Of the restless who walk in a troubled dream;
Like the figures on arras, that gloomily glare,
Stirr'd by the breath of the wintry air,
So seen by the dying lamp's fitful light,

Lifeless, but life-like, and awful to sight;
As they seem, through the dimness, about to come down
From the shadowy wall where their images frown;
Fearfully flitting to and fro,
As the gusts on the tapestry come and go.
" If not for love of me be given
Thus much, then, for the love of heaven —
Again I say — that turban tear
From off thy faithless brow, and swear
Thine injured country's sons to spare,
Or thou art lost; and never shalt see —
Not earth — that 's past — but heaven or me.
If this thou dost accord, albeit
A heavy doom 't is thine to meet,
That doom shall half absolve thy sin,
And mercy's gate may receive thee within:
But pause one moment more, and take
The curse of Him thou didst forsake;
And look once more to heaven, and see
Its love forever shut from thee.
There is a light cloud by the moon —
'T is passing, and will pass full soon —
If, by the time its vapory sail
Hath ceased her shaded orb to veil,
Thy heart within thee is not changed,
Then God and man are both avenged;
Dark will thy doom be, darker still
Thine immortality of ill."

Alp look'd to heaven, and saw on high
The sign she spake of in the sky;

But his heart was swollen, and turn'd aside
By deep interminable pride.
This first false passion of his breast
Roll'd like a torrent o'er the rest.
He sue for mercy! *He* dismay'd
By wild words of a timid maid!
He, wrong'd by Venice, vow to save
Her sons, devoted to the grave!
No — though that cloud were thunder's worst,
And charged to crush him — let it burst!

He look'd upon it earnestly,
Without an accent of reply;
He watch'd it passing; it is flown;
Full on his eye the clear moon shone,
And thus he spake — " Whate'er my fate,
I am no changeling — 't is too late:
The reed in storms may bow and quiver,
Then rise again; the tree must shiver.
What Venice made me, I must be,
Her foe in all, save love to thee:
But thou art safe: oh, fly with me! "
He turn'd, but she is gone!
Nothing is there but the column stone.
Hath she sunk in the earth, or melted in air?
He saw not — he knew not — but nothing is there

THE ASSAULT.

(SIEGE OF CORINTH, Stanzas 22–27.)

LIGHTLY and brightly breaks away
The Morning from her mantle gray,
And the Noon will look on a sultry day.
Hark to the trump, and the drum,
And the mournful sound of the barbarous horn,
And the flap of the banners, that flit as they 're borne,
And the neigh of the steed, and the multitude's hum,
And the clash, and the shout, "They come! they come!"
The horsetails are pluck'd from the ground, and the
　　sword
From its sheath; and they form, and but wait for the word.
Tartar, and Spahi, and Turcoman,
Strike your tents, and throng to the van;
Mount ye, spur ye, skirr the plain,
That the fugitive may flee in vain,
When he breaks from the town; and none escape,
Aged or young, in the Christian shape;
While your fellows on foot, in a fiery mass,
Bloodstain the breach through which they pass.
The steeds are all bridled, and snort to the rein;
Curved is each neck, and flowing each mane;
White is the foam of their champ on the bit:
The spears are uplifted; the matches are lit;
The cannon are pointed, and ready to roar,
And crush the wall they have crumbled before:
Forms in his phalanx each Janizar;

Alp at their head; his right arm is bare,
So is the blade of his scimitar;
The khan and the pachas are all at their post;
The vizier himself at the head of the host.
When the culverin's signal is fired, then on;
Leave not in Corinth a living one —
A priest at her altars, a chief in her halls,
A hearth in her mansions, a stone on her walls.
God and the prophet — Alla Hu!
Up to the skies with that wild halloo!
"There the breach lies for passage, the ladder to scale;
And your hands on your sabres, and how should ye fail?
He who first downs with the red cross may crave
His heart's dearest wish; let him ask it, and have!"
Thus utter'd Coumourgi, the dauntless vizier;
The reply was the brandish of sabre and spear,
And the shout of fierce thousands in joyous ire: —
Silence — hark to the signal — fire!

   *   *   *   *   *   *

The rampart is won, and the spoil begun,
And all but the after carnage done.
But here and there, where 'vantage ground
Against the foe may still be found,
Desperate groups of twelve or ten
Make a pause, and turn again —
With banded backs against the wall
Fiercely stand, or fighting fall.

There stood an old man — his hairs were white,
But his veteran arm was full of might:
So gallantly bore he the brunt of the fray,

The dead before him, on that day,
In a semicircle lay;
Still he combated unwounded,
Though retreating, unsurrounded.
Many a scar of former fight
Lurk'd beneath his corslet bright;
But of every wound his body bore,
Each and all had been ta'en before:
Though aged, he was so iron of limb,
Few of our youth could cope with him.
Still the old man stood erect,
And Alp's career a moment check'd.
" Yield thee, Minotti; quarter take,
For thine own, thy daughter's sake."
" Never, renegado, never !
Though the life of thy gift would last forever."

" Francesca ! — Oh, my promised bride !
Must she too perish by thy pride? "
" She is safe." — " Where? where? " — " In heaven;
From whence thy traitor soul is driven —
Far from thee, and undefiled."
Grimly then Minotti smiled,
As he saw Alp staggering bow
Before his words, as with a blow.

" Oh God ! when died she? " — " Yesternight —
Nor weep I for her spirit's flight:
None of my pure race shall be
Slaves to Mahomet and thee —
Come on ! "— That challenge is in vain —

Alp 's already with the slain!
While Minotti's words were wreaking
More revenge in bitter speaking
Than his falchion's point had found
Had the time allow'd to wound,
From within the neighboring porch
Of a long defended church,
Where the last and desperate few
Would the failing fight renew,
The sharp shot dash'd Alp to the ground.
Ere an eye could view the wound
That crash'd through the brain of the infidel,
Round he spun, and down he fell.

PARISINA.

(PARISINA, Stanzas 1, 2.)

IT is the hour when from the boughs
   The nightingale's high note is heard:
It is the hour when lovers' vows
   Seem sweet in every whisper'd word;
And gentle winds, and waters near,
Make music to the lonely ear.
Each flower the dews have lightly wet,
And in the sky the stars are met,
And on the wave is deeper blue,
And on the leaf a browner hue,
And in the heaven that clear obscure,
So softly dark, and darkly pure,
Which follows the decline of day,
As twilight melts beneath the moon away.

But it is not to list to the waterfall
That Parisina leaves her hall,
And it is not to gaze on the heavenly light
That the lady walks in the shadow of night;
And if she sits in Este's bower,
'T is not for the sake of its full-blown flower —
She listens — but not for the nightingale —
Though her ear expects as soft a tale.
There glides a step through the foliage thick,
And her cheek grows pale — and her heart beats quick.
There whispers a voice through the rustling leaves,
And her blush returns, and her bosom heaves:
A moment more — and they shall meet —
'T is past — her lover 's at her feet.

THE LAST OF EZZELIN.

(LARA, Canto ii. Stanza 24.)

UPON that night (a peasant's is the tale)
A Serf that cross'd the intervening vale,
When Cynthia's light almost gave way to morn,
And nearly veil'd in mist her waning horn —
A Serf, that rose betimes to thread the wood,
And hew the bough that bought his children's food,
Past by the river that divides the plain
Of Otho's lands and Lara's broad domain:
He heard a tramp — a horse and horseman broke
From out the wood — before him was a cloak

Wrapt round some burthen at his saddle-bow,
Bent was his head, and hidden was his brow.
Roused by the sudden sight at such a time,
And some foreboding that it might be crime,
Himself unheeded watch'd the stranger's course,
Who reach'd the river, bounded from his horse,
And lifting thence the burthen which he bore,
Heaved up the bank, and dash'd it from the shore,
Then paused, and look'd, and turn'd, and seem'd to
    watch,
And still another hurried glance would snatch,
And follow with his step the stream that flow'd,
As if even yet too much its surface show'd.
At once he started — stoop'd; around him strown
The winter floods had scatter'd heaps of stone;
Of these the heaviest thence he gather'd there,
And slung them with a more than common care.
Meantime the Serf had crept to where unseen
Himself might safely mark what this might mean;
He caught a glimpse, as of a floating breast,
And something glitter'd starlike on the vest;
But ere he well could mark the buoyant trunk,
A massy fragment smote it, and it sunk:
It rose again, but indistinct to view,
And left the waters of a purple hue,
Then deeply disappear'd: the horseman gazed
Till ebb'd the latest eddy it had raised;
Then turning, vaulted on his pawing steed,
And instant spurr'd him into panting speed.
His face was mask'd — the features of the dead,
If dead it were, escaped the observer's dread;

But if in sooth a star its bosom bore,
Such is the badge that knighthood ever wore,
And such 't is known Sir Ezzelin had worn
Upon the night that led to such a morn.

[handwritten annotation: see circumstances ... and in ordering ... circumstance ... which ...]

MAZEPPA'S RIDE.

(MAZEPPA, Stanzas 9–17.)

" BRING forth the horse " ! — the horse was brought;
   In truth he was a noble steed,
   A Tartar of the Ukraine breed,
Who look'd as though the speed of thought
Were in his limbs; but he was wild,
   Wild as the wild deer, and untaught,
With spur and bridle undefiled —
   'T was but a day he had been caught;
And snorting, with erected mane,
And struggling fiercely, but in vain,
In the full foam of wrath and dread
To me the desert-born was led:
They bound me on, that menial throng,
Upon his back with many a thong;
Then loosed him with a sudden lash —
Away ! — away ! — and on we dash ! —
Torrents less rapid and less rash.

Away ! — away ! — My breath was gone —
I saw not where he hurried on:
'T was scarcely yet the break of day,
And on he foam'd — away ! — away ! —

The last of human sounds which rose,
As I was darted from my foes,
Was the wild shout of savage laughter,
Which on the wind came roaring after
A moment from that rabble rout:
With sudden wrath I wrench'd my head,
    And snapt the cord, which to the mane
    Had bound my neck in lieu of rein,
And, writhing half my form about,
Howl'd back my curse; but 'midst the tread,
The thunder of my courser's speed,
Perchance they did not hear nor heed:
It vexes me — for I would fain
Have paid their insult back again.
I paid it well in after days:
There is not of that castle gate,
Its drawbridge and portcullis' weight,
Stone, bar, moat, bridge, or barrier left;
Nor of its fields a blade of grass,
    Save what grows on a ridge of wall,
    Where stood the hearth-stone of the hall;
And many a time ye there might pass,
Nor dream that e'er that fortress was:
I saw its turrets in a blaze,
Their crackling battlements all cleft,
    And the hot lead pour down like rain
From off the scorch'd and blackening roof,
Whose thickness was not vengeance-proof.
    They little thought that day of pain,
When launch'd as on the lightning's flash,
They bade me to destruction dash,

That one day I should come again,
With twice five thousand horse, to thank
  The Count for his uncourteous ride.
They play'd me then a bitter prank,
  When, with the wild horse for my guide,
They bound me to his foaming flank:
At length I play'd them one as frank —
For time at last sets all things even —
  And if we do but watch the hour,
  There never yet was human power
Which could evade, if unforgiven,
The patient search and vigil long
Of him who treasures up a wrong.

Away, away, my steed and I,
  Upon the pinions of the wind,
  All human dwellings left behind ;
We sped like meteors through the sky,
When with its crackling sound the night
Is checker'd with the northern light :
Town — village — none were on our track,
  But a wild plain of far extent,
And bounded by a forest black ;
  And, save the scarce seen battlement
On distant heights of some strong hold,
Against the Tartars built of old,
No trace of man.   The year before
A Turkish army had march'd o'er ;
And where the Spahi's hoof hath trod,
  The verdure flies the bloody sod : —
The sky was dull, and dim, and gray,

And a low breeze crept moaning by —
I could have answer'd with a sigh —
But fast we fled, away, away —
And I could neither sigh nor pray ;
And my cold sweat-drops fell like rain
Upon the courser's bristling mane ;
But, snorting still with rage and fear,
He flew upon his far career :
At times I almost thought, indeed,
He must have slacken'd in his speed ;
But no — my bound and slender frame
  Was nothing to his angry might,
And merely like a spur became :
Each motion which I made to free
My swoln limbs from their agony
  Increased his fury and affright :
I tried my voice, — 't was faint and low,
But yet he swerved as from a blow ;
And, starting to each accent, sprang
As from a sudden trumpet's clang :
Meantime my cords were wet with gore,
Which, oozing through my limbs, ran o'er ;
And in my tongue the thirst became
A something fierier far than flame.

We near'd the wild wood — 't was so wide,
I saw no bounds on either side ;
'T was studded with old sturdy trees,
That bent not to the roughest breeze
Which howls down from Siberia's waste,
And strips the forest in its haste, —

But these were few, and far between
Set thick with shrubs more young and green,
Luxuriant with their annual leaves,
Ere strown by those autumnal eves
That nipt the forest's foliage dead,
Discolor'd with a lifeless red,
Which stands thereon like stiffen'd gore
Upon the slain when battle 's o'er,
And some long winter's night hath shed
Its frost o'er every tombless head,
So cold and stark the raven's beak
May peck unpierced each frozen cheek :
'T was a wild waste of underwood,
And here and there a chestnut stood,
The strong oak, and the hardy pine ;
    But far apart — and well it were,
Or else a different lot were mine —
    The boughs gave way, and did not tear
My limbs; and I found strength to bear
My wounds, already scarr'd with cold —
My bonds forbade to loose my hold.
We rustled through the leaves like wind,
Left shrubs, and trees, and wolves behind ;
By night I heard them on the track,
Their troop came hard upon our back,
With their long gallop, which can tire
The hound's deep hate, and hunter's fire :
Where'er we flew they follow'd on,
Nor left us with the morning sun ;
Behind I saw them, scarce a rood,
At day-break winding through the wood,

And through the night had heard their feet
Their stealing, rustling step repeat.
Oh ! how I wish'd for spear or sword,
At least to die amidst the horde,
And perish — if it must be so —
At bay, destroying many a foe.
When first my courser's race begun,
I wish'd the goal already won ;
But now I doubted strength and speed.
Vain doubt ! his swift and savage breed
Had nerved him like the mountain-roe ;
Nor faster falls the blinding snow
Which whelms the peasant near the door
Whose threshold he shall cross no more,
Bewilder'd with the dazzling blast,
Than through the forest-paths he past —
Untired, untamed, and worse than wild ;
All furious as a favor'd child
Balk'd of its wish ; or fiercer still —
A woman piqued — who has her will.

The wood was past ; 't was more than noon,
But chill the air, although in June ;
Or it might be my veins ran cold —
Prolong'd endurance tames the bold ;
And I was then not what I seem,
But headlong as a wintry stream,
And wore my feelings out before
I well could count their causes o'er :
And what with fury, fear, and wrath,
The tortures which beset my path,

Cold, hunger, sorrow, shame, distress,
Thus bound in nature's nakedness;
Sprung from a race whose rising blood
When stirr'd beyond its calmer mood,
And trodden hard upon, is like
The rattle-snake's in act to strike,
What marvel if this worn-out trunk
Beneath its woes a moment sunk?
The earth gave way, the skies roll'd round,
I seem'd to sink upon the ground;
But err'd, for I was fastly bound.
My heart turn'd sick, my brain grew sore,
And throbb'd awhile, then beat no more;
The skies spun like a mighty wheel;
I saw the trees like drunkards reel,
And a slight flash sprang o'er my eyes,
Which saw no farther: he who dies
Can die no more than then I died.
O'ertortured by that ghastly ride,
I felt the blackness come and go,
And strove to wake; but could not make
My senses climb up from below:
I felt as on a plank at sea,
When all the waves that dash o'er thee,
At the same time upheave and whelm,
And hurl thee towards a desert realm.
My undulating life was as
The fancied lights that flitting pass
Our shut eyes in deep midnight, when
Fever begins upon the brain;
But soon it pass'd, with little pain,

But a confusion worse than such:
I own that I should deem it much,
Dying, to feel the same again;
And yet I do suppose we must
Feel far more ere we turn to dust:
No matter; I have bared my brow
Full in Death's face — before — and now.

My blood reflow'd, though thick and chill;
My heart began once more to thrill;
Methought the dash of waves was nigh;
There was a gleam too of the sky,
Studded with stars;—it is no dream;
The wild horse swims the wilder stream!
The bright broad river's gushing tide
Sweeps, winding onward, far and wide,
And we are half-way, struggling o'er
To yon unknown and silent shore.
The waters broke my hollow trance,
And with a temporary strength
My stiffen'd limbs were rebaptized.
My courser's broad breast proudly braves,
And dashes off the ascending waves,
And onward we advance!
We reach the slippery shore at length,
A haven I but little prized,
For all behind was dark and drear,
And all before was night and fear.
How many hours of night or day
In those suspended pangs I lay,
I could not tell; I scarcely knew
If this were human breath I drew.

With glossy skin, and dripping mane,
And reeling limbs, and reeking flank,
 The wild steed's sinewy nerves still strain
Up the repelling bank.
 We gain the top: a boundless plain
 Spreads through the shadow of the night,
  And onward, onward, onward, seems,
  Like precipices in our dreams,
To stretch beyond the sight;
And here and there a speck of white,
 Or scatter'd spot of dusky green,
In masses broke into the light,
As rose the moon upon my right.
 But nought distinctly seen
In the dim waste would indicate
The omen of a cottage gate;
No twinkling taper from afar
Stood like a hospitable star;
Not even an ignis-fatuus rose
To make him merry with my woes:
 That very cheat had cheer'd me then!
Although detected, welcome still,
Reminding me, through every ill,
 Of the abodes of men.

Onward we went — but slack and slow.
 His savage force at length o'erspent,
The drooping courser, faint and low,
 All feebly foaming went.
A sickly infant had had power
To guide him forward in that hour;

But useless all to me.
His new-born tameness nought avail'd,
My limbs were bound; my force had fail'd,
  Perchance, had they been free.
With feeble effort still I tried
To rend the bonds so starkly tied —
  But still it was in vain;
My limbs were only wrung the more,
And soon the idle strife gave o'er,
  Which but prolong'd their pain.
The dizzy race seem'd almost run;
Some streaks announced the coming sun —
  How slow, alas! he came!
Methought that mist of dawning gray
Would never dapple into day;
How heavily it roll'd away —
  Before the eastern flame
Rose crimson, and deposed the stars,
And call'd the radiance from their cars,
And fill'd the earth, from his deep throne,
With lonely lustre, all his own.

Up rose the sun; the mists were curl'd
Back from the solitary world
Which lay around — behind — before;
What booted it to traverse o'er
Plain, forest, river? Man nor brute,
Nor dint of hoof, nor print of foot,
Lay in the wild luxuriant soil;
No sign of travel — none of toil;
The very air was mute;

And not an insect's shrill small horn,
Nor matin bird's new voice was borne
From herb nor thicket.   Many a werst,
Panting as if his heart would burst,
The weary brute still stagger'd on;
And still we were — or seem'd — alone:
At length, while reeling on our way,
Methought I heard a courser neigh,
From out yon tuft of blackening firs.
Is it the wind those branches stirs?
No, no! from out the forest prance
   A trampling troop; I see them come!
In one vast squadron they advance!
   I strove to cry — my lips were dumb.
The steeds rush on in plunging pride;
But where are they the reins to guide?
A thousand horse — and none to ride!
With flowing tail, and flying mane,
Wide nostrils — never stretch'd by pain,
Mouths bloodless to the bit or rein,
And feet that iron never shod,
And flanks unscarr'd by spur or rod,
A thousand horse, the wild, the free,
Like waves that follow o'er the sea,
   Came thickly thundering on,
As if our faint approach to meet;
The sight re-nerved my courser's feet,
A moment staggering, feebly fleet,
A moment, with a faint low neigh,
   He answer'd, and then fell;
With gasps and glazing eyes he lay,

And reeking limbs immovable,
     His first and last career is done.
On came the troop — they saw him stoop,
   They saw me strangely bound along
   His back with many a bloody thong:
They stop — they start — they snuff the air,
Gallop a moment here and there,
Approach, retire, wheel round and round,
Then plunging back with sudden bound,
Headed by one black mighty steed,
Who seem'd the patriarch of his breed,
   Without a single speck or hair
Of white upon his shaggy hide;
They snort — they foam — neigh — swerve aside,
And backward to the forest fly,
By instinct, from a human eye. —
   They left me there to my despair,
Link'd to the dead and stiffening wretch,
Whose lifeless limbs beneath me stretch,
Relieved from that unwonted weight,
From whence I could not extricate
Nor him nor me — and there we lay
   The dying on the dead!
And there from morn till twilight bound,
I felt the heavy hours toil round,
With just enough of life to see
My last of suns go down on me.

I know no more — my latest dream
   Is something of a lovely star
   Which fix'd my dull eyes from afar,

And went and came with wandering beam,
And of the cold, dull, swimming, dense
Sensation of recurring sense,
And then subsiding back to death,
And then again a little breath,
A little thrill, a short suspense,
    An icy sickness curdling o'er
My heart, and sparks that cross'd my brain —
A gasp, a throb, a start of pain,
    A sigh, and nothing more.

I woke — Where was I? — Do I see
A human face look down on me?
And doth a roof above me close?
Do these limbs on a couch repose?
Is this a chamber where I lie?
And is it mortal yon bright eye,
That watches me with gentle glance?
    I closed my own again once more,
As doubtful that the former trance
    Could not as yet be o'er.
    A slender girl, long-haired, and tall,
Sate watching by the cottage wall;
The sparkle of her eye I caught,
Even with my first return of thought;
For ever and anon she threw
    A prying, pitying glance on me
    With her black eyes so wild and free:
I gazed, and gazed, until I knew
    No vision it could be, —
But that I lived, and was released
From adding to the vulture's feast:

And when the Cossack maid beheld
My heavy eyes at length unseal'd,
She smiled — and I essay'd to speak,
   But failed — and she approach'd, and made
   With lip and finger signs that said,
I must not strive as yet to break
The silence, till my strength should be
Enough to leave my accents free;
And then her hand on mine she laid,
And smooth'd the pillow for my head,
And stole along on tiptoe tread,
   And gently oped the door, and spake
In whispers — ne'er was voice so sweet!
Even music follow'd her light feet; —
   But those she call'd were not awake,
And she went forth; but, ere she past,
Another look on me she cast,
   Another sign she made, to say,
That I had nought to fear, that all
Were near, at my command or call,
   And she would not delay
Her due return: — while she was gone,
Methought I felt too much alone.

She came with mother and with sire —
What need of more? — I will not tire
With long recital of the rest,
Since I became the Cossack's guest.
They found me senseless on the plain —
   They bore me to the nearest hut —
They brought me into life again —
Me — one day o'er their realm to reign!

THE STREAMLET FROM THE CLIFF.

(THE ISLAND, Canto iii. Stanza 3.)

A LITTLE stream came tumbling from the height,
And straggling into ocean as it might,
Its bounding crystal frolick'd in the ray,
And gush'd from cliff to crag with saltless spray;
Close on the wild, wide ocean, yet as pure
And fresh as innocence, and more secure,
Its silver torrent glitter'd o'er the deep,
As the shy chamois' eye o'erlooks the steep,
While far below the vast and sullen swell
Of ocean's alpine azure rose and fell.

THE SHIPWRECK.

(DON JUAN, Canto ii. Stanzas 49–53.)

'T WAS twilight, and the sunless day went down
    Over the waste of waters; like a veil,
Which, if withdrawn, would but disclose the frown
    Of one whose hate is mask'd but to assail.
Thus to their hopeless eyes the night was shown,
    And grimly darkled o'er the faces pale,
And the dim desolate deep: twelve days had Fear
Been their familiar, and now Death was here.

Some trial had been making at a raft,
    With little hope in such a rolling sea,

A sort of thing at which one would have laugh'd,
    If any laughter at such times could be,
Unless with people who too much have quaff'd,
    And have a kind of wild and horrid glee,
Half epileptical, and half hysterical: —
Their preservation would have been a miracle.

At half-past eight o'clock, booms, hencoops, spars,
    And all things, for a chance, had been cast loose,
That still could keep afloat the struggling tars,
    For yet they strove, although of no great use:
There was no light in heaven but a few stars,
    The boats put off o'ercrowded with their crews;
She gave a heel, and then a lurch to port,
And, going down head foremost — sunk, in short.

Then rose from sea to sky the wild farewell —
    Then shriek'd the timid, and stood still the brave, —
Then some leap'd overboard with dreadful yell,
    As eager to anticipate their grave;
And the sea yawn'd around her like a hell,
    And down she suck'd with her the whirling wave,
Like one who grapples with his enemy,
And strives to strangle him before he die.

And first one universal shriek there rush'd,
    Louder than the loud ocean, like a crash
Of echoing thunder; and then all was hush'd,
    Save the wild wind and the remorseless dash
Of billows; but at intervals there gush'd,
    Accompanied with a convulsive splash,
A solitary shriek, the bubbling cry
Of some strong swimmer in his agony.

HAIDÉE.

(DON JUAN, Canto ii. Stanzas 111–118.)

How long in his damp trance young Juan lay
  He knew not, for the earth was gone for him,
And Time had nothing more of night nor day
  For his congealing blood, and senses dim;
And how this heavy faintness past away
  He knew not, till each painful pulse and limb,
And tingling vein seem'd throbbing back to life,
For Death, though vanquish'd, still retired with strife.

His eyes he open'd, shut, again unclosed,
  For all was doubt and dizziness; he thought
He still was in the boat, and had but dozed,
  And felt again with his despair o'erwrought,
And wish'd it death in which he had reposed,
  And then once more his feelings back were brought,
And slowly by his swimming eyes was seen
A lovely female face of seventeen.

'T was bending close o'er his, and the small mouth
  Seem'd almost prying into his for breath;
And, chafing him, the soft warm hand of youth
  Recall'd his answering spirits back from death;
And bathing his chill temples, tried to soothe
  Each pulse to animation, till beneath
Its gentle touch and trembling care, a sigh
To these kind efforts made a low reply.

Then was the cordial pour'd, and mantle flung
   Around his scarce-clad limbs; and the fair arm
Raised higher the faint head which o'er it hung;
   And her transparent cheek, all pure and warm,
Pillow'd his death-like forehead; then she wrung
   His dewy curls, long drench'd by every storm;
And watch'd with eagerness each throb that drew
A sigh from his heaved bosom — and hers, too.

And lifting him with care into the cave,
   The gentle girl, and her attendant, — one
Young, yet her elder, and of brow less grave,
   And more robust of figure, — then begun
To kindle fire, and as the new flames gave
   Light to the rocks that roof'd them, which the sun
Had never seen, the maid, or whatsoe'er
She was, appear'd distinct, and tall, and fair.

Her brow was overhung with coins of gold,
   That sparkled o'er the auburn of her hair,
Her clustering hair, whose longer locks were roll'd
   In braids behind; and though her stature were
Even of the highest for a female mould,
   They nearly reach'd her heel; and in her air
There was a something which bespoke command,
As one who was a lady in the land.

Her hair, I said, was auburn; but her eyes
   Were black as death, their lashes the same hue,
Of downcast length, in whose silk shadows lies
   Deepest attraction; for when to the view

Forth from its raven fringe the full glance flies,
   Ne'er with such force the swiftest arrow flew;
'T is as the snake late coil'd, who pours his length,
And hurls at once his venom and his strength.

Her brow was white and low, her cheek's pure dye
   Like twilight rosy still with the set sun;
Short upper lip — sweet lips! that make us sigh
   Ever to have seen such; for she was one
Fit for the model of a statuary
   (A race of mere impostors, when all 's done —
I 've seen much finer women, ripe and real,
Than all the nonsense of their stone ideal).

———

HAIDÉE AGAIN.

(DON JUAN, Canto iii. Stanzas 70–75.)

OF all the dresses I select Haidée's:
   She wore two jelicks — one was of pale yellow;
Of azure, pink, and white was her chemise —
   'Neath which her breast heaved like a little billow;
With buttons form'd of pearls as large as peas,
   All gold and crimson shone her jelick's fellow,
And the striped white gauze baracan that bound her
Like fleecy clouds about the moon flow'd round her.

One large gold bracelet clasp'd each lovely arm,
   Lockless — so pliable from the pure gold
That the hand stretch'd and shut it without harm,
   The limb which it adorn'd its only mould;

So beautiful — its very shape would charm,
  And clinging as if loath to lose its hold,
The purest ore enclosed the whitest skin
That e'er by precious metal was held in.

Around, as princess of her father's land,
  A like gold bar above her instep roll'd
Announced her rank; twelve rings were on her hand;
  Her hair was starr'd with gems; her veil's fine fold
Below her breast was fasten'd with a band
  Of lavish pearls, whose worth could scarce be told;
Her orange silk full Turkish trousers furl'd
About the prettiest ankle in the world.

Her hair's long auburn waves down to her heel
  Flow'd like an Alpine torrent which the sun
Dyes with his morning light, — and would conceal
  Her person if allow'd at large to run,
And still they seem resentfully to feel
  The silken fillet's curb, and sought to shun
Their bonds whene'er some Zephyr caught began
To offer his young pinion as her fan.

Round her she made an atmosphere of life,
  The very air seem'd lighter from her eyes,
They were so soft and beautiful, and rife
  With all we can imagine of the skies,
And pure as Psyche ere she grew a wife —
  Too pure even for the purest human ties;
Her overpowering presence made you feel
It would not be idolatry to kneel.

Her eyelashes, though dark as night, were tinged
   (It is the country's custom), but in vain;
For those large black eyes were so blackly fringed,
   The glossy rebels mock'd the jetty stain,
And in their native beauty stood avenged:
   Her nails were touch'd with henna; but again
The power of art was turn'd to nothing, for
They could not look more rosy than before.

———

AURORA RABY.

(Don Juan, Canto xv. Stanzas 43–47.)

AND then there was — but why should I go on,
   Unless the ladies should go off? — there was
Indeed a certain fair and fairy one,
   Of the best class, and better than her class, —
Aurora Raby, a young star who shone
   O'er life, too sweet an image for such glass,
A lovely being, scarcely form'd or moulded,
A rose with all its sweetest leaves yet folded;

Rich, noble, but an orphan: left an only
   Child to the care of guardians good and kind;
But still her aspect had an air so lonely!
   Blood is not water; and where shall we find
Feelings of youth like those which overthrown lie
   By death, when we are left, alas! behind,
To feel, in friendless palaces, a home
Is wanting, and our best ties in the tomb?

Early in years, and yet more infantine
    In figure, she had something of sublime
In eyes which sadly shone, as seraphs' shine.
    All youth — but with an aspect beyond time;
Radiant and grave — as pitying man's decline;
    Mournful — but mournful of another's crime,
She look'd as if she sate by Eden's door,
And grieved for those who could return no more.

She was a Catholic, too, sincere, austere,
    As far as her own gentle heart allow'd,
And deem'd that fallen worship far more dear
    Perhaps because 't was fall'n: her sires were proud
Of deeds and days when they had fill'd the ear
    Of nations, and had never bent or bow'd
To novel power; and as she was the last,
She held their old faith and old feelings fast.

She gazed upon a world she scarcely knew,
    As seeking not to know it; silent, lone,
As grows a flower, thus quietly she grew,
    And kept her heart serene within its zone.
There was awe in the homage which she drew;
    Her spirit seem'd as seated on a throne
Apart from the surrounding world, and strong
In its own strength — most strange in one so young!

III.

DRAMATIC.

MANFRED AND THE SEVEN SPIRITS.

(MANFRED, Act i. Scene i.)

MANFRED *alone. — Scene, a Gothic Gallery. — Time,
Midnight.*

Man. THE lamp must be replenish'd, but even then
It will not burn so long as I must watch:
My slumbers — if I slumber — are not sleep,
But a continuance of enduring thought,
Which then I can resist not: in my heart
There is a vigil, and these eyes but close
To look within; and yet I live, and bear
The aspect and the form of breathing men.
But grief should be the instructor of the wise;
Sorrow is knowledge: they who know the most
Must mourn the deepest o'er the fatal truth,
The Tree of Knowledge is not that of Life.
Philosophy and science, and the springs
Of wonder, and the wisdom of the world,
I have essay'd, and in my mind there is
A power to make these subject to itself —
But they avail not: I have done men good,
And I have met with good even among men —
But this avail'd not: I have had my foes,
And none have baffled, many fallen before me —
But this avail'd not: Good, or evil, life,
Powers, passions, all I see in other beings,
Have been to me as rain unto the sands,
Since that all-nameless hour.   I have no dread,

And feel the curse to have no natural fear,
Nor fluttering throb, that beats with hopes or wishes,
Or lurking love of something on the earth. —
Now to my task. —

                 Mysterious Agency!
Ye spirits of the unbounded Universe!
Whom I have sought in darkness and in light —
Ye, who do compass earth about, and dwell
In subtler essence — ye, to whom the tops
Of mountains inaccessible are haunts,
And earth's and ocean's caves familiar things —
I call upon ye by the written charm
Which gives me power upon you —— Rise! appear!

                                   [A pause.

They come not yet. — Now by the voice of him
Who is the first among you — by this sign,
Which makes you tremble — by the claims of him
Who is undying, — Rise! appear! —— Appear!

                                   [A pause.

If it be so. — Spirits of earth and air,
Ye shall not thus elude me: by a power,
Deeper than all yet urged, a tyrant-spell,
Which had its birthplace in a star condemn'd,
The burning wreck of a demolish'd world,
A wandering hell in the eternal space;
By the strong curse which is upon my soul,
The thought which is within me and around me,
I do compel ye to my will. — Appear!

    *[A star is seen at the darker end of the gallery: it is
       stationary ; and a voice is heard singing.*

FIRST SPIRIT.

Mortal! to thy bidding bow'd,
From my mansion in the cloud,
Which the breath of twilight builds,
And the summer's sunset gilds
With the azure and vermilion,
Which is mix'd for my pavilion;
Though thy quest may be forbidden,
On a star-beam I have ridden;
To thine adjuration bow'd,
Mortal — be thy wish avow'd!

Voice of the SECOND SPIRIT.

Mont Blanc is the Monarch of mountains;
  They crown'd him long ago
On a throne of rocks, in a robe of clouds,
  With a diadem of snow.
Around his waist are forests braced,
  The Avalanche in his hand;
But ere it fall, that thundering ball
  Must pause for my command.
The Glacier's cold and restless mass
  Moves onward day by day;
But I am he who bids it pass,
  Or with its ice delay.
I am the spirit of the place,
  Could make the mountain bow
And quiver to his cavern'd base —
  And what with me wouldst *Thou?*

Voice of the THIRD SPIRIT.

In the blue depth of the waters,
   Where the wave hath no strife,
Where the wind is a stranger,
   And the sea-snake hath life,
Where the Mermaid is decking
   Her green hair with shells;
Like the storm on the surface
   Came the sound of thy spells;
O'er my calm Hall of Coral
   The deep echo roll'd —
To the Spirit of Ocean
   Thy wishes unfold!

FOURTH SPIRIT.

Where the slumbering earthquake
   Lies pillow'd on fire,
And the lakes of bitumen
   Rise boilingly higher;
Where the roots of the Andes
   Strike deep in the earth,
As their summits to heaven
   Shoot soaringly forth;
I have quitted my birthplace,
   Thy bidding to bide —
Thy spell hath subdued me,
   Thy will be my guide!

FIFTH SPIRIT.

I am the Rider of the wind,
   The Stirrer of the storm ;
The hurricane I left behind
   Is yet with lightning warm ;
To speed to thee, o'er shore and sea
   I swept upon the blast :
The fleet I met sail'd well, and yet
    'T will sink ere night be past.

SIXTH SPIRIT.

My dwelling is the shadow of the night,
Why doth thy magic torture me with light?

SEVENTH SPIRIT.

The star which rules thy destiny
Was ruled, ere earth began, by me :
It was a world as fresh and fair
As e'er revolved round sun in air ;
Its course was free and regular,
Space bosom'd not a lovelier star.
The hour arrived — and it became
A wandering mass of shapeless flame,
A pathless comet, and a curse,
The menace of the universe ;
Still rolling on with innate force,
 Without a sphere, without a course,

A bright deformity on high,
The monster of the upper sky!
And thou! beneath its influence born —
Thou worm! whom I obey and scorn —
Forced by a power (which is not thine,
And lent thee but to make thee mine)
For this brief moment to descend,
Where these weak spirits round thee bend
And parley with a thing like thee —
What wouldst thou, Child of Clay! with me?

The SEVEN SPIRITS.

Earth, ocean, air, night, mountains, winds, thy star,
    Are at thy beck and bidding, Child of Clay!
Before thee at thy quest their spirits are —
    What wouldst thou with us, son of mortals — say?

Man. Forgetfulness ——
First Spirit.   Of what — of whom — and why?
Man. Of that which is within me; read it there —
Ye know it, and I cannot utter it.
Spirit. We can but give thee that which we possess:
Ask of us subjects, sovereignty, the power
O'er earth, the whole, or portion, or a sign
Which shall control the elements, whereof
We are the dominators, each and all,
These shall be thine.
Man.   Oblivion, self-oblivion —
Can ye not wring from out the hidden realms
Ye offer so profusely what I ask?

Spirit.   It is not in our essence, in our skill;
But — thou mayest die.
   Man.   Will death bestow it on me?
   Spirit.   We are immortal, and do not forget ;
We are eternal ; and to us the past
Is, as the future, present.   Art thou answer'd?
   Man.   Ye mock me — but the power which brought
             ye here
Hath made you mine.   Slaves, scoff not at my will!
The mind, the spirit, the Promethean spark,
The lightning of my being, is as bright,
Pervading, and far darting as your own,
And shall not yield to yours, though coop'd in clay!
Answer, or I will teach you what I am.
   Spirit.   We answer as we answer'd ; our reply
Is even in thine own words.
   Man.   Why say ye so?
   Spirit.   If, as thou say'st, thine essence be as ours,
We have replied in telling thee, the thing
Mortals call death hath nought to do with us.
   Man.   I then have call'd ye from your realms in
             vain ;
Ye cannot, or ye will not, aid me.
   Spirit.   Stay ;
What we possess we offer ; it is thine :
Bethink ere thou dismiss us, ask again —
Kingdom, and sway, and strength, and length of days —
   Man.   Accursed! what have I to do with days?
They are too long already. — Hence — begone !
   Spirit.   Yet pause : being here, our will would do
             thee service;

Bethink thee, is there then no other gift
Which we can make not worthless in thine eyes?

 Man. No, none; yet stay — one moment, ere we
    part —
I would behold ye face to face. I hear
Your voices, sweet and melancholy sounds,
As music on the waters; and I see
The steady aspect of a clear large star;
But nothing more. Approach me as ye are,
Or one, or all, in your accustom'd forms.

 Spirit. We have no forms, beyond the elements
Of which we are the mind and principle:
But choose a form — in that we will appear.

 Man. I have no choice; there is no form on earth
Hideous or beautiful to me. Let him,
Who is most powerful of ye, take such aspect
As unto him may seem most fitting — Come!

Seventh Spirit. (*Appearing in the shape of a beautiful
   female figure.*) Behold!

 Man. Oh God! if it be thus, and *thou*
Art not a madness and a mockery,
I yet might be most happy. I will clasp thee,
And we again will be —— [*The figure vanishes.*
     My heart is crush'd!
     [MANFRED *falls senseless.*

(*A Voice is heard in the Incantation which follows.*)

  When the moon is on the wave,
   And the glow-worm in the grass,

And the meteor on the grave,
  And the wisp on the morass ;
When the falling stars are shooting,
And the answer'd owls are hooting,
And the silent leaves are still
In the shadow of the hill,
Shall my soul be upon thine,
With a power and with a sign.

Though thy slumber may be deep,
Yet thy spirit shall not sleep ;
There are shades which will not vanish,
There are thoughts thou canst not banish ;
By a power to thee unknown,
Thou canst never be alone;
Thou art wrapt as with a shroud,
Thou art gather'd in a cloud;
And forever shalt thou dwell
In the spirit of this spell.

Though thou seest me not pass by,
Thou shalt feel me with thine eye
As a thing that, though unseen,
Must be near thee, and hath been;
And when in that secret dread
Thou hast turn'd around thy head,
Thou shalt marvel I am not
As thy shadow on the spot,
And the power which thou dost feel
Shall be what thou must conceal.

And a magic voice and verse
Hath baptized thee with a curse;
And a spirit of the air
Hath begirt thee with a snare;
In the wind there is a voice
Shall forbid thee to rejoice;
And to thee shall Night deny
All the quiet of her sky;
And the Day shall have a sun,
Which shall make thee wish it done.

MANFRED ON THE CLIFFS.

(MANFRED, Act i. Scene 2.)

The Mountain of the Jungfrau. — Time, Morning. —
MANFRED *alone upon the Cliffs.*

Man.   THE spirits I have raised abandon me —
The spells which I have studied baffle me —
The remedy I reck'd of tortured me.
I lean no more on super-human aid;
It hath no power upon the past, and for
The future, till the past be gulf'd in darkness,
It is not of my search. — My mother Earth!
And thou fresh breaking Day, and you, ye Mountains,
Why are ye beautiful?   I cannot love ye.
And thou, the bright eye of the universe,
That openest over all, and unto all
Art a delight — thou shin'st not on my heart.

And you, ye crags, upon whose extreme edge
I stand, and on the torrent's brink beneath
Behold the tall pines dwindled as to shrubs
In dizziness of distance; when a leap,
A stir, a motion, even a breath, would bring
My breast upon its rocky bosom's bed
To rest forever — wherefore do I pause?
I feel the impulse — yet I do not plunge;
I see the peril — yet do not recede;
And my brain reels — and yet my foot is firm:
There is a power upon me which withholds,
And makes it my fatality to live;
If it be life to wear within myself
This barrenness of spirit, and to be
My own soul's sepulchre, for I have ceased
To justify my deeds unto myself —
The last infirmity of evil.   Ay,
Thou winged and cloud-cleaving minister,

                        [*An eagle passes.*

Whose happy flight is highest into heaven,
Well may'st thou swoop so near me — I should be
Thy prey, and gorge thine eaglets; thou art gone
Where the eye cannot follow thee; but thine
Yet pierces downward, onward, or above,
With a pervading vision. — Beautiful!
How beautiful is all this visible world!
How glorious in its action and itself!
But we, who name ourselves its sovereigns, we,
Half dust, half deity, alike unfit
To sink or soar, with our mix'd essence make
A conflict of its elements, and breathe

The breath of degradation and of pride,
Contending with low wants and lofty will,
Till our mortality predominates,
And men are — what they name not to themselves,
And trust not to each other.   Hark! the note,
　　　[*The Shepherd's pipe in the distance is heard.*
The natural music of the mountain reed —
For here the patriarchal days are not
A pastoral fable — pipes in the liberal air,
Mixt with the sweet bells of the sauntering herd;
My soul would drink those echoes. — Oh, that I were
The viewless spirit of a lovely sound.
A living voice, a breathing harmony,
A bodiless enjoyment — born and dying
With the blest tone which made me!

　　　Enter from below a CHAMOIS HUNTER.

Chamois Hunter.　　　　　　**Even so**
This way the chamois leapt: her nimble feet
Have baffled me; my gains to-day will scarce
Repay my break-neck travail. — What is here?
Who seems not of my trade, and yet hath reach'd
A height which none even of our mountaineers,
Save our best hunters, may attain: his garb
Is goodly, his mien manly, and his air
Proud as a free-born peasant's, at this distance —
I will approach him nearer.
　　　Man. (not perceiving the other).   To be thus —
Gray-hair'd with anguish, like these blasted pines,
Wrecks of a single winter, barkless, branchless,
A blighted trunk upon a cursèd root,

Which but supplies a feeling to decay —
And to be thus, eternally but thus,
Having been otherwise ! Now furrow'd o'er
With wrinkles, plough'd by moments, not by years
And hours — all tortured into ages — hours
Which I outlive ! — Ye toppling crags of ice !
Ye avalanches, whom a breath draws down
In mountainous o'erwhelming, come and crush me !
I hear ye momently above, beneath,
Crash with a frequent conflict; but ye pass,
And only fall on things that still would live;
On the young flourishing forest, or the hut
And hamlet of the harmless villager.

   C. Hun.   The mists begin to rise up from the valley;
I 'll warn him to descend, or he may chance
To lose at once his way and life together.

   Man.   The mists boil up around the glaciers; clouds
Rise curling fast beneath me, white and sulphury,
Like foam from the roused ocean of deep Hell,
Whose every wave breaks on a living shore,
Heap'd with the damn'd like pebbles. — I am giddy.

   C. Hun.   I must approach him cautiously; if near,
A sudden step will startle him, and he
Seems tottering already.

   Man.   Mountains have fallen,
Leaving a gap in the clouds, and with the shock
Rocking their Alpine brethren; filling up
The ripe green valleys with destruction's splinters;
Damming the rivers with a sudden dash,
Which crush'd the waters into mist, and made
Their fountains find another channel — thus,

Thus, in its old age, did Mount Rosenberg —
Why stood I not beneath it?

   C. Hun.   Friend! have a care,
Your next step may be fatal! — for the love
Of Him who made you, stand not on that brink!

   Man. (*not hearing him*).   Such would have been for
          me a fitting tomb;
My bones had then been quiet in their depth ;
They had not then been strewn upon the rocks
For the wind's pastime — as thus — thus they shall be —
In this one plunge. — Farewell, ye opening heavens !
Look not upon me thus reproachfully —
Ye were not meant for me — Earth ! take these atoms !

     [*As* MANFRED *is in the act to spring from the cliff,*
       the CHAMOIS HUNTER *seizes and retains him*
       with a sudden grasp.

   C. Hun. Hold, madman !—though aweary of thy life,
Stain not our pure vales with thy guilty blood.
Away with me —— I will not quit my hold.

   Man.   I am most sick at heart — nay, grasp me not —
I am all feebleness — the mountains whirl
Spinning around me —— I grow blind —— What art
        thou?

   C. Hun.   I 'll answer that anon. — Away with me —
The clouds grow thicker —— there — now lean on me —
Place your foot here — here, take this staff, and cling
A moment to that shrub — now give me your hand,
And hold fast by my girdle — softly — well —
The Châlet will be gain'd within an hour —
Come on, we 'll quickly find a surer footing,
And something like a pathway, which the torrent

Hath wash'd since winter. — Come, 't is bravely done —
You should have been a hunter. — Follow me.

> [*They descend the rocks.*

THE WITCH OF THE ALPS.

(MANFRED, Act ii. Scene 2.)

A lower Valley in the Alps. — A Cataract.

Enter MANFRED.

IT is not noon — the sunbow's rays still arch
The torrent with the many hues of heaven,
And roll the sheeted silver's waving column
O'er the crag's headlong perpendicular,
And fling its lines of foaming light along,
And to and fro, like the pale courser's tail,
The Giant steed, to be bestrode by Death,
As told in the Apocalypse.   No eyes
But mine now drink this sight of loveliness;
I should be sole in this sweet solitude,
And with the Spirit of the place divide
The homage of these waters. — I will call her.

> [MANFRED *takes some of the water into the palm
> of his hand, and flings it into the air, mutter-
> ing the adjuration. After a pause, the* WITCH
> OF THE ALPS *rises beneath the arch of the sun-
> bow of the torrent.*

Beautiful Spirit! with thy hair of light,
And dazzling eyes of glory, in whose form

The charms of earth's least mortal daughters grow
To an unearthly stature, in an essence
Of purer elements; while the hues of youth, —
Carnation'd like a sleeping infant's cheek,
Rock'd by the beating of her mother's heart,
Or the rose tints, which summer's twilight leaves
Upon the lofty glacier's virgin snow,
The blush of earth embracing with her heaven, —
Tinge thy celestial aspect, and make tame
The beauties of the sunbow which bends o'er thee.
Beautiful Spirit! in thy calm clear brow,
Wherein is glass'd serenity of soul,
Which of itself shows immortality,
I read that thou wilt pardon to a Son
Of Earth, whom the abstruser powers permit
At times to commune with them — if that he
Avail him of his spells — to call thee thus,
And gaze on thee a moment.
  Witch.   Son of Earth!
I know thee, and the powers which give thee power;
I know thee for a man of many thoughts,
And deeds of good and ill, extreme in both,
Fatal and fated in thy sufferings.
I have expected this — what would'st thou with me?
 Man. To·look upon thy beauty — nothing further.
The face of the earth hath madden'd me, and I
Take refuge in her mysteries, and pierce
To the abodes of those who govern her —
But they can nothing aid me.   I have sought
From them what they could not bestow, and now
I search no further.

Witch. What could be the quest
Which is not in the power of the most powerful,
The rulers of the invisible?
   Man. A boon;
But why should I repeat it? 't were in vain.
   Witch. I know not that; let thy lips utter it.
   Man. Well, though it torture me, 't is but the same;
My pang shall find a voice.   From my youth upwards
My spirit walk'd not with the souls of men,
Nor look'd upon the earth with human eyes;
The thirst of their ambition was not mine,
The aim of their existence was not mine;
My joys, my griefs, my passions, and my powers,
Made me a stranger; though I wore the form,
I had no sympathy with breathing flesh,
Nor midst the creatures of clay that girded me
Was there but one who —— but of her anon.
I said with men, and with the thoughts of men,
I held but slight communion; but instead,
My joy was in the Wilderness, to breathe
The difficult air of the iced mountain's top,
Where the birds dare not build, nor insect's wing
Flit o'er the herbless granite; or to plunge
Into the torrent, and to roll along
On the swift whirl of the new breaking wave
Of river-stream, or ocean, in their flow.
In these my early strength exulted; or
To follow through the night the moving moon,
The stars and their development; or catch
The dazzling lightnings till my eyes grew dim;
Or to look, list'ning, on the scatter'd leaves,

While Autumn winds were at their evening song.
These were my pastimes, and to be alone;
For if the beings, of whom I was one, —
Hating to be so, — cross'd me in my path,
I felt myself degraded back to them,
And was all clay again.   And then I dived,
In my lone wanderings, to the caves of death,
Searching its cause in its effect; and drew
From wither'd bones, and skulls, and heap'd up dust,
Conclusions most forbidden.   Then I pass'd
The nights of years in sciences untaught,
Save in the old time; and with time and toil,
And terrible ordeal, and such penance
As in itself hath power upon the air,
And spirits that do compass air and earth,
Space, and the peopled infinite, I made
Mine eyes familiar with Eternity,
Such as, before me, did the Magi, and
He who from out their fountain-dwellings raised
Eros and Anteros, at Gadara,
As I do thee; — and with my knowledge grew
The thirst of knowledge, and the power and joy
Of this most bright intelligence, until ——
 Witch.   Proceed.
 Man.   Oh! I but thus prolong'd my words,
Boasting these idle attributes, because
As I approach the core of my heart's grief —
But to my task.   I have not named to thee
Father or mother, mistress, friend, or being,
With whom I wore the chain of human ties;
If I had such, they seem'd not such to me —

Yet there was one ——

   Witch.   Spare not thyself — proceed.

   Man.   She was like me in lineaments — her eyes,
Her hair, her features, all, to the very tone
Even of her voice, they said were like to mine;
But soften'd all, and temper'd into beauty;
She had the same lone thoughts and wanderings,
The quest of hidden knowledge, and a mind
To comprehend the universe: nor these
Alone, but with them gentler powers than mine,
Pity, and smiles, and tears — which I had not;
And tenderness — but that I had for her;
Humility — and that I never had.
Her faults were mine — her virtues were her own —
I loved her, and destroy'd her!

   Witch.   With thy hand?

   Man. Not with my hand, but heart — which broke
          her heart —
It gazed on mine, and wither'd. I have shed
Blood, but not hers — and yet her blood was shed —
I saw — and could not stanch it.

   Witch.   And for this —
A being of the race thou dost despise,
The order which thine own would rise above,
Mingling with us and ours, thou dost forego
The gifts of our great knowledge, and shrink'st back
To recreant mortality —— Away!

   Man. Daughter of Air! I tell thee, since that hour —
But words are breath — look on me in my sleep,
Or watch my watchings — Come and sit by me!
My solitude is solitude no more,

But peopled with the Furies; — I have gnash'd
My teeth in darkness till returning morn,
Then curst myself till sunset; — I have pray'd
For madness as a blessing — 't is denied me.
I have affronted death — but in the war
Of elements the waters shrunk from me,
And fatal things pass'd harmless — the cold hand
Of an all-pitiless demon held me back,
Back by a single hair, which would not break.
In fantasy, imagination, all
The affluence of my soul — which one day was
A Crœsus in creation — I plunged deep,
But, like an ebbing wave, it dash'd me back
Into the gulf of my unfathom'd thought.
I plunged amidst mankind — Forgetfulness
I sought in all, save where 't is to be found,
And that I have to learn; — my sciences,
My long-pursued and superhuman art,
Is mortal here — I dwell in my despair —
And live — and live forever.

   Witch.   It may be
That I can aid thee.

   Man.   To do this thy power
Must wake the dead, or lay me low with them.
Do so — in any shape — in any hour —
With any torture — so it be the last.

   Witch.   That is not in my province; but if thou
Wilt swear obedience to my will, and do
My bidding, it may help thee to thy wishes.

   Man.   I will not swear — Obey! and whom? the spirits
Whose presence I command, and be the slave

Of those who served me — Never!
   Witch.   Is this all ?
Hast thou no gentler answer? — Yet bethink thee,
And pause ere thou rejectest.
   Man.   I have said it.
   Witch.   Enough! — I may retire then — say!
   Man.   Retire!
                [*The* WITCH *disappears.*
   Man. (alone). We are the fools of time and terror:
          Days
Steal on us and steal from us; yet we live,
Loathing our life, and dreading still to die.
In all the days of this detested yoke —
This vital weight upon the struggling heart,
Which sinks with sorrow, or beats quick with pain,
Or joy that ends in agony or faintness —
In all the days of past and future, for
In life there is no present, we can number
How few — how less than few — wherein the soul
Forbears to pant for death, and yet draws back
As from a stream in winter, though the chill
Be but a moment's.   I have one resource
Still in my science — I can call the dead,
And ask them what it is we dread to be:
The sternest answer can but be the Grave,
And that is nothing; — if they answer not —
The buried Prophet answered to the Hag
Of Endor; and the Spartan Monarch drew
From the Byzantine maid's unsleeping spirit
An answer and his destiny — he slew
That which he loved, unknowing what he slew,

And died unpardon'd — though he call'd in aid
The Phyxian Jove, and in Phigalia roused
The Arcadian Evocators to compel
The indignant shadow to depose her wrath,
Or fix her term of vengeance — she replied
In words of dubious import, but fulfill'd.
If I had never lived, that which I love
Had still been living; had I never loved,
That which I love would still be beautiful —
Happy and giving happiness.   What is she?
What is she now? — a sufferer for my sins —
A thing I dare not think upon — or nothing.
Within few hours I shall not call in vain —
Yet in this hour I dread the thing I dare:
Until this hour I never shrunk to gaze
On spirit, good or evil — now I tremble,
And feel a strange cold thaw upon my heart.
But I can act-even what I most abhor,
And champion human fears. — The night approaches.
                              [*Exit.*

ASTARTE.

(MANFRED, Act ii. Scene 4.)

*The Hall of Arimanes. — Arimanes on his Throne,
a Globe of Fire, surrounded by the Spirits.*

Enter the DESTINIES *and* NEMESIS ;   *then* MANFRED.

A Spirit.   What is here?
A mortal ! — Thou most rash and fatal wretch !

Bow down and worship!

   Second Spirit.   I do know the man —

A Magian of great power, and fearful skill!

   Third Spirit. Bow down and worship, slave! —

        What, know'st thou not

Thine and our Sovereign? — Tremble, and obey!

   All the Spirits. Prostrate thyself, and thy condemnèd

        clay,

Child of the Earth! or dread the worst.

   Man.   I know it;

And yet ye see I kneel not.

   Fourth Spirit.   'T will be taught thee.

   Man. 'T is taught already; — many a night on the

        earth,

On the bare ground, have I bow'd down my face,

And strew'd my head with ashes; I have known

The fulness of humiliation, for

I sunk before my vain despair, and knelt

To my own desolation.

   Fifth Spirit.   Dost thou dare

Refuse to Arimanes on his throne

What the whole earth accords, beholding not

The terror of his Glory? — Crouch! I say.

   Man. Bid *him* bow down to that which is above him,

The overruling Infinite — the Maker

Who made him not for worship — let him kneel,

And we will kneel together.

   The Spirits.   Crush the worm!

Tear him in pieces! —

   First Destiny.   Hence! Avaunt! — he 's mine.

Prince of the Powers invisible! This man

Is of no common order, as his port
And presence here denote; his sufferings
Have been of an immortal nature, like
Our own; his knowledge, and his powers and will,
As far as is compatible with clay,
Which clogs the ethereal essence, have been such
As clay hath seldom borne; his aspirations
Have been beyond the dwellers of the earth,
And they have only taught him what we know —
That knowledge is not happiness, and science
But an exchange of ignorance for that
Which is another kind of ignorance.
This is not all — the passions, attributes
Of earth and heaven, from which no power, nor being,
Nor breath from the worm upwards is exempt,
Have pierced his heart; and in their consequence
Made him a thing, which I, who pity not,
Yet pardon those who pity.   He is mine,
And thine, it may be — be it so, or not,
No other Spirit in this region hath
A soul like his — or power upon his soul.
   Nemesis.   What doth he here then?
   First Des.   Let him answer that.
   Man.   Ye know what I have known; and without
        'power
I could not be amongst ye: but there are
Powers deeper still beyond — I come in quest
Of such, to answer unto what I seek.
   Nem.   What would'st thou?
   Man.   Thou canst not reply to me.
Call up the dead — my question is for them.

Nem.   Great Arimanes, doth thy will avouch
The wishes of this mortal?
   Ari.   Yea.
   Nem.   Whom would'st thou
Uncharnel?
   Man.   One without a tomb — call up
Astarte.

NEMESIS.

     Shadow! or Spirit!
       Whatever thou art,
    Which still doth inherit
       The whole or a part
    Of the form of thy birth,
       Of the mould of thy clay,
    Which return'd to the earth,
       Re-appear to the day!
    Bear what thou borest,
       The heart and the form,
    And the aspect thou worest
       Redeem from the worm.
   Appear! — Appear! — Appear!
   Who sent thee there requires thee here!
   [*The Phantom of* ASTARTE *rises and stands
     in the midst.*
  Man.   Can this be death? there 's bloom upon her
     cheek;
But now I see it is no living hue,
But a strange hectic — like the unnatural red
Which Autumn plants upon the perish'd leaf.
It is the same! Oh, God! that I should dread

To look upon the same — Astarte ! — No,
I cannot speak to her — but bid her speak —
Forgive me or condemn me.

NEMESIS.

By the power which hath broken
    The grave which enthrall'd thee,
Speak to him who hath spoken,
    Or those who have call'd thee !

Man.   She is silent,
And in that silence I am more than answer'd.
    Nem.   My power extends no further.   Prince of air !
It rests with thee alone — command her voice.
    Ari.   Spirit — obey this sceptre !
    Nem.   Silent still !
She is not of our order, but belongs
To the other powers.   Mortal ! thy quest is vain,
And we are baffled also.
    Man.   Hear me, hear me —
Astarte ! my beloved ! speak to me :
I have so much endured — so much endure —
Look on me ! the grave hath not changed thee more
Than I am changed for thee.   Thou lovedst me
Too much, as I loved thee : we were not made
To torture thus each other, though it were
The deadliest sin to love as we have loved.
Say that thou loath'st me not — that I do bear
This punishment for both — that thou wilt be
One of the blessed — and that I shall die ;
For hitherto all hateful things conspire

To bind me in existence — in a life
Which makes me shrink from immortality —
A future like the past.   I cannot rest.
I know not what I ask, nor what I seek:
I feel but what thou art — and what I am;
And I would hear yet once before I perish
The voice which was my music — Speak to me!
For I have call'd on thee in the still night,
Startled the slumbering birds from the hush'd boughs,
And woke the mountain wolves, and made the caves
Acquainted with thy vainly echoed name,
Which answer'd me — many things answer'd me —
Spirits and men — but thou wert silent all.
Yet speak to me! I have outwatch'd the stars,
And gazed o'er heaven in vain in search of thee.
Speak to me! I have wander'd o'er the earth,
And never found thy likeness — Speak to me!
Look on the fiends around — they feel for me:
I fear them not, and feel for thee alone —
Speak to me! though it be in wrath; — but say —
I reck not what — but let me hear thee once —
This once — once more!

    Phantom of Astarte.   Manfred!

    Man.   Say on, say on —
I live but in the sound — it is thy voice!

    Phan.   Manfred!   To-morrow ends thine earthly ills
Farewell!

    Man.   Yet one word more — am I forgiven?

    Phan.   Farewell!

    Man.   Say, shall we meet again?

    Phan.   Farewell!

Man.   One word for mercy!   Say, thou lovest me.
Phan.   Manfred!

> [*The Spirit of* ASTARTE *disappears.*

Nem.   She 's gone, and will not be recall'd;
Her words will be fulfill'd.   Return to the earth.

A Spirit.   He is convulsed — This is to be a mortal
And seek the things beyond mortality.

Another Spirit.   Yet, see, he mastereth himself, and
          makes
His torture tributary to his will.
Had he been one of us, he would have made
An awful spirit.

Nem.   Hast thou further question
Of our great sovereign, or his worshippers?

Man.   None.

Nem.   Then for a time farewell.

Man.   We meet then!   Where?   On the earth? —
Even as thou wilt: and for the grace accorded
I now depart a debtor.   Fare ye well!

> [*Exit* MANFRED.

MANFRED'S FAREWELL TO THE SUN.

(MANFRED, Act iii. Scene 2.)

> GLORIOUS Orb! the idol

Of early nature, and the vigorous race
Of undiseased mankind, the giant sons
Of the embrace of angels, with a sex
More beautiful than they, which did draw down
The erring spirits who can ne'er return —

Most glorious orb! that wert a worship, ere
The mystery of thy making was reveal'd!
Thou earliest minister of the Almighty,
Which gladden'd, on their mountain tops, the hearts
Of the Chaldean shepherds, till they pour'd
Themselves in orisons! Thou material God,
And representative of the Unknown —
Who chose thee for His shadow! Thou chief star,
Centre of many stars! which mak'st our earth
Endurable, and temperest the hues
And hearts of all who walk within thy rays!
Sire of the seasons! Monarch of the climes,
And those who dwell in them! for near or far,
Our inborn spirits have a tint of thee
Even as our outward aspects; — thou dost rise,
And shine, and set in glory. Fare thee well!
I ne'er shall see thee more. As my first glance
Of love and wonder was for thee, then take
My latest look: thou wilt not beam on one
To whom the gifts of life and warmth have been
Of a more fatal nature. He is gone:
I follow.

MANFRED'S END.

(MANFRED, Act iii. Scene 4.)

Interior of a Tower. MANFRED *alone.*

THE stars are forth, the moon above the tops
Of the snow-shining mountains. — Beautiful!
I linger yet with Nature, for the night

Hath been to me a more familiar face
Than that of man; and in her starry shade
Of dim and solitary loveliness,
I learn'd the language of another world.
I do remember me, that in my youth,
When I was wandering, — upon such a night
I stood within the Coliseum's wall,
Midst the chief relics of almighty Rome;
The trees which grew along the broken arches
Waved dark in the blue midnight, and the stars
Shone through the rents of ruin; from afar
The watchdog bay'd beyond the Tiber; and
More near from out the Cæsar's palace came
The owl's long cry, and, interruptedly,
Of distant sentinels the fitful song
Begun and died upon the gentle wind.
Some cypresses beyond the time-worn breach
Appear'd to skirt the horizon, yet they stood
Within a bowshot. — Where the Cæsars dwelt,
And dwell the tuneless birds of night, amidst
A grove which springs through levell'd battlements,
And twines its roots with the imperial hearths,
Ivy usurps the laurel's place of growth; —
But the gladiator's bloody Circus stands,
A noble wreck in ruinous perfection !
While Cæsar's chambers, and the Augustan halls,
Grovel on earth in indistinct decay.
— And thou didst shine, thou rolling moon, upon
All this, and cast a wide and tender light,
Which soften'd down the hoar austerity
Of rugged desolation, and fill'd up,

As 't were anew, the gaps of centuries;
Leaving that beautiful which still was so,
And making that which was not, till the place
Became religion, and the heart ran o'er
With silent worship of the great of old! —
The dead, but sceptred sovereigns, who still rule
Our spirits from their urns. —

                            'T was such a night!
'T is strange that I recall it at this time;
But I have found our thoughts take wildest flight
Even at the moment when they should array
Themselves in pensive order.

Enter the ABBOT.

   Abbot.   My good lord!
I crave a second grace for this approach;
But yet let not my humble zeal offend
By its abruptness — all it hath of ill
Recoils on me; its good in the effect
May light upon your head — could I say *heart* —
Could I touch *that*, with words or prayers, I should
Recall a noble spirit which hath wander'd,
But is not yet all lost.
   Man.   Thou know'st me not;
My days are number'd, and my deeds recorded:
Retire, or 't will be dangerous — Away!
   Abbot.   Thou dost not mean to menace me?
   Man.   Not I;
I simply tell thee peril is at hand,
And would preserve thee.
   Abbot.   What dost thou mean?

Man.   Look there!
What dost thou see?
   Abbot.   Nothing.
   Man.   Look there, I say,
And steadfastly; — now tell me what thou seest?
   Abbot.   That which should shake me, — but I fear it
        not —
I see a dusk and awful figure rise,
Like an infernal god, from out the earth;
His face wrapt in a mantle, and his form
Robed as with angry clouds; he stands between
Thyself and me — but I do fear him not.
   Man.   Thou hast no cause — he shall not harm thee —
        but
His sight may shock thine old limbs into palsy.
I say to thee — Retire!
   Abbot.   And I reply —
Never — till I have battled with this fiend: —
What doth he here?
   Man.   Why — ay — what doth he here? —
I did not send for him, — he is unbidden.
   Abbot.   Alas! lost mortal! what with guests like these
Hast thou to do?   I tremble for thy sake:
Why doth he gaze on thee, and thou on him?
Ah! he unveils his aspect: on his brow
The thunder-scars are graven; from his eye
Glares forth the immortality of hell —
Avaunt! —
   Man.   Pronounce — what is thy mission?
   Spirit.   Come!
   Abbot.   What art thou, unknown being? answer! —
        speak!

Spirit.   The genius of this mortal. — Come! 't is time.

Man.   I am prepared for all things, but deny
The power which summons me.   Who sent thee here?

Spirit.   Thou 'lt know anon — Come! come!

Man.   I have commanded
Things of an essence greater far than thine,
And striven with thy masters.   Get thee hence!

Spirit.   Mortal! thine hour is come — Away! I say.

Man.   I knew, and know my hour is come, but not
To render up my soul to such as thee:
Away! I 'll die as I have lived — alone.

Spirit.   Then I must summon up my brethren. — Rise !

                               [*Other spirits rise up.*

Abbot.   Avaunt! ye evil ones! — Avaunt! I say, —
Ye have no power where piety hath power,
And I do charge ye in the name——

Spirit.   Old man!
We know ourselves, our mission, and thine order;
Waste not thy holy words on idle uses,
It were in vain: this man is forfeited.
Once more I summon him — Away! away!

Man.   I do defy ye, — though I feel my soul
Is ebbing from me, yet I do defy ye;
Nor will I hence, while I have earthly breath
To breathe my scorn upon ye — earthly strength
To wrestle, though with spirits; what ye take
Shall be ta'en limb by limb.

Spirit.   Reluctant mortal!
Is this the Magian who would so pervade
The world invisible, and make himself
Almost our equal? — Can it be that thou

Art thus in love with life? the very life
Which made thee wretched!
    Man.   Thou false fiend, thou liest!
My life is in its last hour, — *that* I know,
Nor would redeem a moment of that hour;
I do not combat against death, but thee
And thy surrounding angels; my past power
Was purchased by no compact with thy crew,
But by superior science — penance — daring —
And length of watching — strength of mind — and skill
In knowledge of our fathers — when the earth
Saw men and spirits walking side by side,
And gave ye no supremacy: I stand
Upon my strength — I do defy — deny —
Spurn back, and scorn ye! —
    Spirit.   But thy many crimes
Have made thee ——
    Man.   What are they to such as thee?
Must crimes be punish'd but by other crimes,
And greater criminals? — Back to thy hell!
Thou hast no power upon me, *that* I feel;
Thou never shalt possess me, *that* I know:
What I have done is done; I bear within
A torture which could nothing gain from.thine:
The mind which is immortal makes itself
Requital for its good or evil thoughts —
Is its own origin of ill and end —
And its own place and time — its innate sense,
When stripp'd of this mortality, derives
No color from the fleeting things without;
But is absorb'd in sufferance or in joy,

Born from the knowledge of its own desert.
Thou didst not tempt me, and thou couldst not tempt me;
I have not been thy dupe, nor am thy prey —
But was my own destroyer, and will be
My own hereafter. — Back, ye baffled fiends!
The hand of death is on me — but not yours!

                            [*The Demons disappear.*

  Abbot.   Alas! how pale thou art — thy lips are white —
And thy breast heaves — and in thy gasping throat
The accents rattle. — Give thy prayers to Heaven —
Pray — albeit but in thought, — but die not thus.
  Man.   'T is over — my dull eyes can fix thee not;
But all things swim around me, and the earth
Heaves as it were beneath me. Fare thee well —
Give me thy hand.
  Abbot.   Cold — cold — even to the heart —
But yet one prayer — Alas! how fares it with thee?
  Man. Old man! 't is not so difficult to die.

                          [MANFRED *expires*

DYING SPEECH OF THE DOGE OF VENICE.

(MARINO FALIERO, Act v. Scene 3.)

I SPEAK to Time and to Eternity,
Of which I grow a portion, not to man.
Ye elements! in which to be resolved
I hasten, let my voice be as a spirit
Upon you! Ye blue waves! which bore my banner,
Ye winds! which flutter'd o'er as if you loved it,

And fill'd my swelling sails as they were wafted
To many a triumph!   Thou, my native earth,
Which I have bled for, and thou foreign earth,
Which drank this willing blood from many a wound!
Ye stones, in which my gore will not sink, but
Reek up to Heaven!   Ye skies, which will receive it!
Thou sun! which shinest on these things, and Thou!
Who kindlest and who quenchest suns! — Attest!
I am not innocent — but are these guiltless?
I perish, but not unavenged; far ages
Float up from the abyss of time to be,
And show these eyes, before they close, the doom
Of this proud city, and I leave my curse
On her and hers forever! —— Yes, the hours
Are silently engendering of the day,
When she, who built 'gainst Attila a bulwark,
Shall yield, and bloodlessly and basely yield
Unto a bastard Attila, without
Shedding so much blood in her last defence
As these old veins, oft drain'd in shielding her,
Shall pour in sacrifice.   She shall be bought
And sold, and be an appanage to those
Who shall despise her! — She shall stoop to be
A province for an empire, petty town
In lieu of capital, with slaves for senates,
Beggars for nobles, panders for a people!
Then when the Hebrew 's in thy palaces,
The Hun in thy high places, and the Greek
Walks o'er thy mart, and smiles on it for his!
When thy patricians beg their bitter bread
In narrow streets, and in their shameful need

Make their nobility a plea for pity!
Then, when the few who still retain a wreck
Of their great fathers' heritage shall fawn
Round a barbarian Vice of Kings' Vice-gerent,
Even in the palace where they sway'd as sovereigns,
Even in the palace where they slew their sovereign,
Proud of some name they have disgraced, or sprung
From an adulteress boastful of her guilt
With some large gondolier or foreign soldier,
Shall bear about their bastardy in triumph
To the third spurious generation;—when
Thy sons are in the lowest scale of being,
Slaves turn'd o'er to the vanquish'd by the victors,
Despised by cowards for greater cowardice,
And scorn'd even by the vicious for such vices
As in the monstrous grasp of their conception
Defy all codes to image or to name them;
When all the ills of conquer'd states shall cling thee,
Vice without splendor, sin without relief
Even from the gloss of love to smooth it o'er,
But in its stead, coarse lusts of habitude,
Prurient yet passionless, cold studied lewdness,
Depraving nature's frailty to an art;—
When these and more are heavy on thee, when
Smiles without mirth, and pastimes without pleasure,
Youth without honor, age without respect,
Meanness and weakness, and a sense of woe
'Gainst which thou wilt not strive, and dar'st not murmur.
Have made thee last and worst of peopled deserts—
Then, in the last gasp of thine agony,
Amidst thy many murders, think of *mine!*

Thou den of drunkards with the blood of princes!
Gehenna of the waters! thou sea Sodom!
Thus I devote thee to the infernal gods!
Thee and thy serpent seed!

DEATH OF SALEMENES.

(SARDANAPALUS, Act v. Scene 1.)

To MYRRHA *and* BALEA, *enter Soldiers, bearing in*
SALEMENES *wounded, with a broken Javelin in his
Side : they seat him upon one of the Couches which
furnish the Apartment.*

Myr.   Oh, Jove!
Bal.   Then all is over.
Sal.   That is false.
Hew down the slave who says so, if a soldier.
Myr.   Spare him — he 's none: a mere court butterfly,
That flutters in the pageant of a monarch.
Sal.   Let him live on, then.
Myr.   So wilt thou, I trust.
Sal.   I fain would live this hour out, and the event,
But doubt it.   Wherefore did ye bear me here?
Sol.   By the king's order. When the javelin struck you,
You fell and fainted: 't was his strict command
To bear you to this hall.
Sal.   'T was not ill done:
For seeming slain in that cold dizzy trance,
The sight might shake our soldiers — but — 't is vain,
I feel it ebbing!

Myr.   Let me see the wound;
I am not quite skilless: in my native land
'T is part of our instruction.   War being constant,
We are nerved to look on such things.

Sol.   Best extract
The javelin.

Myr.   Hold! no, no, it cannot be.

Sal.   I am sped, then!

Myr.   With the blood that fast must follow
The extracted weapon, I do fear thy life.

Sal.   And I *not* death.   Where was the king when you
Convey'd me from the spot where I was stricken?

Sol.   Upon the same ground, and encouraging
With voice and gesture the dispirited troops
Who had seen you fall, and falter'd back.

Sal.   Whom heard ye
Named next to the command?

Sol.   I did not hear.

Sal.   Fly, then, and tell him, 't was my last request
That Zames take my post until the junction,
So hoped for, yet delay'd, of Ofratanes,
Satrap of Susa.   Leave me here: our troops
Are not so numerous as to spare your absence.

Sol.   But prince ——

Sal.   Hence, I say! Here 's a courtier and
A woman, the best chamber company.
As you would not permit me to expire
Upon the field, I 'll have no idle soldiers
About my sick couch.   Hence! and do my bidding!

                         [*Exeunt the Soldiers.*

Myr.   Gallant and glorious spirit! must the earth
So soon resign thee?

Sal.   Gentle Myrrha, 't is
The end I would have chosen had I saved
The monarch or the monarchy by this.
As 't is, I have not outlived them.
  Myr.   You wax paler.
  Sal.   Your hand; this broken weapon but prolongs
My pangs, without sustaining life enough,
To make me useful: I would draw it forth,
And my life with it, could I but hear how
The fight goes.

      Enter SARDANAPALUS *and Soldiers.*

Sar.   My best brother !
Sal.   And the battle
Is lost?
  Sar. (despondingly).   You see *me here.*
  Sal.   I 'd rather see you *thus !*
    [*He draws out the weapon from the wound, and
       dies.*

DEATH OF JACOPO FOSCARI.

(TWO FOSCARI, Act iv. Scene I.)

To JACOPO FOSCARI, MARINA, *and the* DOGE,
enter an Officer and Guards.

Off.   Signor ! the boat is at the shore — the wind
Is rising — we are ready to attend you.
  Jac. Fos.   And I to be attended.   Once more, father
Your hand !

Doge.   Take it.   Alas! how thine own trembles!

Jac. Fos.   No — you mistake; 't is yours that shakes,
        my father,

Farewell!

Doge.   Farewell!   Is there aught else?

Jac. Fos.   No — nothing.

                                [To the Officer.

Lend me your arm, good signor.

Offi.   You turn pale —

Let me support you — paler — ho! some aid there!
Some water!

Mar.   Ah, he is dying!

Jac. Fos.   Now, I 'm ready —

My eyes swim strangely — where 's the door?

Mar.   Away!

Let me support him — my best love!   Oh, God!
How faintly beats this heart — this pulse!

Jac. Fos.   The light!

Is it the light? — I am faint.

                [Officer presents him with water.

Offi.   He will be better,

Perhaps, in the air.

Jac. Fos.   I doubt not.   Father — wife —
Your hands.

Mar.   There 's death in that damp clammy grasp.
Oh, God! — My Foscari, how fare you?

Jac. Fos.   Well!

                                [He dies

Offi.   He's gone!

Doge.   He 's free.

Mar.   No — no, he is not dead.

There must be life yet in that heart — he could not
Thus leave me.

    Doge.   Daughter!

    Mar.   Hold thy peace, old man!
I am no daughter now — thou hast no son.
Oh, Foscari!

    Offi.   We must remove the body.

    Mar.   Touch it not, dungeon miscreants! your base
              office
Ends with his life, and goes not beyond murder,
Even by your murderous laws.   Leave his remains
To those who know to honor them.

    Offi.   I must
Inform the signory, and learn their pleasure.

    Doge.   Inform the signory, from *me*, the Doge,
They have no further power upon those ashes:
While he lived, he was theirs, as fits a subject —
Now he is *mine* — my broken-hearted boy!

                          [*Exit Officer.*

    Mar. And I must live!

    Doge.   Your children live, Marina.

    Mar. My children! true — they live, and I must live
To bring them up to serve the state, and die
As died their father.   Oh! what best of blessings
Were barrenness in Venice!   Would my mother
Had been so!

    Doge.   My unhappy children!

    Mar.   What!
You feel it then at last — *you!* — Where is now
The stoic of the state?

    Doge (throwing himself down by the body).   Here!

Mar. Ay, weep on!
I thought you had no tears — you hoarded them
Until they are useless; but weep on! he never
Shall weep more — never, never more.

CAIN AND LUCIFER IN THE ABYSS OF SPACE.

(CAIN, Act ii. Scene 1.)

Cain. Oh, god, or demon, or whate'er thou art,
Is yon our earth?
Lucifer. Dost thou not recognize
The dust which form'd your father?
Cain. Can it be?
Yon small blue circle, swinging in far ether,
With an inferior circlet near it still,
Which looks like that which lit our earthly night?
Is this our Paradise? Where are its walls,
And they who guard them?
Lucifer. Point me out the site
Of Paradise.
Cain. How should I? As we move
Like sunbeams onward, it grows small and smaller,
And as it waxes little, and then less,
Gathers a halo round it, like the light
Which shone the roundest of the stars, when I
Beheld them from the skirts of Paradise:
Methinks they both, as we recede from them,
Appear to join the innumerable stars

Which are around us; and, as we move on,
Increase their myriads.

   Lucifer.   And if there should be
Worlds greater than thine own, inhabited
By greater things, and they themselves far more
In number than the dust of thy dull earth,
Though multiplied to animated atoms,
All living, and all doom'd to death, and wretched,
What wouldst thou think?

   Cain.   I should be proud of thought
Which knew such things.

   Lucifer.   But if that high thought were
Link'd to a servile mass of matter, and,
Knowing such things, aspiring to such things,
And science still beyond them, were chain'd down
To the most gross and petty paltry wants,
All foul and fulsome, and the very best
Of thine enjoyments a sweet degradation,
A most enervating and filthy cheat
To lure thee on to the renewal of
Fresh souls and bodies, all foredoom'd to be
As frail, and few so happy ——

   Cain.   Spirit! I
Know not of death, save as a dreadful thing
Of which I have heard my parents speak, as of
A hideous heritage I owe to them
No less than life; a heritage not happy,
If I may judge, till now. But, spirit! if
It be as thou hast said (and I within
Feel the prophetic torture of its truth),
Here let me die: for to give birth to those

Who can but suffer many years, and die,
Methinks is merely propagating death,
And multiplying murder.

 Lucifer.   Thou canst not
All die — there is what must survive.

 Cain.   The Other
Spake not of this unto my father, when
He shut him forth from Paradise, with death
Written upon his forehead.   But at least
Let what is mortal of me perish, that
I may be in the rest as angels are.

 Lucifer.   *I* am angelic: wouldst thou be as I am?

 Cain.   I know not what thou art: I see thy power,
And see thou show'st me things beyond *my* power.
Beyond all power of my born faculties,
Although inferior still to my desires
And my conceptions.

 Lucifer.   What are they which dwell
So humbly in their pride, as to sojourn
With worms in clay?

 Cain.   And what art thou who dwellest
So haughtily in spirit, and canst range
Nature and immortality — and yet
Seem'st sorrowful?

 Lucifer.   I seem that which I am;
And therefore do I ask of thee, if thou
Would'st be immortal!

 Cain.   Thou hast said, I must be
Immortal in despite of me.   I knew not
This until lately — but since it must be,
Let me, or happy or unhappy, learn
To anticipate my immortality.

Lucifer.   Thou didst before I came upon thee.
Cain.   How?
Lucifer.   By suffering.
Cain.   And must torture be immortal?
Lucifer.   We and thy sons will try.   But now behold!
Is it not glorious?
Cain.   Oh, thou beautiful
And unimaginable ether! and
Ye multiplying masses of increased
And still increasing lights! what are ye? what
Is this blue wilderness of interminable
Air, where ye roll along, as I have seen
The leaves along the limpid streams of Eden?
Is your course measured for ye?   Or do ye
Sweep on in your unbounded revelry
Through an aërial universe of endless
Expansion — at which my soul aches to think —
Intoxicated with eternity?
Oh God! Oh Gods! or whatsoe'er ye are!
How beautiful ye are! how beautiful
Your works, or accidents, or whatsoe'er
They may be!   Let me die, as atoms die,
(If that they die) or know ye in your might
And knowledge!   My thoughts are not in this hour
Unworthy what I see, though my dust is;
Spirit! let me expire, or see them nearer.
     Lucifer.   Art thou not nearer? look back to thine
                    earth!
     Cain.   Where is it?   I see nothing save a mass
Of most innumerable lights.
     Lucifer.   Look there!

Cain.   I cannot see it.
Lucifer.   Yet it sparkles still.
Cain.   That! — yonder!
Lucifer.   Yea.
Cain.   And wilt thou tell me so?
Why, I have seen the fire-flies and fire-worms
Sprinkle the dusky groves and the green banks
In the dim twilight, brighter than yon world
Which bears them.
Lucifer.   Thou hast seen both worms and worlds,
Each bright and sparkling — what dost think of them?
Cain.   That they are beautiful in their own sphere,
And that the night, which makes both beautiful,
The little shining fire-fly in its flight,
And the immortal star in its great course,
Must both be guided.
Lucifer.   But by whom or what?
Cain.   Show me.
Lucifer.   Dar'st thou behold?
Cain.   How know I what
I *dare* behold?   As yet, thou hast shown nought
I dare not gaze on further.
Lucifer.   On, then, with me.

———

CAIN AND ADAH.

(CAIN, Act iii. Scene 1.)

Adah.   HUSH! tread softly, Cain.
Cain.   I will; but wherefore?

Adah.   Our little Enoch sleeps upon yon bed
Of leaves, beneath the cypress.
    Cain.   Cypress! 't is
A gloomy tree, which looks as if it mourn'd
O'er what it shadows; wherefore didst thou choose it
For our child's canopy?
    Adah.   Because its branches
Shut out the sun like night, and therefore seem'd
Fitting to shadow slumber.
    Cain   Ay, the last —
And longest; but no matter — lead me to him.
                         [*They go up to the child.*
How lovely he appears! his little cheeks,
In their pure incarnation, vying with
The rose leaves strewn beneath them.
    Adah.   And his lips, too.
How beautifully parted! No; you shall not
Kiss him, at least not now: he will awake soon——
His hour of mid-day rest is nearly over;
But it were pity to disturb him till
'T is closed.
    Cain.   You have said well; I will contain
My heart till then.   He smiles, and sleeps! — Sleep on
And smile, thou little, young inheritor
Of a world scarce less young: sleep on, and smile!
Thine are the hours and days when both are cheering
And innocent! *thou* hast not pluck'd the fruit —
Thou know'st not thou art naked!   Must the time
Come thou shalt be amerced for sins unknown,
Which were not thine nor mine?   But now sleep on!
His cheeks are reddening into deeper smiles,

And shining lids are trembling o'er his long
Lashes, dark as the cypress which waves o'er them;
Half open, from beneath them the clear blue
Laughs out, although in slumber.   He must dream —
Of what?   Of Paradise! — Ay! dream of it,
My disinherited boy!   'T is but a dream;
For never more thyself, thy sons, nor fathers,
Shall walk in that forbidden place of joy!

 Adah.   Dear Cain!   Nay, do not whisper o'er our son
Such melancholy yearnings o'er the past:
Why wilt thou always mourn for Paradise?
Can we not make another?

  Cain.   **Where?**

  Adah.   **Here, or**
Where'er thou wilt: where'er thou art, I feel not
The want of this so much regretted Eden.
Have I not thee, our boy, our sire, and brother,
And Zillah — our sweet sister, and our Eve,
To whom we owe so much besides our birth?

  Cain.   Yes — death, too, is amongst the debts we owe
    her.

  Adah.   Cain! that proud spirit, who withdrew **thee**
    hence,
Hath sadden'd thine still deeper.   I had hoped
The promised wonders which thou hast beheld,
Visions, thou say'st, of past and present worlds,
Would have composed thy mind into the calm
Of a contented knowledge; but I see
Thy guide hath done thee evil; still I thank him,
And can forgive him all, that he so soon
Hath given thee back to us.

Cain.   So soon?

Adah.   'T is scarcely
Two hours since ye departed: two *long* hours
To *me*, but only *hours* upon the sun.

   Cain.   And yet I have approach'd that sun, and seen
Worlds which he once shone on, and never more
Shall light; and worlds he never lit: methought
Years had roll'd o'er my absence.

   Adah.   Hardly hours.

   Cain.   The mind then hath capacity of time,
And measures it by that which it beholds,
Pleasing or painful; little or almighty.
I had beheld the immemorial works
Of endless beings; skirr'd extinguish'd worlds;
And, gazing on eternity, methought
I had borrow'd more by a few drops of ages
From its immensity: but now I feel
My littleness again.   Well said the spirit,
That I was nothing!

   Adah.   Wherefore said he so?
Jehovah said not that.

   Cain.   No: *he* contents him
With making us the nothing which we are;
And after flattering dust with glimpses of
Eden and Immortality, resolves
It back to dust again — for what?

   Adah.   Thou know'st —
Even for our parents' error.

   Cain.   What is that
To us? they sinn'd, then let *them* die!

   Adah.   Thou hast not spoken well, nor is that thought

Thy own, but of the spirit who was with thee.
Would *I* could die for them, so *they* might live!
   Cain.   Why, so say I — provided that one victim
Might satiate the insatiable of life,
And that our little rosy sleeper there
Might never taste of death nor human sorrow,
Nor hand it down to those who spring from him.
   Adah.   How know we that some such atonement one
                 day
May not redeem our race?
   Cain.   By sacrificing
The harmless for the guilty? what atonement
Were there? why, *we* are innocent: what have we
Done, that we must be victims for a deed
Before our birth, or need have victims to
Atone for this mysterious, nameless sin —
If it be such a sin to seek for knowledge?
   Adah.   Alas! thou sinnest now, my Cain: thy words
Sound impious in mine ears.
   Cain.   Then leave me!
   Adah.   Never,
Though thy God left thee.
   Cain.   Say, what have we here?
   Adah.   Two altars, which our brother Abel made
During thine absence, whereupon to offer
A sacrifice to God on thy return.
   Cain.   And how knew *he*, that *I* would be so ready
With the burnt offerings, which he daily brings
With a meek brow, whose base humility
Shows more of fear than worship, as a bribe
To the Creator?

Adah.   Surely, 't is well done.

Cain.   One altar may suffice; *I* have no offering.

Adah.   The fruits of the earth, the early, beautiful
Blossom and bud, and bloom of flowers, and fruits;
These are a goodly offering to the Lord,
Given with a gentle and a contrite spirit.

Cain.   I have toil'd, and till'd, and sweaten in the
          sun
According to the curse: — must I do more?
For what should I be gentle? for a war
With all the elements ere they will yield
The bread we eat?   For what must I be grateful?
For being dust, and grovelling in the dust,
Till I return to dust?   If I am nothing —
For nothing shall I be an hypocrite,
And seem well-pleased with pain?   For what should I
Be contrite? for my father's sin, already
Expiate with what we all have undergone,
And to be more than expiated by
The ages prophesied, upon our seed.
Little deems our young blooming sleeper, there,
The germs of an eternal misery
To myriads is within him! better 't were
I snatch'd him in his sleep, and dash'd him 'gainst
The rocks, than let him live to —

Adah.   Oh, my God!
Touch not the child — my child! *thy* child!   Oh, Cain!

Cain.   Fear not! for all the stars, and all the power
Which sways them, I would not accost yon infant
With ruder greeting than a father's kiss.

Adah.   Then, why so awful in thy speech?

Cain.   I said,
'T were better that he ceased to live, than give
Life to so much of sorrow as he must
Endure, and, harder still, bequeath; but since
That saying jars you, let us only say —
'T were better that he never had been born.

Adah.   Oh, do not say so! Where were then the joys,
The mother's joys of watching, nourishing,
And loving him?   Soft! he awakes.   Sweet Enoch!

[*She goes to the child.*

Oh Cain! look on him; see how full of life,
Of strength, of bloom, of beauty, and of joy,
How like to me — how like to thee, when gentle,
For *then* we are *all* alike; is 't not so, Cain?
Mother, and sire, and son, our features are
Reflected in each other; as they are
In the clear waters, when *they* are gentle, and
When *thou* art gentle.   Love us, then, my Cain!
And love thyself for our sakes, for we love thee.
Look! how he laughs and stretches out his arms,
And opens wide his blue eyes upon thine,
To hail his father; while his little form
Flutters as wing'd with joy.   Talk not of pain!
The childless cherubs well might envy thee
The pleasures of a parent!   Bless him, Cain!
As yet he hath no words to thank thee, but
His heart will, and thine own too.

Cain.   Bless thee, boy!
If that a mortal blessing may avail thee,
To save thee from the serpent's curse!

  Adah.   It shall.
Surely a father's blessing may avert
A reptile's subtlety.
  Cain.   Of that I doubt;
But bless him ne'er the less.

IV.

SATIRIC.

FAME.

OH, talk not to me of a name great in story;
The days of our youth are the days of our glory;
And the myrtle and ivy of sweet two-and-twenty
Are worth all your laurels, though ever so plenty.

What are garlands and crowns to the brow that is
    wrinkled?
'T is but as a dead-flower with May-dew besprinkled.
Then away with all such from the head that is hoary!
What care I for the wreaths that can *only* give glory?

Oh FAME! — if I e'er took delight in thy praises,
'T was less for the sake of thy high-sounding phrases,
Than to see the bright eyes of the dear one discover
She thought that I was not unworthy to love her.

There chiefly I sought thee, *there* only I found thee;
Her glance was the best of the rays that surround thee;
When it sparkled o'er aught that was bright in my story,
I knew it was love, and I felt it was glory.

———

WRITTEN AFTER SWIMMING FROM SESTOS TO ABYDOS.

IF, in the month of dark December,
   Leander, who was nightly wont
(What maid will not the tale remember?)
   To cross thy stream, broad Hellespont!

If, when the wintry tempest roar'd,
  He sped to Hero, nothing loth,
And thus of old thy current pour'd,
  Fair Venus! how I pity both!

For *me*, degenerate modern wretch,
  Though in the genial month of May,
My dripping limbs I faintly stretch,
  And think I 've done a feat to-day.

But since he cross'd the rapid tide,
  According to the doubtful story,
To woo, — and — Lord knows what beside,
  And swam for Love, as I for Glory;

'T were hard to say who fared the best:
  Sad mortals! thus the Gods still plague you!
He lost his labor, I my jest:
  For he was drown'd, and I 've the ague.

ON MY THIRTY-THIRD BIRTHDAY.

January 22, 1821.

THROUGH life's dull road, so dim and dirty,
I have dragg'd to three and thirty.
What have these years left to me?
Nothing — except thirty-three.

TO MR. MURRAY.

FOR Orford and for Waldegrave
You give much more than me you gave;
Which is not fairly to behave,
          My Murray.

Because if a live dog, 't is said,
Be worth a lion fairly sped,
A *live lord* must be worth *two* dead,
          My Murray.

And if, as the opinion goes,
Verse hath a better sale than prose —
Certes, I should have more than those,
          My Murray.

But now this sheet is nearly cramm'd,
So, if *you will*, *I* sha'n't be shamm'd,
And if you *won't*, *you* may be damn'd,
          My Murray.

———

EPISTLE FROM MR. MURRAY TO DR. POLIDORI.

DEAR DOCTOR, I have read your play.
Which is a good one in its way, —
Purges the eyes and moves the bowels,
And drenches handkerchiefs like towels

With tears, that, in a flux of grief,
Afford hysterical relief
To shatter'd nerves and quicken'd pulses,
Which your catastrophe convulses.

I like your moral and machinery;
Your plot, too, has such scope for scenery;
Your dialogue is apt and smart;
The play's concoction full of art;
Your hero raves, your heroine cries,
All stab, and everybody dies.
In short, your tragedy would be
The very thing to hear and see:
And for a piece of publication,
If I decline on this occasion,
It is not that I am not sensible
To merits in themselves ostensible,
But — and I grieve to speak it — plays
Are drugs — mere drugs, sir — nowadays.
I had a heavy loss by " Manuel," —
Too lucky if it prove not annual, —
And Sotheby, with his " Orestes "
(Which, by the by, the author's best is),
Has lain so very long on hand
That I despair of all demand.
I 've advertised, but see my books,
Or only watch my shopman's looks; —
Still Ivan, Ina, and such lumber,
My back-shop glut, my shelves encumber.

There 's Byron, too, who once did better,
Has sent me, folded in a letter,

A sort of — it's no more a drama
Than Darnley, Ivan, or Kehama;
So alter'd since last year his pen is,
I think he's lost his wits at Venice.
In short, sir, what with one and t' other,
I dare not venture on another.
I write in haste; excuse each blunder;
The coaches through the street so thunder!
My room's so full — we've Gifford here
Reading MS., with Hookham Frere
Pronouncing on the nouns and particles
Of some of our forthcoming Articles.

    The Quarterly — Ah, sir, if you
Had but the genius to review! —
A smart critique upon St. Helena,
Or if you only would but tell in a
Short compass what ——— but, to resume;
As I was saying, sir, the room —
The room's so full of wits and bards,
Crabbes, Campbells, Crokers, Freres and Wards,
And others, neither bards nor wits:—
My humble tenement admits
All persons in the dress of gent.,
From Mr. Hammond to Dog Dent.

    A party dines with me to-day,
All clever men, who make their way;
Crabbe, Malcolm, Hamilton, and Chantrey,
Are all partakers of my pantry.
They're at this moment in discussion
On poor De Staël's late dissolution.

Her book, they say, was in advance —
Pray heaven, she tell the truth of France!
Thus run our time and tongues away. —
But, to return, sir, to your play:
Sorry, sir, but I cannot deal,
Unless 't were acted by O'Neill.
My hands so full, my head so busy,
I 'm almost dead, and always dizzy;
And so, with endless truth and hurry,
Dear Doctor, I am yours,

JOHN MURRAY.

——

TO MR. MURRAY.

STRAHAN, Tonson, Lintot of the times,
Patron and publisher of rhymes,
For thee the bard up Pindus climbs,
    My Murray.

To thee, with hope and terror dumb,
The unfledged MS. authors come;
Thou printest all — and sellest some —
    My Murray.

Upon thy table's baize so green
The last new Quarterly is seen, —
But where is thy new Magazine,
    My Murray?

Along thy sprucest bookshelves shine
The works thou deemest most divine —
The "Art of Cookery," and mine,
    My Murray.

Tours, Travels, Essays, too, I wist
And Sermons to thy mill bring grist;
And then thou hast the "Navy List,"
    My Murray.

And Heaven forbid I should conclude
Without "the Board of Longitude,"
Although this narrow paper would,
    My Murray!

HOLLAND HOUSE.

(From English Bards and Scotch Reviewers.)

ILLUSTRIOUS Holland! hard would be his lot,
His hirelings mention'd, and himself forgot!
Holland, with Henry Petty at his back,
The whipper-in and huntsman of the pack.
Blest be the banquets spread at Holland House,
Where Scotchmen feed, and critics may carouse!
Long, long beneath that hospitable roof
Shall Grub-street dine, while duns are kept aloof.
See honest Hallam lay aside his fork,
Resume his pen, review his Lordship's work,
And, grateful for the dainties on his plate,
Declare his landlord can at least translate!

Dunedin ! view thy children with delight,
They write for food — and feed because they write :
And lest, when heated with the unusual grape,
Some glowing thoughts should to the press escape,
And tinge with red the female reader's cheek,
My lady skims the cream of each critique;
Breathes o 'er the page her purity of soul,
Reforms each error, and refines the whole.

EPILOGUE TO ENGLISH BARDS AND SCOTCH REVIEWERS.

THUS far I 've held my undisturb'd career,
Prepared for rancor, steel'd 'gainst selfish fear:
This thing of rhyme I ne'er disdain'd to own —
Though not obtrusive, yet not quite unknown:
My voice was heard again, though not so loud,
My page, though nameless, never disavow'd;
And now at once I tear the veil away: —
Cheer on the pack ! the quarry stands at bay,
Unscared by all the din of Melbourne house,
By Lambe's resentment, or by Holland's spouse,
By Jeffrey's harmless pistol, Hallam's rage,
Edina's brawny sons and brimstone page.
Our men in buckram shall have blows enough,
And feel they too are "penetrable stuff:"
And though I hope not hence unscathed to go,
Who conquers me shall find a stubborn foe.
The time hath been, when no harsh sound would fall
From lips that now may seem imbued with gall;

Nor fools nor follies tempt me to despise
The meanest thing that crawl'd beneath my eyes:
But now, so callous grown, so changed since youth,
I 've learn'd to think, and sternly speak the truth;
Learn'd to deride the critic's starch decree,
And break him on the wheel he meant for me;
To spurn the rod a scribbler bids me kiss,
Nor care if courts and crowds applaud or hiss:
Nay more, though all my rival rhymesters frown,
I too can hunt a poetaster down;
And, arm'd in proof, the gauntlet cast at once
To Scotch marauder, and to southern dunce.

THE LANDED INTEREST.

(AGE OF BRONZE, Stanza 14.)

ALAS, the country! how shall tongue or pen
Bewail her now *un*country gentlemen?
The last to bid the cry of warfare cease,
The first to make a malady of peace.
For what were all these country patriots born?
To hunt, and vote, and raise the price of corn?
But corn, like every mortal thing, must fall;
Kings, conquerors — and markets most of all.
And must ye fall with every ear of grain?
Why would you trouble Buonaparte's reign?
He was your great Triptolemus; his vices
Destroy'd but realms, and still maintain'd your prices;
He amplified to every lord's content
The grand agrarian aichymy, high *rent*.

Why did the tyrant stumble on the Tartars,
And lower wheat to such desponding quarters?
Why did you chain him on yon isle so lone?
The man was worth much more upon his throne.
True, blood and treasure boundlessly were spilt,
But what of that? the Gaul may bear the guilt;
But bread was high, the farmer paid his way,
And acres told upon the appointed day.
But where is now the goodly audit ale?
The purse-proud tenant, never known to fail?
The farm which never yet was left on hand?
The marsh reclaim'd to most improving land?
The impatient hope of the expiring lease?
The doubling rental? — What an evil's peace!
In vain the prize excites the ploughman's skill,
In vain the Commons pass their patriot bill;
The *landed interest* — (you may understand
The phrase much better leaving out the *land*) —
The land self-interest groans from shore to shore,
For fear that plenty should attain the poor.
Up, up again, ye rents! exalt your notes,
Or else the ministry will lose their votes,
And patriotism, so delicately nice,
Her loaves will lower to the market price;
For ah! " the loaves and fishes," once so high,
Are gone — their oven closed, their ocean dry,
And nought remains of all the millions spent,
Excepting to grow moderate and content.
They who are not so, *had* their turn — and turn
About still flows from Fortune's equal urn;
Now let their virtue be its own reward,
And share the blessings which themselves prepared.

See these inglorious Cincinnati swarm,
Farmers of war, dictators of the farm;
Their ploughshare was the sword in hireling hands,
Their fields manured by gore of other lands;
Safe in their barns, these Sabine tillers sent
Their brethren out to battle — why? for rent!
Year after year they voted cent per cent,
Blood, sweat, and tear-wrung millions — why? for rent!
They roar'd, they dined, they drank, they swore they
   meant
To die for England — why then live? — for rent!
The peace has made one general malcontent
Of these high-market patriots; war was rent!
Their love of country, millions all mis-spent,
How reconcile? by reconciling rent!
And will they not repay the treasures lent?
No: down with everything, and up with rent!
Their good, ill, health, wealth, joy, or discontent,
Being, end, aim, religion — rent, rent, rent!

ITALY.

(BEPPO, Stanzas 41–45.)

WITH all its sinful doings, I must say,
   That Italy 's a pleasant place to me,
Who love to see the sun shine every day,
   And vines (not nail'd to walls) from tree to tree
Festoon'd, much like the back scene of a play,
   Or melodrame, which people flock to see,
When the first act is ended by a dance
In vineyards copied from the south of France.

I like on Autumn evenings to ride out,
   Without being forced to bid my groom be sure
My cloak is round his middle strapp'd about,
   Because the skies are not the most secure;
I know too that, if stopp'd upon my route,
   Where the green alleys windingly allure,
Reeling with *grapes* red wagons choke the way, —
In England 't would be dung, dust, or a dray.

I also like to dine on becaficas,
   To see the Sun set, sure he 'll rise to-morrow,
Not through a misty morning, twinkling weak as
   A drunken man's dead eye in maudlin sorrow,
But with all Heaven t' himself ; that day will break as
   Beauteous as cloudless, not be forced to borrow
That sort of farthing candlelight which glimmers
Where reeking London's smoky caldron simmers.

I love the language, that soft bastard Latin,
   Which melts like kisses from a female mouth,
And sounds as if it should be writ on satin,
   With syllables which breathe of the sweet South,
And gentle liquids gliding all so pat in,
   That not a single accent seems uncouth,
Like our harsh northern whistling, grunting guttural,
Which we 're obliged to hiss, and spit, and sputter all.

I like the women too (forgive my folly),
   From the rich peasant cheek of ruddy bronze,
And large black eyes that flash on you a volley
   Of rays that say a thousand things at once,

To the high dama's brow, more melancholy,
  But clear, and with a wild and liquid glance,
Heart on her lips, and soul within her eyes.
Soft as her clime, and sunny as her skies.

ENGLAND.

(Beppo, Stanzas 47 – 49.)

" England ! with all thy faults I love thee still,"
  I said at Calais, and have not forgot it ;
I like to speak and lucubrate my fill ;
  I like the government (but that is not it) ;
I like the freedom of the press and quill ;
  I like the Habeas Corpus (when we 've got it) ;
I like a parliamentary debate,
Particularly when 't is not too late ;

I like the taxes, when they 're not too many ;
  I like a sea-coal fire, when not too dear ;
I like a beef-steak, too, as well as any ;
  Have no objection to a pot of beer ;
I like the weather, when it is not rainy,
  That is, I like two months of every year.
And so God save the Regent, Church and King !
Which means that I like all and every thing.

Our standing army, and disbanded seamen,
  Poor's rate, Reform, my own, the nation's debt,
Our little riots just to show we are free men,
  Our trifling bankruptcies in the Gazette,

Our cloudy climate, and our chilly women,
  All these I can forgive, and those forget,
And greatly venerate our recent glories,
And wish they were not owing to the Tories

WANTED—A HERO.

(DON JUAN, Canto i. Stanzas 1-5.)

I WANT a hero: an uncommon want,
  When every year and month sends forth a new one,
Till, after cloying the gazettes with cant,
  The age discovers he is not the true one ;
Of such as these I should not care to vaunt,
  I' ll therefore take our ancient friend Don Juan—
We all have seen him, in the pantomime,
Sent to the devil somewhat ere his time.

Vernon, the butcher Cumberland, Wolfe, Hawke,
  Prince Ferdinand, Granby, Burgoyne, Keppel, Howe,
Evil and good, have had their tithe of talk,
  And fill'd their sign-posts then, like Wellesley now ;
Each in their turn like Banquo's monarchs stalk,
  Followers of .fame, " nine farrow " of that sow:
France, too, had Buonaparté and Dumourier
Recorded in the Moniteur and Courier.

Barnave, Brissot, Condorcet, Mirabeau,
  Petion, Clootz, Danton, Marat, La Fayette,
Were French, and famous people, as we know ;

And there were others, scarce forgotten yet,
Joubert, Hoche, Marceau, Lannes, Desaix, Moreau,
   With many of the military set,
Exceedingly remarkable at times,
But not at all adapted to my rhymes.

Nelson was once Britannia's god of war, .
   And still should be so, but the tide is turn'd ;
There 's no more to be said of Trafalgar,
   'T is with our hero quietly inurn'd ;
Because the army 's grown more popular,
   At which the naval people are concern'd ;
Besides, the prince is all for the land-service,
Forgetting Duncan, Nelson, Howe, and Jervis.

Brave men were living before Agamemnon
   And since, exceeding valorous and sage,
A good deal like him too, though quite the same none ;
   But then they shone not on the poet's page,
And so have been forgotten : — I condemn none,
   But can't find any in the present age
Fit for my poem (that is, for my new one) ;
So, as I said, I 'll take my friend Don Juan.

LONDON.

(DON JUAN, Canto x. Stanzas 81, 82.)

THE sun went down, the smoke rose up as from
   A half-unquench'd volcano, o'er a space
Which well beseem'd the " Devil's drawing-room,"
   As some have qualified that wondrous place :
But Juan felt, though not approaching *home,*
   As one who, though he were not of the race,
Revered the soil, of those true sons the mother,
Who butcher'd half the earth, and bullied t' other.

A mighty mass of brick, and smoke, and shipping,
   Dirty and dusky, but as wide as eye
Could reach, with here and there a sail just skipping
   In sight, then lost amidst the forestry
Of masts ; a wilderness of steeples peeping
   On tiptoe through their sea-coal canopy ;
A huge, dun cupola, like a foolscap crown
On a fool's head — and there is London Town !

THINGS SWEET.

(DON JUAN, Canto i. Stanzas 123–127.)

'T IS sweet to hear the watch-dog's honest bark
   Bay deep-mouth'd welcome as we draw near home;
'T is sweet to know there is an eye will mark
   Our coming, and look brighter when we come;

'T is sweet to be awaken'd by the lark,
   Or lull'd by falling waters; sweet the hum
Of bees, the voice of girls, the song of birds,
The lisp of children, and their earliest words.

Sweet is the vintage, when the showering grapes
   In Bacchanal profusion reel to earth
Purple and gushing: sweet are our escapes
   From civic revelry to rural mirth ;
Sweet to the miser are his glittering heaps,
   Sweet to the father is his first-born's birth,
Sweet is revenge — especially to women,
Pillage to soldiers, prize-money to seamen.

Sweet is a legacy, and passing sweet
   The unexpected death of some old lady
Or gentleman of seventy years complete,
   Who 've made "us youth" wait too — too long
     already
For an estate, or cash, or country-seat,
   Still breaking, but with stamina so steady,
That all the Israelites are fit to mob its
Next owner for their double-damn'd post-obits.

'T is sweet to win, no matter how, one's laurels,
   By blood or ink; 't is sweet to put an end
To strife; 't is sometimes sweet to have our quarrels,
   Particularly with a tiresome friend:
Sweet is old wine in bottles, ale in barrels;
   Dear is the helpless creature we defend
Against the world; and dear the schoolboy spot
We ne'er forget, though there we are forgot.

But sweeter still, than this, than these, than all,
   Is first and passionate love — it stands alone,
Like Adam's recollection of his fall;
   The tree of knowledge has been pluck'd — all 's
      known —
And life yields nothing further to recall
   Worthy of this ambrosial sin, so shown,
No doubt in fable, as the unforgiven
Fire which Prometheus filch'd for us from heaven.

LAMBRO'S RETURN.

(Don Juan, Canto iii. Stanzas 27, 29–41.)

He saw his white walls shining in the sun,
   His garden trees all shadowy and green ;
He heard his rivulet's light bubbling run,
   The distant dog-bark ; and perceived between
The umbrage of the wood so cool and dun
   The moving figures, and the sparkling sheen
Of arms (in the East all arm) — and various dyes
Of color'd garbs, as bright as butterflies.

And still more nearly to the place advancing,
   Descending rather quickly the declivity,
Through the waved branches, o'er the greensward
     glancing,
   'Midst other indications of festivity,
Seeing a troop of his domestics dancing
   Like dervises, who turn as on a pivot, he
Perceived it was the Pyrrhic dance so martial,
To which the Levantines are very partial.

And further on a group of Grecian girls,
   The first and tallest her white kerchief waving,
Were strung together like a row of pearls,
   Link'd hand in hand, and dancing ; each too having
Down her white neck long floating auburn curls —
   (The least of which would set ten poets raving) ;
Their leader sang — and bounded to her song,
With choral step and voice, the virgin throng.

And here, assembled cross-legg'd round their trays,
   Small social parties just begun to dine ;
Pilaus and meats of all sorts met the gaze,
   And flasks of Samian and of Chian wine,
And sherbet cooling in the porous vase ;
   Above them their dessert grew on its vine,
The orange and pomegranate nodding o'er,
Dropp'd in their laps, scarce pluck'd, their mellow store.

A band of children, round a snow-white ram,
   There wreathe his venerable horns with flowers ;
While peaceful, as if still an unwean'd lamb,
   The patriarch of the flock all gently cowers
His sober head, majestically tame,
   Or eats from out the palm, or playful lowers
His brow, as if in act to butt, and then
Yielding to their small hands, draws back again.

Their classic profiles, and glittering dresses,
   Their large black eyes, and soft seraphic cheeks,
Crimson as cleft pomegranates, their long tresses,
   The gesture which enchants, the eye that speaks,

The innocence which happy childhood blesses,
    Made quite a picture of these little Greeks ;
So that the philosophical beholder
Sigh'd, for their sakes — that they should e'er grow older.

Afar, a dwarf buffoon stood telling tales
    To a sedate gray circle of old smokers
Of secret treasures found in hidden vales,
    Of wonderful replies from Arab jokers,
Of charms to make good gold and cure bad ails,
    Of rocks bewitch'd that open to the knockers,
Of magic ladies who, by one sole act,
Transform'd their lords to beasts (but that 's a fact).

Here was no lack of innocent diversion
    For the imagination or the senses,
Song, dance, wine, music, stories from the Persian,
    All pretty pastimes in which no offence is;
But Lambro saw all these things with aversion,
    Perceiving in his absence such expenses,
Dreading that climax of all human ills,
The inflammation of his weekly bills.

Ah! what is man? what perils still environ
    The happiest mortals even after dinner —
A day of gold from out an age of iron
    Is all that life allows the luckiest sinner;
Pleasure (whene'er she sings, at least) 's a siren,
    That lures, to flay alive, the young beginner;
Lambro's reception at his people's banquet
Was such as fire accords to a wet blanket.

He — being a man who seldom used a word
    Too much, and wishing gladly to surprise
(In general he surprised men with the sword)
    His daughter — had not sent before to advise
Of his arrival, so that no one stirr'd ;
    And long he paused to re-assure his eyes,
In fact much more astonish'd than delighted,
To find so much good company invited.

He did not know (alas ! how men will lie)
    That a report (especially the Greeks)
Avouch'd his death (such people never die),
    And put his house in mourning several weeks, —
But now their eyes and also lips were dry;
    The bloom, too, had return'd to Haidée's cheeks.
Her tears, too, being return'd into their fount,
She now kept house upon her own account.

Hence all this rice, meat, dancing, wine, and fiddling,
    Which turn'd the isle into a place of pleasure;
The servants all were getting drunk or idling,
    A life which made them happy beyond measure.
Her father's hospitality seem'd middling,
    Compared with what Haidée did with his treasure;
'T was wonderful how things went on improving,
While she had not one hour to spare from loving.

Perhaps you think in stumbling on this feast
    He flew into a passion, and in fact
There was no mighty reason to be pleased;
    Perhaps you prophesy some sudden act,

The whip, the rack, or dungeon at the least,
　To teach his people to be more exact,
And that, proceeding at a very high rate,
He show'd the royal *penchants* of a pirate.

You 're wrong. — He was the mildest manner'd man
　That ever scuttled ship or cut a throat;
With such true breeding of a gentleman,
　You never could divine his real thought;
No courtier could, and scarcely woman can
　Gird more deceit within a petticoat;
Pity he loved adventurous life's variety,
He was so great a loss to good society.

A STORMED CITY.

(DON JUAN, Canto viii. Stanzas 123–127.)

ALL that the mind would shrink from of excesses;
　All that the body perpetrates of bad;
All that we read, hear, dream, of man's distresses;
　All that the devil would do if run stark mad;
All that defies the worst which pen expresses;
　All by which hell is peopled, or as sad
As hell — mere mortals who their power abuse —
Was here (as heretofore and since) let loose.

If here and there some transient trait of pity
　Was shown, and some more noble heart broke through
Its bloody bond, and saved, perhaps, some pretty
　Child, or an aged, helpless man or two —

What 's this in one annihilated city,
  Where thousand loves, and ties, and duties grow?
Cockneys of London! Muscadins of Paris!
Just ponder what a pious pastime war is.

Think how the joys of reading a Gazette
  Are purchased by all agonies and crimes:
Or if these do not move you, don't forget
  Such doom may be your own in after-times.
Meantime the Taxes, Castlereagh, and Debt,
  Are hints as good as sermons, or as rhymes.
Read your own hearts and Ireland's present story
Then feed her famine fat with Wellesley's glory.

But still there is unto a patriot nation,
  Which loves so well its country and its king,
A subject of sublimest exultation —
  Bear it, ye Muses, on your brightest wing!
Howe'er the mighty locust, Desolation,
  Strip your green fields, and to your harvests cling,
Gaunt famine never shall approach the throne —
Though Ireland starve, great George weighs twenty stone

But let me put an end unto my theme:
  There was an end of Ismail — hapless town!
Far flash'd her burning towers o'er Danube's stream,
  And redly ran his blushing waters down.
The horrid war-whoop and the shriller scream
  Rose still; but fainter were the thunders grown:
Of forty thousand who had mann'd the wall,
Some hundreds breathed — the rest were silent all!

EXHORTATION TO MR. WILBERFORCE.

(Don Juan, Canto xiv. Stanzas 82–84.)

O Wilberforce! thou man of black renown,
   Whose merit none enough can sing or say,
Thou hast struck one immense Colossus down,
   Thou moral Washington of Africa!
But there's another little thing, I own,
   Which you should perpetrate some summer's day,
And set the other half of earth to rights;
You have freed the *blacks* — now pray shut up the whites.

Shut up the bald-coot bully Alexander!
   Ship off the Holy Three to Senegal;
Teach them that " sauce for goose is sauce for gander,"
   And ask them how *they* like to be in thrall?
Shut up each high heroic salamander,
   Who eats fire gratis (since the pay 's but small);
Shut up — no, *not* the King, but the Pavilion,
Or else 't will cost us all another million.

Shut up the world at large, let Bedlam out;
   And you will be perhaps surprised to find
All things pursue exactly the same route,
   As now with those of *soi-disant* sound mind.
This I could prove beyond a single doubt,
   Were there a jot of sense among mankind;
But till that *point d'appui* is found, alas!
Like Archimedes, I leave earth as 't was.

EXHORTATION TO MRS. FRY.

(DON JUAN, Canto x. Stanzas 85–87.)

OH Mrs. Fry! Why go to Newgate?   Why
   Preach to poor rogues?   And wherefore not begin
With Carlton, or with other houses?   Try
   Your hand at harden'd and imperial sin.
To mend the people 's an absurdity.
   A jargon, a mere philanthropic din,
Unless you make their betters better: — Fy!
I thought you had more religion, Mrs. Fry.

Teach them the decencies of good threescore;
   Cure them of tours, hussar and highland dresses;
Tell them that youth once gone returns no more,
   That hired huzzas redeem no land's distresses;
Tell them Sir William Curtis is a bore,
   Too dull even for the dullest of excesses,
The witless Falstaff of a hoary Hal,
A fool whose bells have ceased to ring at all.

Tell them, though it may be perhaps too late
   On life's worn confine, jaded, bloated, sated,
To set up vain pretences of being great,
   'T is not so to be good; and be it stated,
The worthiest kings have ever loved least state;
   And tell them —— But you won't, and I have prated
Just now enough; but by and by I 'll prattle
Like Roland's horn in Roncesvalles' battle.

SATAN CLAIMS, AT HEAVEN'S GATE, GEORGE THE THIRD.

(VISION OF JUDGMENT, Stanzas 42-49.)

" LOOK to the earth, I said, and say again:
  When this old, blind, mad, helpless, weak, poor worm
Began in youth's first bloom and flush to reign,
  The world and he both wore a different form,
And much of earth and all the watery plain
  Of ocean call'd him king: through many a storm
His isles had floated on the abyss of time;
For the rough virtues chose them for their clime.

" He came to his sceptre young; he leaves it old:
  Look to the state in which he found his realm,
And left it; and his annals too behold,
  How to a minion first he gave the helm;
How grew upon his heart a thirst for gold,
  The beggar's vice, which can but overwhelm
The meanest hearts; and for the rest, but glance
Thine eye along America and France.

" 'T is true, he was a tool from first to last
  (I have the workmen safe); but as a tool
So let him be consumed. From out the past
  Of ages, since mankind have known the rule
Of monarchs — from the bloody rolls amass'd
  Of sin and slaughter — from the Cæsar's school,
Take the worst pupil; and produce a reign
More drench'd with gore, more cumber'd with the slain.

" He ever warr'd with freedom and the free:
　　Nations as men, home subjects, foreign foes,
So that they utter'd the word 'Liberty!'
　　Found George the Third their first opponent.　Whose
History was ever stain'd as his will be
　　With national and individual woes?
I grant his household abstinence; I grant
His neutral virtues, which most monarchs want;

" I know he was a constant consort; own
　　He was a decent sire, and middling lord.
All this is much, and most upon a throne;
　　As temperance, if at Apicius' board,
Is more than at an anchorite's supper shown.
　　I grant him all the kindest can accord;
And this was well for him, but not for those
Millions who found him what oppression chose.

" The New World shook him off: the Old yet groans
　　Beneath what he and his prepared, if not
Completed: he leaves heirs on many thrones
　　To all his vices, without what begot
Compassion for him — his tame virtues; drones
　　Who sleep, or despots who have now forgot
A lesson which shall be re-taught them, wake
Upon the thrones of earth; but let them quake!

" Five millions of the primitive, who hold
　　The faith which makes ye great on earth, implored
A *part* of that vast *all* they held of old, —
　　Freedom to worship — not alone your Lord,

Michael! but you; and you, Saint Peter! Cold
    Must be your souls, if you have not abhorr'd
The foe to Catholic participation
In all the license of a Christian nation.

"True! he allow'd them to pray God; but as
    A consequence of prayer, refused the law
Which would have placed them upon the same base
    With those who did not hold the saints in awe." —
But here Saint Peter started from his place,
    And cried, "You may the prisoner withdraw:
Ere heaven shall ope her portals to this Guelph,
While I am guard, may I be damn'd myself!"

THE SEX.

(CHILDE HAROLD, Canto ii. Stanza 34.)

NOT much he kens, I ween, of woman's breast,
Who thinks that wanton thing is won by sighs;
What careth she for hearts when once possess'd?
Do proper homage to thine idol's eyes,
But not too humbly, or she will despise
Thee and thy suit, though told in moving tropes:
Disguise ev'n tenderness, if thou art wise;
Brisk Confidence still best with woman copes;
Pique her and soothe in turn, soon Passion crowns thy
    hopes.

OUR CHILDREN.

(DON JUAN, Canto iii. Stanzas 59, 60.)

IT is a hard although a common case
 To find our children running restive; — they,
In whom our brightest days we would retrace,
   Our little selves re-form'd in finer clay,
Just as old age is creeping on apace,
   And clouds come o'er the sunset of our day,
They kindly leave us, though not quite alone,
But in good company — the gout or stone.

Yet a fine family is a fine thing
   (Provided they don't come in after dinner);
'T is beautiful to see a matron bring
   Her children up (if nursing them don't thin her);
Like cherubs round an altar-piece they cling
   To the fireside (a sight to touch a sinner)
A lady with her daughters or her nieces
Shine like a guinea and seven-shilling pieces.

SOUL.

(DON JUAN, Canto xiv. Stanzas 70–72.)

HE was a cold, good, honorable man,
   Proud of his birth, and proud of everything;
A goodly spirit for a state divan,
   A figure fit to walk before a king;

Tall, stately, form'd to lead the courtly van
  On birthdays, glorious with a star and string;
The very model of a chamberlain —
And such I mean to make him when I reign.

But there was something wanting on the whole —
  I don't know what, and therefore cannot tell —
Which pretty women — the sweet souls! — call *soul.*
  Certes it was not body; he was well
Proportion'd, as a poplar or a pole,
  A handsome man, that human miracle;
And in each circumstance of love or war
Had still preserved his perpendicular.

Still there was something wanting, as I 've said —
  That undefinable "*Je ne sais quoi,*"
Which, for what I know, may of yore have led
  To Homer's Iliad, since it drew to Troy
The Greek Eve, Helen, from the Spartan's bed;
  Though on the whole, no doubt, the Dardan boy
Was much inferior to King Menelaüs: —
But thus it is some women will betray us.

MOBILITY.

(Don Juan, Canto xvi. Stanzas 96–98.)

——————JUAN, when he cast a glance
On Adeline while playing her grand rôle,
  Which she went through as though it were a dance
(Betraying only now and then her soul

By a look scarce perceptibly askance
Of weariness or scorn), began to feel
Some doubt how much of Adeline was *real;*

So well she acted all and every part
    By turns — with that vivacious versatility,
Which many people take for want of heart.
    They err — 't is merely what is call'd mobility,
A thing of temperament — and not of art,
    Though seeming so from its supposed facility;
And false — though true; for surely they 're sincerest
Who are strongly acted on by what is nearest.

This makes your actors, artists, and romancers,
    Heroes sometimes, though seldom — sages never;
But speakers, bards, diplomatists, and dancers,
    Little that 's great, but much of what is clever;
Most orators, but very few financiers,
    Though all Exchequer chancellors endeavor,
Of late years, to dispense with Cocker's rigors,
And grow quite figurative with their figures.

GREAT NAMES.

(DON JUAN, Canto iii. Stanzas 90–95, and 98–100.)

AND glory long has made the sages smile;
    'T is something, nothing, words, illusion, wind —
Depending more upon the historian's style
    Than on the name a person leaves behind:

Troy owes to Homer what whist owes to Hoyle:
　The present century was growing blind
To the great Marlborough's skill in giving knocks,
Until his late Life by Archdeacon Coxe.

Milton 's the prince of poets — so we say;
　A little heavy, but no less divine:
An independent being in his day —
　Learn'd, pious, temperate in love and wine;
But his life falling into Johnson's way,
　We 're told this great high priest of all the Nine
Was whipt at college — a harsh sire — odd spouse,
For the first Mrs. Milton left his house.

All these are, *certes*, entertaining facts,
　Like Shakspeare's stealing deer, Lord Bacon's bribes;
Like Titus' youth, and Cæsar's earliest acts;
　Like Burns (whom Doctor Currie well describes);
Like Cromwell's pranks; — but although truth exacts
　These amiable descriptions from the scribes,
As most essential to their hero's story,
They do not much contribute to his glory.

All are not moralists, like Southey, when
　He prated to the world of " Pantisocrasy; "
Or Wordsworth unexcised, unhired, who then
　Season'd his pedlar poems with democracy;
Or Coleridge, long before his flighty pen
　Let to the Morning Post its aristocracy;
When he and Southey, following the same path,
Espoused two partners (milliners of Bath).

Such names at present cut a convict figure,
  The very Botany Bay in moral geography;
Their loyal treason, renegado rigor,
  Are good manure for their more bare biography.
Wordsworth's last quarto, by the way, is bigger
  Than any since the birthday of typography;
A drowsy frowsy poem, call'd the " Excursion,"
Writ in a manner which is my aversion.

He there builds up a formidable dyke
  Between his own and others' intellect;
But Wordsworth's poem, and his followers, like
  Joanna Southcote's Shiloh, and her sect,
Are things which in this century don't strike
  The public mind — so few are the elect;
And the new births of both their stale virginities
Have proved but dropsies, taken for divinities.

We learn from Horace, " Homer sometimes sleeps; "
  We feel without him, Wordsworth sometimes wakes, —
To show with what complacency he creeps,
  With his dear " *Waggoners*," around his lakes.
He wishes for " a boat " to sail the deeps —
  Of ocean? — No, of air; and then he makes
Another outcry for " a little boat,"
And drivels seas to set it well afloat.

If he must fain sweep o'er the ethereal plain,
  And Pegasus runs restive in his " Waggon,"
Could he not beg the loan of Charles's Wain?
  Or pray Medea for a single dragon?

Or if too classic for his vulgar brain,
   He fear'd his neck to venture such a nag on,
And he must needs mount nearer to the moon,
Could not the blockhead ask for a balloon?

" Pedlars," and " Boats," and " Waggons!" Oh! ye
       shades
   Of Pope and Dryden, are we come to this?
That trash of such sort not alone evades
   Contempt, but from the bathos' vast abyss
Floats scumlike uppermost, and these Jack Cades
   Of sense and song above your graves may hiss! —
The " little boatman," and his " Peter Bell,"
Can sneer at him who drew " Achitophel!"

POETICAL COMMANDMENTS.

(DON JUAN, Canto i. Stanzas 204–206.)

IF ever I should condescend to prose,
   I 'll write poetical commandments, which
Shall supersede beyond all doubt all those
   That went before; in these I shall enrich
My text with many things that no one knows,
   And carry precept to the highest pitch:
I'll call the work " Longinus o'er a Bottle,
Or, Every Poet his *own* Aristotle."

Thou shalt believe in Milton, Dryden, Pope;
   Thou shalt not set up Wordsworth, Coleridge, Southey;
Because the first is crazed beyond all hope,
   The second drunk, the third so quaint and mouthy:

With Crabbe it may be difficult to cope,
  And Campbell's Hipprocrene is somewhat drouthy:
Thou shalt not steal from Samuel Rogers, nor
Commit — flirtation with the muse of Moore.

Thou shalt not covet Mr. Sotheby's Muse,
  His Pegasus, nor any thing that 's his;
Thou shalt not bear false witness like "the Blues" —
  (There 's one, at least, is very fond of this);
Thou shalt not write, in short, but what I choose:
  This is true criticism, and you may kiss —
Exactly as you please, or not — the rod;
But if you don't I'll lay it on, by G—d!

BYRON AND HIS CONTEMPORARIES.

(DON JUAN, Canto xi. Stanzas 53–60.)

JUAN knew several languages — as well
  He might — and brought them up with skill, in time
To save his fame with each accomplish'd belle,
  Who still regretted that he did not rhyme.
There wanted but this requisite to swell
  His qualities (with them) into sublime:
Lady Fitz-Frisky and Miss Mævia Mannish,
Both long'd extremely to be sung in Spanish.

However, he did pretty well, and was
  Admitted as an aspirant to all
The coteries, and, as in Banquo's glass,
  At great assemblies or in parties small,

He saw ten thousand living authors pass,
 That being about their average numeral;
Also the eighty "greatest living poets,"
As every paltry magazine can show *its*.

In twice five years the "greatest living poet,"
 Like to the champion in the fisty ring,
Is call'd on to support his claim, or show it,
 Although 't is an imaginary thing.
Even I — albeit I 'm sure I did not know it,
 Nor sought of foolscap subjects to be king, —
Was reckon'd a considerable time,
The grand Napoleon of the realms of rhyme.

But Juan was my Moscow, and Faliero
 My Leipsic, and my Mont Saint Jean seems Cain:
"La Belle Alliance" of dunces down at zero,
 Now that the Lion 's fall'n, may rise again:
But I will fall at least as fell my hero;
 Nor reign at all, or as a *monarch* reign;
Or to some lonely isle of gaolers go,
With turncoat Southey for my turnkey Lowe.

Sir Walter reign'd before me; Moore and Campbell
 Before and after; but now grown more holy,
The Muses upon Sion's hill must ramble
 With poets almost clergymen, or wholly;
And Pegasus hath a psalmodic amble
 Beneath the very Reverend Rowley Powley,
Who shoes the glorious animal with stilts,
A modern Ancient Pistol — by the hilts!

Then there 's my gentle Euphues; who, they say,
   Sets up for being a sort of *moral me;*
He 'll find it rather difficult some day
   To turn out both, or either, it may be.
Some persons think that Coleridge hath the sway;
   And Wordsworth has supporters, two or three;
And that deep-mouth'd Bœotian " Savage Landor "
Has taken for a swan rogue Southey's gander.

John Keats, who was kill'd off by one critique,
   Just as he really promised something great,
If not intelligible, without Greek
   Contrived to talk about the gods of late
Much as they might have been supposed to speak.
   Poor fellow!   His was an untoward fate;
'T is strange the mind, that very fiery particle,
Should let itself be snuff'd out by an article.

The list grows long of live and dead pretenders
   To that which none will gain — or none will know
The conqueror at least; who, ere time renders
   His last award, will have the long grass grow
Above his burnt-out brain, and sapless cinders.
   If I might augur, I should rate but low
Their chances; — they 're too numerous, like the thirty
Mock tyrants, when Rome's annals wax'd but dirty.

POETICAL PRODUCTION.

(Don Juan, Canto xiv. Stanzas 10, 11.)

I HAVE brought this world about my ears, and eke
   The other; that 's to say, the clergy — who
Upon my head have bid their thunders break
   In pious libels by no means a few.
And yet I can't help scribbling once a week,
   Tiring old readers, nor discovering new.
In youth I wrote because my mind was full,
And now because I feel it growing dull.

But " why then publish?" — There are no rewards
   Of fame or profit when the world grows weary.
I ask in turn, — Why do you play at cards?
   Why drink? Why read? — To make some hour less
      dreary.
It occupies me to turn back regards
   On what I 've seen or ponder'd, sad or cheery;
And what I write I cast upon the stream,
To swim or sink — I have had at least my dream.

THE LIGHTER SIDE.

(Don Juan, Canto iv. Stanzas 3, 4.)

As boy, I thought myself a clever fellow,
   And wish'd that others held the same opinion;
They took it up when my days grew more mellow,
   And other minds acknowledged my dominion:

Now my sere fancy '' falls into the yellow
    Leaf,'' and Imagination droops her pinion,
And the sad truth which hovers o'er my desk
Turns what was once romantic to burlesque.

And if I laugh at any mortal thing,
    'T is that I may not weep; and if I weep,
'T is that our nature cannot always bring
    Itself to apathy, for we must steep
Our hearts first in the depths of Lethe's spring,
    Ere what we least wish to behold will sleep;
Thetis baptized her mortal son in Styx;
A mortal mother would on Lethe fix.

THE END.

Lightning Source UK Ltd.
Milton Keynes UK
UKOW020623210513

211006UK00004B/99/P

9 781171 896357